'With clarity, courage, and intellectual rigour, Victoria Baskerville's transactional analysis is rendered intersectionally, as a practice deeply rooted in socially contextualized, ethical relatedness. Her intelligent voice is personal and unpretentious, yet theoretically and clinically astute. I'm gratified that she has made such good use of my concept of radical openness, thoughtfully weaving it into her vision and bringing vitality to both clinical and conceptual examples. I hope practitioners of all orientations will avail themselves of the wisdom this book offers. It is a generous, timely, and important contribution'.

Anton Hart, PhD, *FABP, FIPA, Psychologist - Psychoanalyst and author*

'This book is a vibrant and essential addition to contemporary transactional analysis and the broader fields of counselling and psychotherapy. Written with passion and fluidity, it embodies the personal, radical, relational, and systemic dynamics within and around us. The narrative will compel readers to reflect on and reassess their philosophies, theories, and practices as both professionals and citizens. Baskerville intertwines lived experience, critical theory, and clinical insight to examine power, privilege, and identity in consulting, training, and collective spaces. This thoroughly researched and informative book is both inspiring and educational'.

Karen Minikin, *Psychotherapist and author*

'What Victoria Baskerville has done with this excellent book is to craft a tome which brings transactional analysis into the 21st century. The strength of Baskerville's beautifully written text is in its embrace of intersectional and decolonial theories – it challenges many of the colonised adaptations that our profession has allowed itself to be co-opted by. By inviting readers of intersectional difference to this theoretical table, there is an important opportunity to explore creatively and decolonise our adapted colonial identities. Baskerville's eloquent, sensitive, patient, and measured work deserves to find its place amongst the annals of TA literature as transactional analysis embraces and grows from the decolonial richness of the methods and ideas presented here'.

Dr Dwight Turner, *Psychotherapist and author*

The cover image speaks to the author, Victoria Baskerville, of ancestral memory and interconnection. The web of oppressions and supremacies – silencing. And the hope in returning to earth – through collective liberation – a transformational awakening.

Contemporary Transactional Analysis Through an Intersectional Lens

This book takes the reader on a decolonising journey from the radical roots of transactional analysis to intersectional transactional analysis on the ground, challenging social constructs and constructed truths.

Contemporary Transactional Analysis Through an Intersectional Lens: Deconstruction and Reconstruction of Theory and Practice, is framed by social, cultural, political, and historical contexts, and accounts for systemic oppression – the onslaught of colonisation, supremacies, and systemic racism – which has not been adequately addressed in TA and psychotherapy. Victoria Baskerville draws on social justice and the role of activism, influenced by queer theory, critical race theory, and critical disability studies, to challenge binary social constructs and further contemporary practice. This book amplifies voices of the marginalised and the complexity of intersectional power dynamics, and honours our ancestry and the responsibility we hold as coloniser or colonised – and in many instances, both. Reflecting on the idea that 'all oppression is connected', it invites the opening up of mind and heart through the practice of radically open and non-defended dialogue, the call to move from 'I' to 'we' – a collective awakening – and asking, in each unique encounter: who holds the power? And, ultimately, what is my part in this intersectional dyad?

This book will be an important resource for psychotherapists, counsellors, transactional analysts, and other mental health professionals, students, and educators taking the decolonising journey.

Victoria Baskerville (she/her) is an Intersectional Psychotherapist based in multidiverse East London, UK. She founded TA East London Institute, bringing a lens of intersectionality, aiming to account for social, cultural, and political contexts across theory and practice. She is a passionate activist for decolonising TA and psychotherapy practice.

Innovations in Transactional Analysis: Theory and Practice
Series Editor: William F. Cornell

This book series is founded on the principle of the importance of open discussion, debate, critique, experimentation, and the integration of other models in fostering innovation in all the arenas of transactional analytic theory and practice: psychotherapy, counseling, education, organizational development, health care, and coaching. It will be a home for the work of established authors and new voices.

Working with Dreams in Transactional Analysis
From Theory to Practice for Individuals and Groups
Anna Emanuela Tangolo and Francesca Vignozzi

Conceptualizing Ego States in Transactional Analysis
Three Systems in Interaction
José Grégoire

A Transactional Analysis of Motherhood and Disturbances in the Maternal
Emma Haynes

A Living History of Transactional Analysis Psychotherapy
Engaging Reflectively with Theory and Methodology
Steff Oates and Diana Deaconu

Existential Perspectives in Transactional Analysis
The Development of the Adult Self and the Human Search for Meaning
Rachel Cook

Contemporary Transactional Analysis Through an Intersectional Lens
Deconstruction and Reconstruction of Theory and Practice
Victoria Baskerville

https://www.routledge.com/Innovations-in-Transactional-Analysis-Theory-and-Practice/book-series/INNTA

Contemporary Transactional Analysis Through an Intersectional Lens

Deconstruction and Reconstruction of Theory and Practice

Victoria Baskerville

Routledge
Taylor & Francis Group

LONDON AND NEW YORK

Designed cover image: © Getty Images

First published 2026
by Routledge
4 Park Square, Milton Park, Abingdon, Oxon OX14 4RN

and by Routledge
605 Third Avenue, New York, NY 10158

Routledge is an imprint of the Taylor & Francis Group, an informa business

British Library Cataloguing-in-Publication Data
A catalogue record for this book is available from the British Library

ISBN: 978-1-032-83455-9 (hbk)
ISBN: 978-1-032-83456-6 (pbk)
ISBN: 978-1-003-50942-4 (ebk)

DOI: 10.4324/9781003509424

Typeset in Times New Roman
by KnowledgeWorks Global Ltd.

Access the Support Material: www.routledge.com/9781032834559

For our daughters Eliza and Amelia,

who will continue the journey, with my love, pride and
deep gratitude

Contents

Illustrations

Acknowledgements

I dedicate this book to the marginalised, the visionaries, the pioneers, the activists, the spoken word artists, the poets, and the trailblazers, and all whom dare to put their heads above the parapet. I express my gratitude to the soul healers, to the two spirited peoples, and indigenous communities.

I offer my profound thanks to student colleagues, colleagues, and dear old and new friends in the TA East London community, who have journeyed with me through unknown terrain – risking not knowing – taking the road less travelled... the decolonising journey, all in the hope of deeper connection.

I thank those who have had the courage and willingness to dialogue with me. I thank J. for her generosity and openness back in 2022, and I thank Alexis, Corynne, Jubriel, and Dhruva for their willingness to share their experiences in this book – I thank colleagues who have contributed to the amplified voices, with generosity, openness, and wisdom.

I thank my dear colleagues and friends who have walked alongside me over the years, those who have come and gone, and those who have stayed in my life. You know who you are. I thank my dear first supervisor and now friend, Geoff Hopping, for walking with me for over 25 years, and supervisor Suzanne Boyd for her support always.

I thank those in the wider psychotherapy community who have supported my vision, and I particularly thank dear fellow researchers.

I thank Karen Minikin, Dwight Turner, and Anton Hart for their radical wisdom and for their endorsement of this book, and Keith Tudor and Helen Rowland for continuing the radical vision and encouraging me to centre the political in my writing.

I offer my gratitude to William Cornell for the opportunity to feature in the Innovations Series and for his deep challenges and critical thinking.

I express my deepest gratitude to Ali Bird for her wisdom, generous support, and encouragement in actualising this book.

I end by expressing my profound gratitude to my lifelong partner Catherine and our daughters Eliza and Amelia, for their love, support, and continuous belief in me. I thank my sister Julia for her love and political allyship in challenging the establishment. And my late parents for their encouragement always and knowing how deeply proud they would be.

Chapter 1

Introduction

The journey

I am she/her, cis woman, White, British, Northerner, East Londoner, from the Midlands, 'The Potteries', from a lineage of miners, brought up heterosexual, lesbian, Queer, working class in my DNA, middle class in lifestyle, civil partner, mother, daughter, sister, Methodist, of Irish and Catholic heritage, neurotypical, probably neurodiverse, able-bodied, recently disabled, middle aged, artist, political, activist. An ancestral warrior? – I like to think so – I am Celtic, Norwegian, Viking, French, Basque, Norman. I am all of these and none of these social configurations of being human. I change as my contexts change, while bringing some identities to the fore and sending others into hiding.

These many selves I call the transcultural self, the self that has journeyed for generations before us. The self, holding many cultural and social contexts – presently, historically and ancestrally, held in our DNA, in our bodies and psyche. The self whose ancestors have journeyed across lands, changing and evolving, identifying and being identified, through the social and political constructs of the time.

Some of these identities afford me privilege and others are oppressed. In each moment, I experience a configuration of my unique identity, these shift and change as they overlap in changing contexts. My Whiteness affords me power, constructed by racism and created by White supremacy generations before me. Yet my overlapping intersect of being Queer and working class in my DNA, brings to the fore my oppression.

For all of us these transcultural selves, creating multiple privilege and multiple marginalisation, are played out in the consulting, education, ecological and organisational contexts. As transactional analysts, as we become aware of our intersectional identities, and understand the intersection and internalisation of the discriminatory systems in which we reside, we further the action and release of autonomy both for ourselves and within our relationships with clients, students and colleagues.

I begin this book, then, with profound gratitude to Eric Berne and our ancestors, the transactional analysts, the psychotherapists, and the soul healers precolonisation, the visionaries, the artists and the poets, and the activists.

While honouring what has come before, this book looks to challenge the status quo within transactional analysis and psychotherapy, calling for critical examination

DOI: 10.4324/9781003509424-1

of normative constructs, and the deconstruction and reconstruction of theory and practice through an intersectional lens. It aims to take us back to our radical roots, making transactional analysis current and relevant for the 21st century. It is framed by cultural, social, political, and historical contexts, accounting for systemic oppression and challenging supremacies.

It is also deeply personal. I am mid-way through a journey, one of embodied social, cultural and political self discovery, a journey begun generations before me. A journey of my lived experience – and of being witness to others' journeying through systems and contexts – with the profound desire to connect and belong with self, other, the more-than-human and the planet.

Being deeply personal, I bring with it humility, a knowing and a not knowing, a willingness to cast aside certainty and arrival. I do not profess to be an expert, or to further centre my Whiteness, or even take up a position of allyship to those who are not seeking it. I do not wish to lecture with my passionate words. I wish to lay down my defence and keep my integrity intact. The activism in writing this book emerges from somatic noticing, my discomfort, my grief and my rage, my noticing of the stark exclusion of those who are marginalised.

And so this book is born out of both my privilege in being afforded belonging in the psychotherapy profession and transactional analyst community in my Whiteness, and emerges from my experience of being othered and seeking safety with marginalised peers. It is a journeying together, an embodied experience of living into, an experiencing through an intersectional lens, from the ground up, an emergent process, a sensibility. A walking down the road less travelled… a decolonising process, a questioning and a wondering, a deep disturbance in the harm caused by normative structures.

The aim here is to amplify voices of the marginalised and account for the multi-complexity of intersectional power dynamics in self and with other. Reflecting on the idea that all oppression is connected, the call to move from the 'I' to the 'we', from the individual to the collective – change is in order to challenge the greatest trauma of all time, our dying planet, intersected with social injustice and racial injustice.

Largely, themes of difference have not been accounted for in our theories and practice. Since the killing of George Floyd there has been an increase in the marginalised writing their stories, and therapists of colour coming together to address themes of harm on therapy courses and in consulting rooms. And yet, as a community we have not been used to having dialogue around themes of race and other intersectional difference. Too often there is fear of engaging in the dialogue.

This book goes some way in offering insight into the practice of radically open and non-defended dialogue (Hart, 2017), through curiosity, aiming to raise social responsibility and accountability in our profession.

I am writing this introduction just as Donald Trump has been in office for a few months; we are seeing a surge in right wing politics mirrored across nations, and witnessing catastrophic splits and genocidal violence in parts of the world. There is a risk that this book joins one side of the split – instead, I invite curiosity around the systems we are each born into, the role we each play, and ultimately the responsibility we hold as transactional analysts and psychotherapists to strive for equity and equality.

I am aware of my use of language through the book, the terms I am choosing to use, and the risk of language alienating the reader, or being weaponised in some way. Alongside intersectionality, deconstruction and reconstruction, I will be using words like supremacy and colonisation – the control of one power over other people; and decolonisation – the process of relinquishing control and supremacy, when one way of being is seen as superior.

These words can invite defence. Instead, I invite an exploration of language, an opening up of the complicated relationship we have within systems of power and marginalisation. Moving away from blaming and shaming and inviting an acknowledgement of what is, owning where we sit in the systemic, where there is a possibility of connection and a shared desire to challenge, and to consider what we can collectively do about it.

I invite an openness in reading this book.

And, in this vein of openness, I would like to share a profound awakening I experienced earlier this year.

Some months ago I was invited to belong to a closed WhatsApp reading group reflecting on *Decolonizing Therapy* by Jennifer Mullan (2023).

Mullan begins with, 'My dear colonised therapists'.

When I started to read it I felt disturbed, uncomfortable. I somehow could not tune in. I wasn't able to take in the words. I reverted to the WhatsApp group to shed some light, I became more aware of some members' discomfort with 'White' presence in the group and I decided this was not the space for me to work through my discomfort. I knew it was my responsibility to engage in my intersectional work. Somehow my bodily rhythm was out of sync. I intuitively decided to lie down, to switch to audio, rather than reading, and it was only then that the book made sense to me, that I could truly take in the challenge. In lying down, I surrendered my defences. I allowed in a different experience, different voices. The voice of the colonised. I keenly felt the intersect of my Whiteness, I resisted, and in each breath, I allowed myself to free associate: Whiteness, coloniser, violence, colonised, rage; maybe I allowed the spirit to move me, though would I prefer to say an 'unconscious emerging' – so flowing between colonised and decolonised as I write this. These were the beginnings of my free associations: some out there (systemic oppression); some back then (ancestral); some in here now (systemic enactment) (Chinnock, 2011; Jacobs, 1988; Menninger, 1958).

I experienced a deeper understanding, held in my body – the onslaught of colonisation. I recognised my difference. I profoundly experienced the responsibility I held as the coloniser, and I knew, in my body, in my ancestry, my experience of being colonised. I began to connect more deeply with my pain of disconnection.

So what does it actually mean to decolonise the transactional analysis curriculum – including creating spaces, inviting dialogue among 'all members', imagining and envisioning all intersectional identities – and further knowledge of all systems with respect to what is being taught and how it frames the world?

Decolonising is integral to an inclusive curriculum, and seeks to both recognise and address the legacies of disadvantage, injustice and racism that have arisen from historic global domination and the consequent inherent 'Whiteness'. And here, I also include ideas around the construct of Whiteness colonising itself – through the supremacies of religion, patriarchy, heteronormativity, the binary gender and capitalism.

Eric Berne was born on May 10, 1910, in Montreal, Quebec, Canada, as Eric Lennard Bernstein. The family immigrated to Canada from Poland and Russia. Berne came to the United States in 1935 when he began his internship at Englewood Hospital in New Jersey. After completing his one-year internship in 1936, he began his psychiatric residency at the Psychiatric Clinic of Yale University School of Medicine, where he worked for two years. In 1939, Berne became an American citizen and shortened his name from Eric Lennard Bernstein to Eric Berne.

While it is not possible to talk to Berne/Bernstein. I want to honour all those who have had to colonise their own names in order to fit in. 'Call me by my name' is a chapter in *Therapists Challenging Racism and Oppression* (Zahid & Cooke, 2023), written by Anita Gaspar, a British cis woman of South Asian origin, who tells her story of being misnamed and consequently misidentified as both a student and educator in psychotherapy.

Certainly, I have experienced countless times, racially marginalised and non-White, or 'White other' students and colleagues shortening their names, or replacing their names, in order to 'make their name easier to pronounce' for the normative group. This in itself is an act of colonisation, of being colonised, in order to assimilate, as a way of staying OK in the normative context. It is survivorship, a way of placating power in order to stay safe and belong. When pursuing what name student colleagues may prefer, almost inevitably the person wishes for the group to use their birth name, usually congruent with heritage. Just as Trans people re-name themselves congruent with the gender they are, we must strive to honour each individual's unique identity.

If Berne were alive today, I wonder what he would have to say about the shortening of his own name from Eric Bernstein to Eric Berne. We will never know. I like to imagine, if alive today, Eric Berne would continue to think outside the box, furthering his radical edge, informed by his marginalised lived experience and position of privilege.

The chapters in this book aim to further the ideas of Berne, developing theoretical ideas in line with our current world, accounting for difference, decentralising normative ideas and opening up possibilities for wider and further inclusion, representative of the diverse communities in which we reside. And, ultimately, to invite in all intersectional voices within ourselves, with each other, in our education settings, in our consulting rooms and in our organisations across all fields of transactional analysis.

Deconstruction and reconstruction of theory and practice through an intersectional lens (see Chapter 5) has evolved from the multi-diverse TA East London community – we have taken the journey together (see Chapter 3). Intersectional theory has been born from discussion and dialogue, from the ground up, asking: Who is represented in this theory? How may we develop this diagram to include all identities in the room? What is the lived experience here? Too often the transactional analysis diagrams and theories have excluded and 'othered' many in the room.

The 'Transcultural and Intersectional Ego State Model of the Self' was published in the *Transactional Analysis Journal*, 2022 (Baskerville, 2022). The article has been read nearly 8000 times to date, demonstrating a thirst, a need, and a readiness to attend to intersectional dynamics in self and other, within transactional analysis theory, process and practice. Here (Chapter 4), the Transcultural and Intersectional Ego State Model article is revised offering a 2025 update, reflecting on and accounting for changing social, cultural and political constructs and intersectional identity.

All theory is considered within the context of systemic oppression (Chapter 6), offering a cultural sensitivity to our hypotheses, and bringing an awareness that normative structures continue to influence diagnosis. Diagnoses have reflected social, cultural and political contexts of the time, hand in hand with laws and policy making, and consequently pathologised the racially marginalised, along with the Queer community, and the neurodivergent community – who have also experienced being educated and harmed through normative systems.

Relational transactional analysis (Chapter 7) is considered through a systemic lens, using the Transcultural and Intersectional Ego State Model to explain relational power dynamics and systemic enactment. While the continued practice of radical openness and non-defended dialogue (Hart, 2017) (Chapter 8) enables a profound accounting for the difference between us, a 'living into' the action of intersectional transactional analysis.

Throughout the book activists sit amongst us – Baldwin, Chin, Ellis, Hart, hooks, Lorde, Minikin, Mullan, Rich, Thomas, Turner, Vaid-Menon, among others – calling out to our marginalised selves, inviting in, pleading to the multi-privileged to own their part. The lived experience of activists and the role of activism (Chapter 9) serves to offer a frame for developing contemporary intersectional theory, while accounting for the personal and the political. The personal and political fight in challenging normative social constructs is illustrated by James Baldwin's (1962) quote: 'Not everything that is faced can be changed, but nothing can be changed until it is faced'. It is a quote I have used repeatedly in inviting dialogue around difference and daring to challenge those holding power in the room.

UKCP research (Ahmed et al., 2023; Baskerville, 2023) into exclusivity and inclusivity in training is republished (Chapter 10) focusing on the student experience, and is evidenced rationale for educators to engage in their intersectional work. While excerpts from published interviews and dialogues undertaken with the author over the past five years (Chapter 11) serve to amplify a wide breadth of intersectional voices, including those of students.

And finally, addressing in many ways our greatest challenge of all, the climate crisis (Chapter 12), I look at our urgent task, as transactional analysts, to fully embrace the eco-systemic, by attending to the vital intersection of climate, racial and social injustice.

Deconstructing theory and practice begins with the mind of the practitioner. Decolonising the mind of the practitioner/educator/tutor/psychotherapist/supervisor or student colleagues is in itself complex, as, when we bring the lens of the transcultural and intersectional self, we see that we embody both the coloniser and the colonised. It is often student colleagues and those recently qualified who are ready to take the journey, while long-experienced practitioners can be more deeply entrenched in 'colonised' thinking.

Ultimately, we all have experienced being othered to a lesser or greater degree in our roles as practitioners, as clients, as educators and as students. And so this book is a journeying of deconstruction and reconstruction, inviting awareness of self, the coloniser, and the process of decolonisation.

I end with deep gratitude to all who have walked with me and allowed me to walk with them. I hope that this book will go some way in continuing the journey and envisioning transactional analysis through an intersectional lens, of deconstructing and reconstructing theory and practice, and ultimately decolonising transactional analysis. While accounting for my own personal journey of 25 years working as a relational transactional analyst psychotherapist, I now look forward to seeing the changing face of transactional analysis as it grows to embrace all intersectional difference.

And it will always be a continuing journey, in the certain knowledge that once I think I have arrived I have lost my way.

> We are now faced with the fact that tomorrow is today. We are confronted with the fierce urgency of now. In this unfolding conundrum of life and history, there is such a thing as being too late. This is no time for apathy or complacency. This is a time for vigorous and positive action.
>
> (Martin Luther King, 1963)

References

Ahmed, N., Baskerville, V., Neish, G., & Nelson, V. (2023). UKCP research project final report: Inclusivity and exclusivity in training – The trainees' experience. *The Transactional Analyst*, 13(1), Winter.

Baldwin, J. (1962). Quote from *New York Times,* Jan 14, 1962.

Baskerville, V. (2022). A transcultural and intersectional ego state model of the self: The influence of transcultural and intersectional identity on self and other. *Transactional Analysis Journal, 52*(32), 1–16. http://doi.org/10.1080/03621537.2022.2076398

Baskerville, V. (2023). 'The unseen: How many trainees are feeling left out?' *The New Psychotherapist*, UKCP Magazine, issue 83, Summer 2023.

Chinnock, K. (2011). Relational transactional analysis supervision. *Transactional Analysis Journal, 41*(4), 336–350. https://doi.org/10.1177/036215371104100410

Hart, A. (2017). From multicultural competence to radical openness: A psychoanalytic engagement of otherness. *The American Psychoanalyst, 51*(1), 12–13, 26–27. https://apsa.org/wp-content/uploads/apsaa-publications/vol51no1-TOC/html/vol51no1_09.xhtml

Jacobs, M. (1988). *Psychodynamic counselling in action*. London: Sage.

King, M. L. (1963). Excerpt 'I had a dream speech'. Washington DC.

Menninger, K. (1958). *Theory of psychoanalytic technique*. New York: Basic Books.

Mullan, J. (2023). *Decolonizing therapy – Oppression, historical trauma, and politicizing your practice*. New York: W.W. Norton & Co.

Zahid, N., & Cooke, R. (Eds.) (2023). *Therapists challenging racism and oppression – The unheard voices*. Monmouth UK: PCCS.

Chapter 2

What is transactional analysis through an intersectional lens?

'Intersectionality's focus on social inequality has its roots and development in social justice research and struggle. As an activist project, intersectionality provides analytical tools for framing social justice issues in such a way as to expose how social exclusion or privilege occurs differently in various social positions, and it does this by focusing on the interaction of multiple systems of oppression'.

(Romero, 2018, p. 1)

Transactional analysis has its roots in social psychiatry and social psychology. Intersectionality furthers this social justice vision bringing transactional analysis into the 21st century, in many ways as an act of activism, forging change for individuals, the collective, and the planet. Research has shown that the inclusion of systems of power and social location are central to the understanding of social interactions between individuals in society (Romero, 2018). Arguably, intersectionality brings another much needed lens to transactional analysis seeing the interconnected nature of the self within multiple systems of oppression and privilege. It thereby challenges normative theories and practice – theories which serve to keep the status quo of supremacies and which, in turn, risk entrenching pathology in those who are marginalised. An intersectional lens requires us to open up our hearts and minds around all difference.

I consider perspectives on the question: What is transactional analysis with an intersectional lens? What is the embodiment of intersectionality through the being of transactional analysis? Am I really calling for 'Intersectional Transactional Analysis', or is this just a play on words? And yet, it has been a significant process and journey for me, beginning with the idea of this lens bringing a sharp focus on intersectionality through the process, theory, and practice of transactional analysis. In this, I realised that the focus on intersectionality meant that I was called to do more work on myself, to examine my intersectional lived experience closely and the part I play within systemic racism and oppression. As time has passed, I started to embody intersectionality through every aspect of transactional analysis, now seeing myself as an intersectional transactional analyst or indeed an intersectional psychotherapist.

DOI: 10.4324/9781003509424-2

When putting forward the proposal for this book, I named it 'Intersectional Transactional Analysis'. I was asked if I was proposing a new school within transactional analysis. My first internal response was yes, how can contemporary transactional analysis exist without intersectionality, indeed any therapeutic practice? However, intersectionality cannot be cordoned off as one school of thought. Intersectionality needs to be considered across all schools of transactional analysis be it Classical, Cathexis, Redecision, and Integrative, and indeed across education, organisational, counselling, and psychotherapy fields.

I remember a conversation in the early days of relational TA saying that relational TA could not be packaged in a baked bean tin and that relational TA would mean different things to each practitioner. Thus, transactional analysis with an intersectional lens spans all the schools, theoretical frameworks, fields, and practice. I invite the questions – each time we meet theory, each time we reflect on process, each time we are in a therapeutic dyad, a supervision relationship, a counselling/educational consultation, or an exam process – where is the intersectionality in this? How are we accounting for difference here? Who does this theory/process serve? What is the unconscious bias in this? Where does the privilege and power sit? What parts of self and other are being oppressed? What is being enacted in this intersectional dyad or this organisational setting? What would intersectional radical dialogue look like? Indeed, whose voices are represented in this theory both human and more-than-human (Abram, 1996), in all living beings, in this process, in this relationship? Fundamentally, is a hierarchy of oppression being played out here? The answer is probably yes, as we reside in systems of power and live within many supremacies (Turner, 2023).

Contemporary transactional analysis is called to address social justice themes around power, privilege, and systemic racism and oppression, being congruent with the values and ethics of transactional analysis illustrated in our new common mission statement (EATA-ITAA, 2024). Indeed, this statement sits empty unless we truly address these themes and authentically position intersectionality as an ethical consideration.

Bondi and Fewell (2017) describe the impossibility of separating our personal and political selves in counselling relationships. Beetham (2019) says: 'Intersectional work can be defined as an intentional effort to directly examine the social structures of which we ourselves are part, and it is hard work. Embracing the complexity of privilege, vulnerability, difference and "otherness" is not straightforward. But, as practitioners in a relational profession, I would argue that we cannot avoid reflecting on the social structures that influence and inform how we inhabit and work through these very relationships with our clients and colleagues' (p. 1).

Crenshaw first coined the idea of intersectionality in 1989. In her paper 'Demarginalizing the Intersection of Race and Sex' (Crenshaw, 1989), she defined intersectionality as 'The interconnected nature of social categorizations such as race, class, gender, regarded as creating overlapping, interdependent systems of discrimination or disadvantage'. She acknowledges that intersectionality was a lived experience long before it became a term, powerfully illustrated in the works of activist and

Black, lesbian, scholar and poet Audre Lorde, drawing on her 'concert of voices' alongside hooks, Rich, Baldwin, and other prominent activists (see Chapter 9 for more on the role of activism). 'Lorde not only challenged her contemporaries to think about identity and politics and intersectionality, but also challenged them to value the inner emotional landscape as a core resource in the work of liberation' (Smith, 2021). So, furthering the action and release of autonomy through understanding the internalisation of the discriminatory systems in which we reside.

Crenshaw (2019) says that through an awareness of intersectionality, we can better acknowledge and ground the differences among us, taking account of overlapping identities and experiences, highlighting where cultural selves intersect, and providing a framework with which to assess levels of discrimination. Thus, 'Intersectionality is a lens through which you can see where power comes and collides, where it interlocks and intersects. It's not simply that there's a race problem here, a gender problem here, and a class or LGBTQ problem there. Often that framework erases what happens to people who are subject to all these things' (Crenshaw, 2019, p. 16). Hence, we cannot separate the personal from the political, or the self from the intersectional self.

A colleague voiced her concerns that if focus was on intersectionality in the consulting room, then there would be a loss of personal themes/issues. I would argue they are inseparable; the personal sits within the intersectional experience. An intersectional lens brings the acknowledgement that there is another dimension alive in the room. Consider, for example, a client who presents with a 'Don't be you' injunction passed down from parents and parent figures and cultural introjects – they will inevitably have been influenced by generations of cultural, social, and political contexts and degrees of power and supremacy.

Using myself as an example, I presented with a 'Don't be you' injunction in therapy at 23 years old. In this process, and in transactional analysis training, I quickly learnt this message was received unconsciously from my parents, as early as being in the womb or at the time of conception. Indeed, I drew it many times on my script matrix. It seemed so plausible. My mother and father passed the message on, just as their parents had to them, and I received it and turned it into a belief. However, my family and my ancestors did not live in a vacuum.

Both my parents came from a working-class upbringing; their fathers and grandfathers were miners, they both revered and resented the middle class, they were the underdogs, they knew their place, and it took tremendous determination to stray from their intersectional positioning. Consequently, a 'Don't be you' injunction can be tracked through ancestry: generations of systemic oppression and systemic positioning. Additionally, there will be many other systemic influences beyond class that would have furthered my injunction 'Don't be you', including my history of having to kill off my Irish and Catholic heritage and growing up lesbian at a time when Queer people were not allowed to exist within the law. Script is borne from all who walked before us. Furthering the ideas of counterinjunction – you can exist as long as you are not too Queer, too Black (Turner, 2021) – and adhering to the powers of the colonisers, those with control and power, creating, and upholding all normative ways of being in the world. Arguably, my Whiteness brought a 'you can be you', and yet the shadow of class and history offered another dimension, as did my other intersects, changing through the journey of time and context (Jusik, 2022).

Contemporary transactional analysis with an intersectional lens serves to deconstruct and decolonise our theories and practice by inviting in all voices, identities, and experiences in the world; opening the possibility of attending to multiple oppression, as in marginalised selves, and the impact of multiple privilege on the development of self. When considering our work as practitioners and educators, I embrace Turner's (2021) ideas on privilege and oppression – he cites privilege as having its part in constructing otherness.

As a White practitioner and educator, I have become aware of the impact and the power of my systemic Whiteness and the part I play in creating otherness. I am aware and notice the palpable exclusion of people of colour in White groups. I notice the impact of Whiteness when theories saturated in Whiteness only offer one lens on how to be in the world; a lens rooted in colonisation, so entrenched that Whiteness doesn't see 'it' or does not want to. Whiteness is constructed as holding power alongside other systems of supremacies, set up to exclude and override others. To belong to one of these privileged groups as a TA practitioner brings responsibility and humility, and an awareness of the profound impact of Whiteness on those who live in socially constructed racially marginalised intersects.

Alongside Whiteness and constructing otherness, I consider the transcultural and intersectional self; ideas on the pluralistic nature of intersectionality (Baskerville, 2022; Dhananjaya, 2022), that the oppressor and the oppressed co-exist. Aware that I am the oppressor in my Whiteness and yet oppressed and marginalised in my Queerness, as well as multiple other experiences of being both oppressed and the oppressor. Some, however, will hold multiple power, and it is these voices that hold court in our profession. And it is these privileged voices that hold responsibility in laying down and sharing power, as such there is an urgent need for marginalised lived experiences, stories, and wisdom to be represented in our theories, in our models, in our practice, and in the training room. (See Appendix 1, *ITAA's Intersectionality Focus Group Report*, Baskerville & Nelson, 2021b.)

The evolving of intersectionality was in response to Women's Studies and Critical Race Studies and the critique that White feminism has been elitist and excluding of women of colour, Black women, Queer women, working class women, and so on. Coleman wrote in *Time Magazine* (2019): 'During the 1970s, Black feminist scholar-activists, a number of whom were also LGBTQ, developed theoretical frameworks to serve as a model for other women of colour, to broaden feminism's definition and scope. Throughout the final decades of the 20th century and during the first decade of the 21st, women of colour published many groundbreaking works that highlighted these dynamics. In doing so, they exposed the interlocking systems that define women's lives'.

Fifty years on, and indeed three decades on from Crenshaw coining the term intersectionality, it is still being talked about, accepted as a truth among academics, activists, and is now seeping into counselling, psychotherapy, and transactional analysis. And there is a fear that the idea of intersectionality is becoming accommodated. There is a risk that courses will add intersectionality to the curriculum yet will continue to avoid challenging dialogue around power dynamics and systemic enactment (Baskerville & Douglas, 2021a). The journey and urgency of an intersectional lens will continue to grow as we face further alienation from ourselves, each other, and our planet (Minikin, 2023a).

We have much to learn from the global majority, much to learn around reconnecting with community and land. Thus, an intersectional lens challenges the White, northern hemisphere, patriarchal, colonised, capitalist, individualistic, and all things constructed as normative, to open up to all configurations of being human and 'more-than-human'. More-than-human, first coined by Abram (1996) and embodied by Marshall (2023), highlights that to be intersectional is to consider all aspects of being alive including our interaction with all organisms and living beings. As Isaacs (2020) says: 'More-than-human geographies (MTHG) trace the multiplicity of encounters and entangled relations between humans and non-human others. They explore different ways of sensing and conveying how the human is always "more-than-human," that is, "enmeshed" with other beings, elements, forces, and objects within dynamic assemblages' (p. 1).

Moreover, transactional analysis with an intersectional lens calls for profound self-examination, beyond decontamination, beyond deconfusion of the Child, beyond the realms of the therapeutic relationship, by furthering conscious awareness of social, political, cultural, and historical contexts which sit within us, between us, and collectively. And so, committing to intentionally taking a journey in researching our histories, knowing our cultural narrative, our transcultural journey (Baskerville, 2022), spanning generations (Klosin et al., 2017), in order to name our intersectional identity and to own our intersects of privilege and oppression and where we sit systemically – we become consciously aware of the intersectional map within us and how this intersects with and furthers oppression and supremacy (Collins & Bilge, 2020).

The intersectional self takes us away from the idea of monoculture (Baskerville, 2022) opening up and challenging the binary across identities. Taking us to the transgender dialogue where non-binary identity challenges all the binaries we sit within and between. This was articulated eloquently by a colleague who described their experience of dual heritage and their decision to identify as non-binary as a synthesis of expressing their sense of self. Indeed, Queer theory is a way of thinking and dismantling traditional assumptions about gender and sexual identities, seeing them as socially constructed concepts.

In Kliman's (2010) model 'Intersecting domains of privilege and marginalisation: locating oneself in a social matrix', she proposes that we can have more than 100 socially and culturally constructed identities and that they can change as we age and shift between constructs of oppression and privilege. Kliman introduces a visual tool to help students and professionals explore the influences of multiple, intersecting domains of social privilege and marginalisation in their personal and professional relationships. The model highlights overlooked or minimised differences in relative power and privilege in familial, therapeutic, and supervisory relationships, arousing curiosity about the effects of those differences. It is a consciousness-raising tool to inform students' clinical work, rather than an instrument to use directly with clients, and is intended to draw students' attention to how sharing different areas of relative privilege and marginalisation with each member of a client family can influence one's perceptions and actions with the family as a whole (Falicov, 1995; Hardy & Laszloffy, 2002; Kliman, 2005).

An intersectional lens brings more curiosity around the multi-complexity of difference within cultural constructs and relationships (Hart, 2017), and that radical openness and non-defended dialogue can facilitate making sense of and working through the complexity of difference and projected sameness. (See Appendix 2 for a dialogue illustrating the multi-complexity of difference and sameness.)

Theory and models

Transactional analysis with an intersectional lens brings the inclusion and examination of systemic oppression across all aspects of theoretical ideas and models. Arguably, all aspects of the self sit within and are formed in response to systemic constructs. Furthering the idea of the deconstruction and reconstruction of theory through an intersectional lens (Baskerville, 2023b), I have continued to develop a model (see Chapter 4) that serves to consider the theory, embedded in the social, cultural, and political contexts of the author, and at the time of writing. The invitation is to think creatively, outside of the normative, of colonisation, and to reconstruct as a decolonising process. Eric Berne began the process of deconstruction and reconstruction when he developed the theory and practice of transactional analysis. He wanted to make psychotherapy accessible and so deconstructed language, making concepts and ideas accessible to everyone. However, a man of his time influenced by western/northern hemisphere oppression, he was not immune to colonised influences in his theories, offering a patriarchal, heteronormative, and binary gendered lens.

Contemporary authors have brought in themes of oppression and offered theoretical models, and yet they still fall short of impacting 'mainstream' TA, wherein transactional analysis models, theory, and practice take account of systemic racism and oppression and the complexity of intersectional identity and power dynamics in the development of self in relationship.

Relationship and process

Transactional analysis with an intersectional lens is a relational approach which pays attention to, and accounts for, power and oppression in the dyad, or group, and the complex lived experience of privilege and marginalisation in both the practitioner/educator and the client/student, thus enabling attention to systemic enactment and the socially constructed transference of both parties. The practitioner, moreover, becomes aware of the impact of their power and marginalisation and what they may be projecting on to the client/s.

Without awareness, practitioners holding many intersectional privileges (for example, in the UK, White, heterosexual, middle class) may risk pathologising difference in clients who are multi-marginalised. This could be the outcome of the practitioners' unprocessed intersectional transference. I call it transference, or proactive countertransference, as a way for the practitioner to take ownership of what is out of awareness and unconsciously biased.

The action of processing and dialoging around themes of racism and difference has largely been kept outside of the consulting room. This was evidenced in UKCP research 'Inclusivity and exclusivity in training' (Ahmed et al., 2023; Baskerville, 2023a). Supporting this are the numerous emails I have received from students of colour and Trans students, talking about feeling they have to kill off parts of their identity in training and in the therapeutic relationship (Turner, 2021).

This is further reinforced by the American Psychoanalytic Association (2023) appointing The Holmes Commission to address systemic racism in psychoanalytic training resulting in an exposing and painful report.

'The Commission writes to you at this anxiety-laden time when our national psychoanalytic communities are roiled by experiences among us of race that many, but not all, consider to be painful illustrations of individual and systemic racism. Intense racial divisiveness threatens to devitalize and discredit psychoanalysis. The Executive Summary speaks forcefully to the leadership that is needed in psychoanalysis currently and urgently to help our discipline move forward to achieve racial and other equities across the various dimensions of intersectionality'.

An example of this is when students working on their written exam start to consider that their own cultural and racial contexts and those of their clients may not be understood. Too often I have witnessed students and practitioners who hold more marginalisation in themselves, or who work with multi-marginalised groups, adapting to protect themselves in their writing, or when presenting to a multi-privileged exam board. For example, when a Queer practitioner presents their work with a Trans client, who may be non-binary, in a polygamous relationship, and fears that the marker/s or the exam board may not have lived experience or knowledge and understanding in this area. Or a student of colour is faced with an all White exam board and no attention is paid to systemic power.

An intersectional lens requires us to open up our hearts and minds around all difference, and to consider the real impact of multi-privileged power. It brings an analytical lens to challenge complex social inequalities at the nexus of multiple systems of oppression and privilege and requires the practitioner to partake in the intersectional work on themselves, to work through their systemically driven and unconsciously biased beliefs.

Conclusion

An intersectional lens enables the deconstruction of the White normative construct of transactional analysis and psychotherapy theory and practice.

The development of life script has largely focused on individuals receiving conscious and unconscious messages from parent and parent figures resulting in individuals making life decisions. Cultural script has often been seen as an overlay of messages from the wider culture, usually a monoculture. Drego (1983) identified ways of doing, being, and behaving in particular cultures. Shivanath and Hiremath (2003) developed the cultural self within the context of the psychodynamics of race and the wider White society. Tudor and Summers (2000) went some way to address multiple intersectional selves in their helix model. Hargaden and Sills (2002) developed two diagrams that account for the development and significance of culture on the self and in the therapeutic relationship. The *Transactional Analysis Journal* in 2022, made a call to address the self within systemic oppression; and prolific writers have over decades brought a political lens to transactional analysis, including Batts (1982, 1983), Cornell (2018, 2024), Minikin (2018, 2021, 2023a, 2023b, 2024), Minikin and Rowland (2022), Naughton and Tudor (2006), Rowland and Cornell (2021), Shadbolt (2009, 2017, 2018, 2022), Tudor (2016), Tudor et al. (2022), among others.

An intersectional lens accounts for lived experience and invites all voices, all cultural and social selves, in self, in other, and in the collective. As a result, the development of self, injunctions, and the formation of life script, life positions, structural analysis, transactional analysis proper, transference, and games must be viewed through an intersectional relational systemic lens. This takes forward the ideas of transcultural narrative; intersectional identity, dynamics and enactment; influence of the binary, Queer theory and social constructs; and ultimately the deconstruction and reconstruction of transactional analysis through the practice of radical openness and non-defended dialogue.

The intersectional practitioner enables the recovery of fragmented individuals alienated from community, by repositioning power, and forging collective vision and responsibility. Taking forward Berne's ideas of autonomy, as a vision of collective autonomy, afforded to all configurations of being human, more-than-human, and indeed our planet. As Smith (2021) states: 'Lorde (1983) extended this argument in her essay "There is no hierarchy of oppression" where she insisted that it is impossible to gain a meaningful picture of the life of a person by isolating a single dimension of their identity (e.g., only their gender) and then agitate for a wholesale transformation of their life and the world without regard for the other dimensions of identity that shape one's social experience'.

The self cannot be separated from social, cultural, political, and historical lived experience: the self is the intersectional self.

References

Abram, D. (1996). *The spell of the sensuous: Perception and language in a more-than-human world.* London: Penguin Random House.

Ahmed, N., Baskerville, V., Neish, G., & Nelson, V. (2023). UKCP research project final report: Inclusivity and exclusivity in training – The trainees' experience. *The Transactional Analyst, 13*(1), Winter 2022/23.

American Psychoanalytic Association (2023). The Holmes Commission on Racial Equality in American Psychoanalysis. https://apsa.org/wp-content/uploads/2023/06/Holmes-Commission-Final-Report-2023-Report-rv6-19-23.pdf?ver

Baskerville, V. (2022). A transcultural and intersectional ego state model of the self: The influence of transcultural and intersectional identity on self and other. *Transactional Analysis Journal, 52*(32), 1–16. http://doi.org/10.1080/03621537.2022.2076398

Baskerville, V. (2023a). 'The unseen: How many trainees are feeling left out?' *The New Psychotherapist*, UKCP Magazine, issue 83, Summer 2023.

Baskerville, V. (2023b). Looking at theory: Deconstructing and reconstructing the curriculum. *The Transactional Analyst, 13*(2), Spring 2023.

Baskerville, V., & Douglas, M. (2021a). Intersectionality in TA training. *ITAA The Script* 2021-04. https://membersarea.itaaworld.com/sites/default/files/itaa-pdfs/the-script/script-2021/ITAA%20The%20Script%202021-04.pdf

Baskerville, V., & Nelson, S. (2021b). Intersectionality focus group report. *ITAA The Script* 2021-07. https://membersarea.itaaworld.com/sites/default/files/itaa-pdfs/the-script/script-2021/ITAA%20The%20Script%202021-07.pdf

Batts, V. A. (1982). Modern racism: A TA perspective. *Transactional Analysis Journal, 12*(3), 207–209. https://doi.org/10.1177/036215378201200309

Batts, V. A. (1983). Knowing and changing the cultural script component of racism. *Transactional Analysis Journal, 13*(4), 255–257. https://doi.org/10.1177/036215378301300416

Beetham, T. (2019). Intersectionality and social justice. *Therapy Today, 30*(3), 1.

Bondi, L., & Fewell, J. (2017). Getting personal: A feminist argument for research aligned to therapeutic practice. *Counselling and Psychotherapy Research, 17*(2), 113–122.

Coleman, A. L. (2019). What's intersectionality? Let these scholars explain the theory and its history. *Time Magazine*. March 28, 2019 (updated March 29, 2019) https://time.com/5560575/intersectionality-theory/

Collins, P., & Bilge, S. (2020). *Intersectionality*. Cambridge, UK: Polity Press.

Cornell, W. F. (2018). If it is not for all, it is not for us: Reflections on racism, nationalism, and populism in the United States. *Transactional Analysis Journal, 48*(2), 97–110. https://doi.org/10.1080/03621537.2018.1431460

Cornell, W. F. (2024). In these dark times: Exploring our values as transactional analysts. *Transactional Analysis Journal, 54*(2), 114–125. https://doi.org/10.1080/03621537.2024.2327266

Crenshaw, K. (1989). Demarginalizing the intersection of race and sex: A Black feminist critique of antidiscrimination doctrine, feminist theory and antiracist politics. *University of Chicago Legal Forum*, Issue 1, Article 8. https://scholarship.law.columbia.edu/faculty_scholarship/3007

Crenshaw, K. (2019). 'Reach everyone on the planet': Kimberlé Crenshaw and intersectionality (Gunda Werner Institute in the Heinrich Böll Foundation and the Centre for Intersectional Justice, Eds.) https://eu.boell.org/en/2019/04/28/reach-everyone-planet-kimberle-crenshaw-and-intersectionality

Dhananjaya, D. (2022). We are the oppressor and the oppressed: The interplay between intrapsychic, interpersonal, and societal intersectionality. *Transactional Analysis Journal, 52*(3), 244–258. https://doi.org/10.1080/03621537.2022.2082031

Drego, P. (1983). The cultural parent. *Transactional Analysis Journal*, *13*(4), 224–227. https://doi.org/10.1177/036215378301300404

EATA-ITAA (2024). Joint Common Mission Statement. https://eatanews.org/eata-itaa-common-mission-statement/

Falicov, C. (1995). Training to think culturally: A multidimensional comparative framework. *Family Process*, *34*, 373–388. https://doi.org/10.1111/j.1545-5300.1995.00373.x

Hardy, K. V., & Laszloffy, T. (2002). Couple therapy using a multicultural perspective. In A. S. Gurman & N. Jacobson (Eds.), *Clinical handbook of couple therapy* (3rd ed., pp. 569–593). New York: Guilford Press.

Hargaden, H., & Sills, C. (2002). *Transactional analysis: A relational perspective*. East Sussex: Brunner-Routledge.

Hart, A. (2017). From multicultural competence to radical openness: A psychoanalytic engagement of otherness. *The American Psychoanalyst*, *51*(1), 12–13, 26–27. https://apsa.org/wp-content/uploads/apsaa-publications/vol51no1-TOC/html/vol51no1_09.xhtml

Isaacs, R. (2020). *More-than-human geographies*. Wiley Online Library. https://doi.org/10.1002/9781118786352.wbieg2041

Jusik, P. (2022). Systemic oppression and cultural diversity: Putting flesh on the bones of intercultural competence. *Transactional Analysis Journal*, *52*(3), 209–227. https://doi.org/10.1080/03621537.2022.2076981

Kliman, J. (2005). Many differences, many voices: Toward social justice in family therapy. In M. P. Mirkin, K. Suyemoto, & B. Okun (Eds.), *Psychotherapy with women: Exploring diverse contexts and identities*. New York: Guilford.

Kliman, J. (2010). Intersections of social privilege and marginalization: A visual teaching tool. In *Expanding our social justice practices: Advances in theory and training* (vol. 6, pp. 39–48) [special issue]. Monograph Series. AFTA (American Family Therapy Academy).

Klosin, A., Casas, E., Hidalgo-Carcedo, C., Vavouri, T., & Lehner, B. (2017). Transgenerational transmission of environmental information in *C. elegans*. *Science*, *356*(6335), 320–323. https://pubmed.ncbi.nlm.nih.gov/28428426

Lorde, A. (1983). There is no hierarchy of oppressions. *Bulletin: Homophobia and education*. Council on Interracial Books for Children.

Marshall, H. (2023). A place for the ecological third: Eco-TA in therapeutic practice. *Transactional Analysis Journal*, *53*(1), 93–108. https://doi.org/10.1080/03621537.2023.2152567

Minikin, K. (2018). Radical relational psychiatry: Toward a democracy of mind and people. *Transactional Analysis Journal*, *48*(2), 111–125. https://doi.org/10.1080/03621537.2018.1429287

Minikin, K. (2021). Relative privilege and the seduction of normativity. *Transactional Analysis Journal*, *51*(1), 35–48. https://doi.org/10.1080/03621537.2020.1853349

Minikin, K. (2023a). *Radical-relational perspectives in transactional analysis psychotherapy: Oppression, alienation, reclamation*. London: Routledge.

Minikin, K. (2023b). Commentary on "War: A transactional group analysis" by Keith Tudor. *Transactional Analysis Journal*, *53*(4), 323–327. https://doi.org/10.1080/03621537.2023.2251841

Minikin, K. (2024). The personal and the political. *Transactional Analysis Journal*, *54*(2), 126–135. https://doi.org/10.1080/03621537.2024.2323870

Minikin, K., & Rowland, H. (2022). Letter from the coeditors: Systemic oppression: What part do we play? *Transactional Analysis Journal*, *52*(3), 175–177. https://doi.org/10.1080/03621537.2022.2080263

Naughton, M., & Tudor, K. (2006). Being white. *Transactional Analysis Journal*, *36*(2), 159–171. https://doi.org/10.1177/036215370603600208

Romero, M. (2018). *Introducing intersectionality*. Cambridge, UK: Polity Press.

Rowland, H., & Cornell, W. F. (2021). Gender identity, queer theory, and working with the sociopolitical in counseling and psychotherapy: Why there is no such thing as neutral. *Transactional Analysis Journal*, *51*(1), 19–34. https://doi.org/10.1080/03621537.2020. 1853347

Shadbolt, C. (2009). Sexuality and shame. *Transactional Analysis Journal*, *39*(2), 163–172. https://doi.org/10.1177/036215370903900210

Shadbolt, C. (2017). Dancing in a different country: When the personal is professional. *Transactional Analysis Journal*, *47*(4), 264–275. https://doi.org/10.1177/0362153717719030

Shadbolt, C. (2018). The sorrow of ghosts: The emergence of a traumatized parent ego state. *Transactional Analysis Journal*, *48*(4), 293–307. https://doi.org/10.1080/03621537. 2018.1505127

Shadbolt, C. (2022). The many faces of systemic oppression, power, and privilege: The necessity of self-examination. *Transactional Analysis Journal*, *52*(3), 259–273. https://doi. org/10.1080/03621537.2022.2076411

Shivanath, S., & Hiremath, M. (2003). The psychodynamics of race and culture. In C. Sills & H. Hargaden (Eds.), *Ego states (key concepts in transactional analysis: Contemporary views)* (pp. 169–184). Worcester: Worth Publishing.

Smith, K. (2021). Exploring Audre Lorde's intersectionality https://www.facinghistory.org/ ideas-week/exploring-audre-lordes-intersectionality

Tudor, K. (2016). "We are": The fundamental life position. *Transactional Analysis Journal*, *46*(2), 164–176. https://doi.org/10.1177/0362153716637064

Tudor, K., Green, E., & Brett, E. (2022). Critical whiteness: A transactional analysis of a systemic oppression. *Transactional Analysis Journal*, *52*(3), 193–208. https://doi.org/10. 1080/03621537.2022.2076394

Tudor, K., & Summers, G. (2000). Co-creative transactional analysis. *Transactional Analysis Journal*, *30*(1), 23–40. https://doi.org/10.1177/036215370003000104

Turner, D. (2021). *Intersections of privilege and otherness in counselling and psychotherapy*. London: Routledge.

Turner, D. (2023). *The psychology of supremacy: Imperium*. London: Routledge.

Chapter 3

Evolving an inclusive training

The process of deconstructing and decolonising through an intersectional lens

This chapter offers a two-part story of the evolving of an inclusive transactional analysis and psychotherapy training, and its challenges: from social justice ideas to embodying intersectionality through the veins of process, theory, and practice.

Part one, 'Evolving an inclusive training, sharing some of the journey to establish TA East London Institute holding social justice in every aspect of its being', was originally published in the UKATA publication, *The Transactional Analyst*, (Baskerville, 2021), two years on from TA East London's foundation in January 2019.

Part two tells the story of TA East six years on, addressing the vast challenges and deep learnings in the embodiment of intersectionality through the veins of training.

Reflecting on themes of multi-marginalisation; privilege; the changing social and political contexts; the influence of the White construct which has so often shaped the models of psychotherapy, the exclusive profession; the lack of theory to frame intersectional inclusive practice; the call for political activism; and the influence of the Trans movement to revolutionise ideas and action towards decolonisation.

After much reflection, I have chosen to keep part one as true to the original published article, in order to tell the story of evolving an inclusive training – chronologically telling and logging our journey in 'real' time. In many ways I find part one a little uncomfortable reading it back now, there was, in part, a naivety and perhaps an over-optimistic vision of the challenges and journey ahead. Consequently, with hindsight, I have added in just a few of those challenges and some reflections within part one, aiming to deconstruct and reconstruct the ideas, living into some of those challenges in part two; and staying true to the idea that we will never arrive – to be inclusive is to keep taking the journey.

PART ONE

Evolving an inclusive training: Two years on from establishing TA East London Institute

TA East is a training institute in East London, holding social responsibility and social justice at its core. It is based in a library in the heart of the urban community.

DOI: 10.4324/9781003509424-3

Its vision being to offer equality in real practical terms, by taking action in terms of inclusivity and accessibility. Aiming to offer a training that is representative of our diverse communities, moving away from a monocultural model, challenging unconscious bias, prejudice, and discrimination, and inviting dialogue about difference, while challenging normative ways of being. I will speak to each of the four social justice principles – equity, access, participation, and rights – these four interrelated principles are embodied in the values and ethical guidelines of our local, national, and world organisations.

Equity: To ensure fair distribution of available resources across society, equity is rooted in fairness, freedom from bias and favouritism

Anton Hart (2017), states: 'At the present moment, psychoanalytically-oriented thinkers and practitioners are reminded that they engage in a strange, minority discipline in relation to the world outside. A recognition of this position of otherness could potentially enhance psychoanalysis' ability to reach beyond its (relatively privileged) borders when it comes to thinking about and therapeutically engaging people who are diverse and who are "other." Yet psychoanalysis too often fails to self-reflectively consider on its own minority status, and its own tendency toward homogeneity and conformity' (p. 1).

Psychotherapy rooted in Whiteness and western/northern hemisphere ideology in itself, has contributed to the unconscious shaping of transactional analysis psychotherapy and indeed the other fields.

Berne's core principles – all people are OK, everyone has the capacity to think, and all people can change – are in themselves both inspiring and challenging. However, how do we as transactional analysts offer equity when only the few are afforded the right of equity? How do we hold these core principles in a world that does not believe that all have the right to exist?

In aiming to offer equity, the task of TA East has been to challenge ourselves to think outside the box – to profoundly examine our bias, to take the journey in becoming non-defended, and to invite dialogue at a grassroots level – in emerging a training institute from the community rather than from the top down. This continues to be an extremely challenging task particularly with regard to modelling radical openness and the complexity of the journey in engaging in non-defended dialogue around complex systemic enactments (Hart, 2017).

In doing so I, as the founder, have had to own my White privilege and the power I hold within systemic oppression; I have had to find a different way of reaching out to those who have been, in some way 'othered'. And, as time has progressed, I have had to continually address my Whiteness and projections from others, alongside the parts of my intersectional identity that are marginalised.

This has brought a complexity in going into the community and reaching out to those who don't reach into what have been 'White' institutions because of their experience of systemic racism and oppression. At TA East, we reflected on how we could reach out to the multi-diverse East London urban community. We did this by setting up stalls at community festivals, taking part in community events like art trails, building relationships with voluntary organisations, setting up information stalls in library foyers, facilitating listening posts on the high street and in libraries, networking with local organisations on social media platforms. We began in the community, aiming to emerge a TA psychotherapy training from the community.

We wanted to invite people in who would not have envisaged themselves as training to be TA psychotherapists. We considered the need for a cultural mirror, 'I can see myself...'. We named this in our dialogues, we openly invited, we named the elephant in the room, the predominant Whiteness, we invited the reflection, can I be a part of this community? Am I welcome? We considered how we promoted ourselves, seeing each contribution to this as conscious and unconscious information; we wanted our 'putting ourselves out there' as congruent with fairness, freedom from bias and favouritism. We reflected on the images we used and use of language, we reflected on multilingual script, we considered what gets lost in translation. For example, 'OK', does not exist as a word in many eastern languages, so what does this mean for the 'I'm OK, you're OK' philosophy? We opened up discussions about this – for example, in Bengali the closest translation is 'I'm good, you're good'.

We invited dialogue on the meaning of 'I'm OK, you're OK' across the languages of people we met, on introductory courses, workshops, and in training groups; dialogue enabled discussion about cultural difference and meaning. I was moved by a dialogue between a British Hindu woman and a British Muslim woman discussing 'I'm OK, you're OK' across Gujarati, Hindi, Urdu, and Bengali, concluding that *Namaste* probably offered the essence of TA philosophy: a Hindu greeting meaning 'I bow to the divine in you and you bow to the divine in me'.

Other dialogues ensued, for example, there not being a word for 'depressed' in many eastern languages, as well as different meanings for shame and other terms that have been assumed to be universal. This was the beginning of deconstruction and decolonisation at TA East. (More on this in Chapter 5.)

We further reflected on the way we reached out into communities, beginning by bringing together a multi-diverse team, offering an intersectional lens. When inviting new applicants to join our community, we actively invited them to get involved in its emerging, framed by one of our British Muslim trainees as: 'We are building a village'.

We considered how we invite and shape an inclusive training. Reflecting on where we would place ourselves in the community, on our identity, and cultural way of being.

We wanted to immerse ourselves in social, cultural, and political contexts.

We began by renting a room in the heart of a busy and diverse East London library, located among books, computers, and people. This space enabled us to live our values of being in touch with the urban community. From the room, if we stand on tip-toe, we can look through the window and see into the main library and the community can see us; for me this is significant, looking in and looking out, looking out into the world, we can see you and you can see us, visible and accessible. The beginning of the decolonising process (Mullan, 2023).

When visited by a psychotherapy colleague, prior to beginning the training, she wondered if this was boundaried enough. This challenged my daring to think outside the box, could a training in a busy library work? Of course, at times, though rarely, there are interruptions; on one occasion an elderly Black British man who had passed me on the library stairs earlier, entered the training room with a string of garlic to treat my knees – at first my internal response was to hush him out of the room. However, I consider these necessary interruptions, reminding ourselves of being connected with and in touch with the wider community and world.

Alongside this, we considered fees and have put them as low as is possible in London, offering bursaries and encouraging bursaries from our national and international organisations. We are also aware of relative privilege and understand that TA training will not be accessible to all, this is evidenced by people who approach us in the library, we offer free spaces on the 101 course and are committed to working towards some full bursary training space each year on clinical trainings.

Access: To ensure all people have access to services regardless of age, gender, ethnicity, class, sexuality, disability, etc

Social and economic factors are an integral consideration when reflecting on access. People from marginalised groups are less likely to access psychotherapy and transactional analysis training due to histories of inequality, racism, and discrimination, leading to socioeconomic disadvantage. However, it's important to flag up Aileen Alleyne's (2011) comments: 'Working from the premise that every Black person is scarred by the mark of oppression and therefore engages life from this basic fault position is wholly presumptuous'. This is where the lens of intersectionality has become so integral, demonstrating that we each hold multiple marginalised and privilege identities.

The Oxford English Dictionary (2014) defines discrimination as, 'unjust or prejudicial treatment of different categories of people, especially on the grounds of race, age, or sex'; similarly, with discrimination, oppression is defined as, 'prolonged cruel or unjust treatment, or exercise of authority'. Thompson (1998), argues that oppression is one of the basic outcomes of discrimination. As the dictionary definition implies, it is the prejudice that leads to an overt negative behaviour and treatment of members of minoritised groups that also produces oppression, in terms of human rights, resources, and equal opportunities.

At TA East we own that not all social groups will access formal transactional analysis training however much we lower fees and offer bursaries. We embrace Berne's vision of transactional analysis, as not only a depth therapy but as a psychoeducational model, accessible to all. Thus, we have built relationships with local councils, who fund and promote activities across the London boroughs. Libraries, in recent times, have had to reinvent themselves, they have become community centres, in the heart of diverse communities offering a breadth of information and support for the communities they serve.

Housing ourselves in the library keeps TA East in touch with the wider community. On a Saturday the library is busy with activity, people reading, chatting, using computers, we are often approached by individuals enquiring about what we are doing or asking to join us. A Black British homeless man, who shelters in the library doorway, approached me in the library, asking me what we were doing. I explained the course and some of the theory of transactional analysis, he was intrigued and came to the library the following Saturday for a further conversation. He challenged the pathologising of men like him in the realm of mental health. We had an open dialogue about White and middle class privilege and the oppression he experienced. He later attended some taster sessions and once again I was reminded of the exclusive profession we reside in.

Anti-discriminatory practice can be defined as promoting diversity, self esteem, and the realisation of an individual's potential while encouraging the recognition of the value of difference and engendering a positive identity within groups which exist in different communities. TA East has been moving away from an individualistic model to a collective model which does not separate the individual from community, society, the systemic, other living things, and our planet.

So how do those who are multi-marginalised equally access the training and curriculum? How is difference valued and promoted?

This begins with meeting individuals where they are, being willing to invite and hear their cultural narrative, while challenging our fixed frame of references of who comes into training. I am reminded of many years ago, when a West African supervisee, training at a TA Institute, turned up on my doorstep on a day off when I was cleaning my windows. I looked at her in surprise and said we are meeting next Thursday at 2 pm. She said, 'I know, I was in the area so I thought I'd come now, shall I help clean your windows?'

I was challenged and stirred, did she not know that psychotherapists meet at set times and adhere to clear boundaries? As time went on, I heard her story, an asylum seeker, sleeping on floors, walking 17 miles across the city each weekend to attend training. We tussled, I held on to my White introjects and western/ northern hemisphere lens of psychotherapy; one day she handed me a book titled '*I wish to inform you that tomorrow you and your children will be killed*', a book describing her experience as a victim of genocide. As I recall the moment, my heart pounds, my realisation of this woman's story versus my cultural expectations and colonised lens. This woman didn't complete her training, I will always wonder about her.

At TA East we have a long way to go regarding access. I have focused largely on ethnicity, there is much to say about other cultural needs around age, gender, class, sexuality, disability, etc. For example, our courses are not currently BSL signed, this is an area we hope to achieve funding for. We want to invite younger people in, more men, we want to be informed around gender fluidity and sexuality, we want to invite those in whose experience is working class. We actively and rigorously continue to challenge our bias. We now see the journey as more crucial, doing the work on ourselves, while sitting with the stark reality of polarised communities locally, nationally, globally, and indeed in our organisations.

As transactional analysts we are called for undefended examination of the way we offer training and the curriculum, examining how theory and practice have been socially and culturally constructed. At TA East we aim to develop access to the training and curriculum through radical openness, as described by Hart (2017), challenging our unconscious bias, offering an intersectional lens not as an add-on. This leads to reflecting on participation.

Participation: To enable people to participate in decisions which affect their lives

Intersectionality developed by Kimberlé Crenshaw (Crenshaw, 1989) identifies the multiple oppressions individuals endure. As described above, my supervisee experienced multiple oppression: being a victim of genocide, an asylum seeker, Black, a woman, and socioeconomically challenged.

If we are truly offering access, participation, and anti-discrimination, then an intersectional lens needs to be considered in the way we offer and facilitate training, and the way we offer participation in the curriculum.

Intersectionality enables more complex understanding of the transcultural nature of our communities. Arguably, alongside race and nationality, we each house different cultural selves, many of us live across different cultures, both historically and presently. Taking time to hear the others' transcultural narrative enables careful consideration of multi-oppression.

At TA East the scene is set for an open dialogue about difference and cultural selves. This is clear in the publicity, the first meetings before application, and in the forming of training groups.

Anton Hart (2017) states: 'In order to penetrate the surface of such intractable things as prejudice and discrimination, a stance of curiosity and openness is required… to examine both the resistances to, and the necessity for, psychoanalytic engagement – and prioritisation – of issues of otherness, difference and diversity'.

Michelle Obama (2018), while on tour promoting her book *Becoming*, highlights the importance of people being able to share their stories, to define themselves by their histories and experience, rather than, in her words their 'stats', what qualifications they have and what they've achieved.

While watching her I was struck by her and other Black people's openness in talking about race and racism. An openness which is not often experienced among White people. White people don't often talk about race, with other White people or in mixed cultural groups, often invitations to do so are met with defence, 'what has this got to do with me?', 'what's the problem?', etc., demonstrating White fragility (DiAngelo, 2018) and the continued centring of Whiteness.

At TA East, in forming the team, we have taken time to hear each other's cultural narrative, rather than a description of academic and work achievement. This in itself is challenging and stirring, uncomfortable as well as exhilarating. Yet it is profoundly necessary in order to see the other. Setting the scene for realness rather than the manifestations of projections resulting in unconscious bias and discrimination.

Early on students are invited to bring cultural objects representative of self, they are invited to take time to tell the group their transcultural story. Inviting a healthy interest and dialogue about difference.

Students with more privilege struggled with this, wondering what represented their cultural selves. All seemed to challenge preconceptions, and this set the scene for further dialogue, including White group members owning their discounting of their Whiteness and putting cultural difference on to the other, thus 'othering' those who are not from the 'normative' culture.

Participating in the curriculum

'The curriculum' could certainly sit under the other headings of equity, access, or rights, however I have placed it under the 'participation' heading to illustrate the cocreational nature of the curriculum – that is, people participate in its development. At TA East every meeting with theory and process brings in a cultural, social, historical, and political lens. Trainers in their planning and teaching, are invited to engage in a non-defensive dialogue in the deconstruction and reconstruction of the theory and curriculum, alongside students who are openly encouraged to contribute to and challenge the evolving and shaping of the curriculum.

When considering the curriculum and participation, we begin with dialogue between trainers/educators at the planning stage of each training unit. Asking what is my countertransferential response to this theory? When was this theory written? What was going on in the world at the time of writing? What was the cultural and social context? (More on this in Chapter 6.)

Out of the dialogue comes the uncovering of unconscious bias – what is stirred in me?; what is stirred in you?; what triggers my defence?

When teaching a unit on sexuality and gender, the planning group began by informing themselves and researching current language and ways of defining and understanding sexuality and gender. All three trainers/educators identified as non-heterosexual and were taken back to their individual frame of reference around language, triggering pain and trauma.

When reflecting on historical, social, and political contexts we considered the impact of gay sex being illegal from the 16th century through to 1967; homosexuality having been classified as a DSM diagnosis and then a sea change, more recently, when homophobia has been classified.

We reflected on language used: 'queer' for example, which pre-1980s was used as a way of denigrating gay men; in the early 1990s reclaimed as a political statement, queer meaning out and proud; and now, 30 years later, Queer being a way of describing and encompassing all the breadth of diversity across gender, sex and sexuality.

When teaching original theory, we teach it as it was originally intended, rooted in its time, bringing in the social, cultural, political, and historical lens to deconstruct, we analyse the theory in the context of now, representing all the diversities. So, in considering the script matrix we name the heteronormative lens, we consider all the differing family configurations and gender identities and pronouns. We reflect on how we may reconstruct the model. We invite open dialogue; we welcome discomfort and meet defence with empathy and challenge, offering a rigorous anti-discriminatory lens. (See Chapter 5 on deconstructing and reconstructing the curriculum.)

So how do we offer participation in the curriculum, which offers equity, access, and rights alongside? We begin with the premise that students bring their cultural stories and their lineage, their experience and knowledge; and that each person has lived experience to contribute to the curriculum, theory and practice, offering a co-creational approach and process. Moving away from the trainers/educators being the experts, where students are stripped down of any previous knowledge, inviting a transferential dynamic and hierarchy.

Tudor and Summers (2000) state: 'Co-creative transactional analysis emphasises the importance of present-centred human development rather than past-centred'. Essentially, we have applied these ideas to the training room, inviting every student and educator to contribute their ideas and share power in actualising the curriculum. 'This reduces the possibility of inappropriate infantilising of adult .... trainees, which can develop when growth is predominantly defined within a Parent–Child frame of reference' (p. 23).

Thus, a co-creational model sets the scene and enables students to challenge and contribute to the theory, by paying attention to both the conscious and unconscious process; inviting a parallel process to that of the trainers at planning stage – returning to the concept of looking in and looking out. I need you as much as you need me, I need the other to challenge me, *I am both the trainer and the trainee, the educator and the student*, we need each other to stay current, not to assume cultural and social experience, to stay in touch with what is going on in the world of our clients. Tudor and Summers (2000) state: 'The implication of this approach is that when two people converse or engage with one another in some way, something comes into existence which is a product of neither of them exclusively. There is a shared field, a common communicative home, which is mutually constructed' (p. 23).

Following the killing of George Floyd, the protests against institutionalised racism and the mass uprising of Black Lives Matter, I discovered that the TA East foundation year, who communicate by WhatsApp between training weekends, shared and then came together and discussed a podcast and writing by Dr Dwight Turner (2021) who speaks of racism being a problem of Whiteness rather than a Black problem and the legacy of centuries of racism that remains largely unaddressed within our professions. Here they took their authority and responsibility to dialogue and make sense of their experience, dialoguing about Whiteness and Blackness.

TA East's challenge is to widen participation. Interestingly, we have been asked, on a few occasions by White middle class people, if the training is open to them. This is an interesting take on positive discrimination. Our training is open to all and invites social awareness and responsibility, aiming to develop a training that is representative of the *breadth* of the community we live in, including all cultural and social groups that value difference.

In this we are mindful of honouring cultural and religious festivals in the planning stage, ensuring, for example, we respect times of fasting for Ramadan, and consider how we structure time consciously and unconsciously, ensuring equal participation.

Rights: To protect individual liberties and human rights

To deny people their human rights is to challenge their very humanity.

(Nelson Mandela, 1990)

Human rights are embodied in our TA national (UKATA), European (EATA), and world (ITAA) organisations. Our world organisation pledges its dedication to promoting the highest calibre of conduct among members, stating: 'As an organisation, the ITAA recognises its social responsibility to set the ethical standards for all members in order to advance the welfare of society through common values and moral principles of mutual respect and ethical actions'.

The ITAA's code of practice (2014) has largely been adapted from the EATA *Ethics Manual* and the Universal Declaration of Human Rights (1948), it states its frame of reference is also congruent with the existential and philosophical perspective of transactional analysis. The ITAA states: 'Values are the fundamental basis on which human beings promote their own personal development and fulfilment as well as that of others. Values include reference to natural law that informs how people behave respectfully toward self and others'. It outlines five values including, dignity of human beings, self-determination, health, security and mutuality and then brings them into action through its ethical principles, including respect, empowerment, protection, responsibility and commitment in relationship; while addressing the following groups: clients, self as practitioner, trainees, colleagues, and human environment/community. At TA East we see that we have a responsibility to facilitate dialogue around rights, ethical standards, and code of practice through a systemic and intersectional lens, considering how we embody and live these values.

The continuing challenge to walk the talk

At TA East we are continually challenged to walk the talk, to look out into the world, as well as look in, to hold social justice and activism as central to our being. We are actively making a stand against systemic racism, discrimination, and oppression. We are called to and embrace the commitment to develop a working understanding of equality and diversity. UKCP (2017) standards of education and training states the need for 'critical understanding of cultural, racial, socio-economic, gendered, heteronormative and dis/ability bias in the theory and culture of psychotherapy and when it is necessary to challenge these biases' (p. 6).

In real terms this requires a conscious determination to examine our biases. This has begun with a dialogue among the TA East team around intersectional identity and manifestations of privilege and oppression. We see this as a needed process passed from educators, to students, to clients, to the wider world in a parallel dialogue about otherness.

As an organisation we offer a willingness to continually examine our frame of reference and to risk a different experience, alongside individual and collective social responsibility, offering an Adult to Adult relationship and co-created dynamic (Tudor & Summers, 2000).

Furthermore, like other psychotherapies, transactional analysis in the UK has moved to a largely individualistic model, offering most often individual therapy. At TA East there is a call to a greater move towards valuing group TA therapy, as originally pioneered by Berne, enabling more access and giving a voice to collective culture and dynamics. We are challenging ourselves to stay current, as the world and transcultural identities continue to evolve.

In short, at TA East, central to our being is social justice and responsibility: we are a community, evolving from the community, for the community of East London.

PART TWO

Evolving an inclusive training: Six years on from establishing TA East London Institute

Six years on from establishing TA East London Institute, the landscape has changed but the challenge and vision for an inclusive training continues to gain momentum with vigour, passion, fight; and, at times, hopeless reflection, fuelled by stories of students and tutors' lived experience of intersectional identity within systemic oppression. The journey of embodying intersectionality through every aspect of being at TA East brings many, many challenges as well as a profound sense that we will never arrive but continue to take the journey.

The Covid-19 pandemic

The Covid-19 pandemic forced us out of the East London library and like many others threw us into the unknown world of facilitating TA psychotherapy training online. This change challenged our very being, our vision that the urban and the community were at the core of our existence. We saw ourselves as street, on the street, in the community for the community. Overnight we became a part of the wider world TA community, which for some marked greater inclusion and for others the notion of greater accessibility. However, this was not the experience of many in the TA East community.

The world had changed, and the outside environment became a threat to our very existence. East London, a built-up city area with many areas of social deprivation, became one of the greatest casualties of the pandemic. Outside mortuaries became a part of the landscape and fear of death was palpable. Those in poor socio-economic areas, with multi-marginalisation were the most affected, not having the privilege of the then UK government's furlough scheme, many having to continue to go to work in the services sector.

Moving online was not a choice, but a necessity and indeed a way to 'stay connected' yet this brought many challenges, one of which I can now describe as digital poverty.

Defined by the UK Digital Poverty Evidence Review (Digital Poverty Alliance, 2022) as 'the inability to interact with the online world fully, when, where, and how an individual needs to'.

In many cases moving online demonstrated the social economic divide in our TA community and indeed the TA East community, those with digital access versus those experiencing digital poverty and of course all the experiences in between. Many did not have laptops or tablets, some borrowed from their children's schools, others used their phones, which was challenging over a 12-hour period. Alongside this accessing good enough WIFI was a problem; but the biggest challenge was private space in student homes, particularly for those living in small spaces with family members, those in collective homes with family members passing by in the background, and those who were single parents with children knocking on the door, bursting in, and wanting and needing their parent. Some took to sitting in their car, others emptied, in order to occupy, under-stair cupboards. This certainly did not feel privileged or accessible and indeed facilitated a disconnect alongside a yearning to connect.

As the pandemic ensued, TA East clung on to its identity, risking becoming like any other London 'normative' psychotherapy institute. We were no longer in the community, reaching out and inviting in. Indeed, a student challenged that we were becoming colonised. I felt defensive at the time and on reflection, it was insightful. Prospective students began to find us, sought us out, via the website, more multi-privileged students started to come in and there was a sense of loss of momentum for an inclusive training, reflecting East London's diversity. We asked how do we return to the community?

By chance I came across a local community radio station, this became the catalyst needed and got us back into networking with libraries and local community groups via Twitter and Facebook. Monday mornings at 10 am became an hourly slot to reach communities offering support and psychoeducation through TA concepts (Woodstreetradio, 2020).

Alongside this, we began to offer online psychoeducation groups for a local charity supporting carers of children with disabilities and Autism. Indeed, these groups became an important reminder of the profound insight of Eric Berne (1961, 1966) in making psychotherapy ideas and practice accessible to all through psychoeducation. When at a disability festival a few years later I unknowingly met an attendee of the group who was representing the charity. Making conversation I said, 'We ran some support groups for your charity during the pandemic'. 'I know', she said, 'I was in one of them, it was life changing for me, it saved my marriage, I learnt to share my feelings, my husband and I talk about things now'. Wow, in that moment I knew that the path we were taking was worth taking.

On March 8, 2021, the pandemic restrictions were slowly being lifted in England. On this day, with renewed hope and freedom, I had a sudden urge to visit Green Street in the London Borough of Newham, about ten minutes away from where I live and TA East places itself. My last teaching job resided in a school on Green Street, where the demographic of the area includes 95 percent of South Asian origin. Green Street in my memory was a vibrant street full of colour, with shop windows adorned with Saris, Indian gold, and wedding attire, and street markets full of okra, rainbow fish, and Bengali fruits. While smells of sugar cane, Indian sweets, and spice filled the air.

I longed to return to its vibrancy and dressed up for the occasion in my red blazer. Stepping out of the car and arriving on Green Street I had a rude awakening, I starkly experienced my multiple privilege and felt the palpable catastrophic death and loss in the environment. The place had lost its life force, chronic despair lurked in the air. Many set up stalls on the street and all wore masks, I heard story after story of multiple loss, fathers, mothers, children, siblings, aunts, uncles, cousins, harrowing multiple losses in families. I became acutely conscious of my privilege, my red blazer, and my ignorance.

Phenomenologically I was taken to a new depth in my vision for TA East, reminded of the limits of my vision. Reminded of the colonised construct of psychotherapy practice and training. Reminded of the class divide, reminded of systemic oppression and racism, reminded of the onslaught of capitalism, in my being, in my body. We had to get back to street.

A new home

Surprisingly, with an unconscious call to the universe, came an opportunity to move TA East into a community building in the heart of East London, Leyton. A place where we still reside.

Residing in the community building is intentional, indeed every aspect of our being serves to decolonise and embody the lived experience of intersectionality in transactional analysis training. Therefore, we deliberately house ourselves in a building on a busy high street reflective of diverse communities, alongside the bustle of Turkish restaurants, Portuguese and eastern European coffee shops, Halal burger bars, Caribbean cuisine, and Italian delis; heavy with traffic and double-decker buses. The building is an old town hall, which once included council offices and a council chamber, as well as having prison cells in the basement. Photographs in the corridors demonstrate 120 years of history in and alongside the community. The building holds the palpable story of the social, cultural, and political. We intentionally immerse ourselves in the social and political context, in a building now full of charities, community, and social enterprise projects. The Night Porter, a previously homeless man, resides in the basement.

Themes of inclusion and exclusion manifest in the physical space, particularly around gender differences and the provision for differing gender identities and thus the need of a non-binary toilet/bathroom. This, in itself, became another fight with the 'normative' system and the unconscious bias and prejudice of the building management. Alongside the breadth of neurodiversity needs – the need for movement, the need for stillness, the brightness of the lights, the noise volume in the room with high ceilings, the positioning of screens, the seating – calling for a sensitivity, calling for a social model of inclusion, again challenging every aspect of our being. Inviting us to consider the collective responsibility for each individual (Oliver, 1983).

Many ask 'when will you get your own building?'. We won't, I say. We welcome and need the discomfort, the palpable history of political struggle, the interruptions, even the disturbance. We manage these complexities.

This decolonises and indeed deconstructs the space and invites more intersectional voices and connections, holding our value of looking in and looking out, reminiscent of the ideas around the therapeutic dyad: in here, out there, and back then (Chinnock, 2011; Jacobs, 1988; Menninger, 1958).

Furthermore, we network locally and continue to go into the community to invite students in, we actively seek to include. We travel around the borough visiting synagogues, faith groups, women's groups, refugee groups, community projects, and partake in fringe events and local collaborations. We offer workshops in high street cafes, we visit libraries, and we meet people. More recently one of our students invited us to the Hare Krishna temple for a TA East retreat day where we compared the *Bhagavad Gita Holy Book* (2003) to our TA existential philosophy.

Six years on we understand the enormity of the task

Six years on we understand the enormity of the task of 'inclusion' and representation. There is a sense that we are a movement as much as we are an institute. A movement that seeks to address the inequalities in the psychotherapy profession and indeed in the transactional analysis community. This has taken us to a deeper reflection on our learnings and challenges, our embodiment of intersectional theory and practice through the veins of our evolving.

Institutionally, we continue to walk unknown territory. We have had to challenge continually why we do what we do and what we have introjected, thereby challenging ourselves to deconstruct and to decolonise 'our own minds' as we pursue and forge this different path.

Surprisingly, and not surprisingly, some have inferred, expressed, and assumed TA East is an institute for those who are 'different', congruent with the belief that difference is somehow an add-on or separate to Whiteness. This arguably is unconscious othering and excluding – a microaggression (Cousins & Diamond, 2021).

At TA East we aim to 'invite in' all difference, indeed all intersectional configurations and identities in being human. We aim to sit among and work 'within difference' (Khan, 2023), and so sharing our transcultural narratives, telling our stories presently, historically, and ancestrally, not as a one-off but over and over again, putting ourselves in touch with the changing landscapes of our lives and intrapsychic narratives. And so, knowing where we each sit within systemic oppression and to own the intersectional parts of self that are oppressed and the parts of self that are privileged (Baskerville, 2022).

Students come to evolve social, cultural, and political awareness

As we have become established, students come to evolve social, cultural, and political awareness in transactional analysis psychotherapy training and are interested in furthering intersectional inclusive practice.

This said, not 'all' will be included due to the cost of the training journey. We have had to face the reality of financial privilege, particularly with the added cost of personal therapy and supervision. Arguably, all who come have a degree of privilege and relative privilege (Minikin, 2021).

If we are congruently seeking 'to include all voices' this needs to be addressed through funding and larger and full bursaries. This raises the capitalist structure of the predominately private psychotherapy profession; and in transactional analysis the hierarchical qualification structure (Baker, 2024), which also plays a role in limiting a breadth of intersectional voices. Many are excluded. We hope as TA East evolves, we will develop a structure that strives for more inclusion.

Not immune to systemic enactment

By authentically inviting all difference into the room at TA East, we have had to face the painful realisation that we are not immune to systemic enactment and that systemic enactments are alive in every process. At TA East we have consciously decided to bring difference into the room, contrary to many students' lived experience of having to exclude aspects of their difference. This in itself brings responsibility (Ahmed et al., 2023, UKCP Research, Baskerville, 2023a).

TA East is a microcosm of the world where there are many splits happening including catastrophic conflicts and wars. Sitting in groups there are students of Jewish descent sitting across from and alongside those of Muslim descent and those who leave early to march for Palestine. There is fear and fight in the room and a need for dialogue to make the space safe. There are Russian students and Ukrainian asylum seekers, sitting witnessing each other's stories, stories of running from missiles, stories of feeling unsafe in being Russian in the UK right now.

There are non-binary people wondering if they can truly exist in the group, longing to belong and waiting for others to become more socially aware around gender fluidity; there are different views around Trans youth, there is a tension between discrimination and a willingness to learn, there are native British speakers and many for whom English is a second language. Some bring their generational stories of mothers travelling across landscapes and countries to find safety, stories of the partition, the onslaught of the British Empire and Windrush; the harm, the trauma, and the rage. Then comes the class splits sitting across race, often going unnamed. Asking what gets lost in translation?

This is the challenge and the responsibility. Some have met these enactments with chronic disappointment, having arrived with the deep desire to be included in their difference. Inclusion involves all of us. Each of us doing the work collectively and individually, moreover, having a willingness to work through and dialogue around our differences, the projections, the splits, the othering, and the challenges.

Lacking an integrated theoretical framework, to make sense of intersectional identity and intersectional dynamics within transactional analysis

A number of transactional analysts, over the years, have kept the radical flame going through activism in their writing, challenging normative constructs and systemic oppression. Notwithstanding this, undertaking a decolonising journey, offering transactional analysis training with an intersectional lens, while lacking an integrated theoretical framework to make sense of intersectional identity and dynamics within the psychotherapeutic, counselling, organisational, or educational setting is challenging. Therefore, I actively journeyed to further and formalise our ideas around deconstructing and reconstructing original and normative theory through an intersectional lens, informed by Queer theory.

In October 2022, the *Transactional Analysis Journal*, published a themed issue, 'Systemic oppression, what part do we play?' edited by Minikin and Rowland (2022). Here, alongside others including Dhananjaya (2022), Jusik (2022), Filipache (2022), Shadbolt (2022), and Tudor et al. (2022), my 'Transcultural and Intersectional Ego State Model' was published (Baskerville, 2022). This model offered an explicit frame for TA East and other institutes, bringing intersectional, historical, social, cultural, and political contexts to transactional analysis ego state theory. (See Chapter 4 for an updated model.)

In Autumn 2023, I published a model (Baskerville, 2023b), tried and tested with students and colleagues, to deconstruct and reconstruct original theory through an intersectional lens. (See Chapter 5 for an updated deconstruction and reconstruction model.)

Similarly, Marshall and Jordan (2010) developed the idea of taking counselling and psychotherapy outside which serves to deconstruct the notion that therapy has to be offered within the social construct, behind closed doors, within an external boundary. The idea of working outside truly reconnects humans to the planet and to all living beings, seeing the external boundary as the circumference of our natural world. (See Chapter 12 for more on Eco-TA and the eco-systemic.)

Evolving an intersectional team

One of our major necessities and challenges has been evolving an intersectional team and finding trainers who want to join us and who are willing to take the journey – decolonising their minds, theory, and practice – learning while walking on new territory. The team is called to take that journey with each other and with and alongside students, being both a tutor and a student, in teaching and learning, as well as bringing ourselves consciously and unconsciously as both the transactional analyst/psychotherapist and the client. The ability to hold a multi-diverse group, while attending to power dynamics, facilitating radically open and non-defensive dialogue, and deconstructing and reconstructing theory are not inconsiderable challenges. To teach at TA East is to keep doing the work around unconscious bias through social and political awareness. (See Chapter 8 for an exploration of radically open and non-defended dialogue.)

The influence of activism and creativity

And there has been a need to look outside academia, out into the wider world to reach the edge of activism, where political activists have been, and are, fiercely challenging all structures of supremacy. In this we have drawn on political activism to support, influence, and evolve our decolonised thinking, theory, and practice. This has included activists using the spoken word and poetry as a way of profoundly deconstructing the way we offer and receive healing.

Queer theory and activism have been instrumental in fiercely challenging social constructs and the binary across identities, challenging ideas around autonomy and collective liberation. (See Chapter 9 for the influence of activists.)

Alongside this is the decolonisation of assessment processes with an intersectional and neurodiverse lens, inviting learning journals and presentations through creative forms. And recently we took the step to invite Year 4 students to 'write' their assignment in another form, along with advocating for this in the UKCP registration assessment process.

The proof is in the pudding

Notwithstanding these considerable challenges, the proof is in the pudding. We are now experiencing groups having profound dialogue around difference, enabling deeper connection and the healing of wounds. We are starting to see generations of TA East students taking their place as practitioners in the TA community and psychotherapy profession. Students who are offering intersectional, culturally sensitive therapy as an act of social justice in the world. In dialogue with tutors and students alike, I own that the future of TA East would be furthered by greater representation in a bigger infrastructure. In time, more and more students will come back and take their rightful place as tutors and leaders of the community. Importantly, there is an overwhelming sense of belonging at TA East, a sense of community, and experiencing taking the journey collectively, proudly expressed in various testimonies.

Six generations of students on, we are gaining momentum and there seems to be a sea change in the wider community towards integrating and accounting for historical, social, cultural, and political contexts. This is reflected in the new joint mission statement of EATA and the ITAA. World webinars are addressing some of these themes that hopefully will be integrated into every aspect of learning rather than just an add-on.

Not surprisingly, TA East continues to take the journey in deconstructing decades and centuries of the colonisation of psychotherapy as a 'normative' pursuit, challenged by Berne's own original radical vision.

Central to the being of TA East is the awareness that 'all oppression is connected' (Chin, 2014), the idea that to oppress one cultural group is to oppress all cultural groups. And that when one cultural group is being oppressed, we are all oppressed. And so this is the journey of TA East, to keep striving and fighting for all inclusion. We will continue to find our way through the changing cultural, social, and political contexts and indeed our changing planet and what this means for all living things that reside on it and with it; and ultimately how we meet our clients within the breadth of their intersectional being.

References

Ahmed, N., Baskerville, V., Neish, G., & Nelson, V. (2023). UKCP research project final report: Inclusivity and exclusivity in training, the trainees' experience. *The Transactional Analyst, 13*(1), Winter 2022/23.

Alleyne, A. (2011). Overcoming racism, discrimination and oppression in psychotherapy. Cited in Lago, C. (2011). *The handbook of transcultural counselling and psychotherapy.* NY: Open University Press.

Baker, J. (2024). Time for a change? A review of transactional analysis psychotherapy training and examinations with consideration to adopting a more inclusive and nondiscriminatory approach. *Transactional Analysis Journal, 54*(1), 78–90. https://doi.org/10.1080/03621537.2023.2286577

Baskerville, V. (2021). Evolving an inclusive training. *The Transactional Analyst, 11*(4), 5–9.

Baskerville, V. (2022). A transcultural and intersectional ego state model of the self: The influence of transcultural and intersectional identity on self and other. *Transactional Analysis Journal, 52*(3), 228–243. https://doi.org/10.1080/03621537.2022.2076398

Baskerville, V. (2023a). 'The unseen: How many trainees are feeling left out?' *The New Psychotherapist*, UKCP Magazine. Summer 2023, issue 83.

Baskerville, V. (2023b). Deconstructing and reconstructing the curriculum. *The Transactional Analyst, 13*(2), 19–25.

Berne, E. (1961). *Transactional analysis in psychotherapy.* NY: Grove Press.

Berne, E. (1966). *Principles of group treatment.* Oxford: OUP.

Bhagavad Gita Holy Book (2003). *Penguin classics.* London: Penguin Random House.

Chin, S. (2014). 'All oppression is connected' [Video]. https://www.pbslearningmedia.org/resource/fp17.lgbtq.oppression/all-oppression-isconnected/

Chinnock, K. (2011). Relational transactional analysis supervision. *Transactional Analysis Journal*, *41*(4), 336–350. https://doi.org/10.1177/036215371104100410

Cousins, S., & Diamond, B. (2021). *Making sense of microaggressions*. UK: Open Voices Publishers.

Crenshaw, K. (1989). Demarginalizing the intersection of race and sex: A Black feminist critique of antidiscrimination doctrine, feminist theory and antiracist politics. *University of Chicago Legal Forum*, Issue 1, Article 8. https://scholarship.law.columbia.edu/faculty_scholarship/3007

Dhananjaya, D. (2022). We are the oppressor and the oppressed: The interplay between intrapsychic, interpersonal, and societal intersectionality. *Transactional Analysis Journal*, *52*(3), 244–258. https://doi.org/10.1080/03621537.2022.2082031

DiAngelo, R. (2018). *White fragility*. Boston, US: Beacon Press.

Digital Poverty Alliance. (2022). https://digitalpovertyalliance.org/uk-digital-poverty-evidence-review/

Filipache, I. (2022). Shattered dignity and unsymbolized past: Facing the legacy of a totalitarian system. *Transactional Analysis Journal*, *52*(3), 178–192. https://doi.org/10.1080/03621537.2022.2076416

Hart, A. (2017). From multicultural competence to radical openness: A psychoanalytic engagement of otherness. *The American Psychoanalyst*, *51*(1), 12–13, 26–27. https://apsa.org/wp-content/uploads/apsaa-publications/vol51no1-TOC/html/vol51no1_09.xhtml

ITAA. (2014). ITAA Code of Ethics - ITAA Code of Ethical Conduct and ITAA Ethics Procedures Manual. https://itaaworld.com/wp-content/uploads/2023/05/12-5-14Revised-Ethics_0.pdf

Jacobs, M. (1988). *Psychodynamic counselling in action*. London: Sage.

Jusik, P. (2022). 'Systemic oppression and cultural diversity: Putting flesh on the bones of intercultural competence'. *Transactional Analysis Journal*. *52*(12), 1–9. https://doi.org/10.1080/03621537.2022.2076981

Khan, M. (2023). *Working within diversity. A reflective guide to anti-oppressive practice in counselling and psychotherapy*. London: Jessica Kingsley Publishers.

Mandela, N. (1990). Excerpt from Mandela Speech to Joint Meeting of Congress.

Marshall, H., & Jordan, M. (2010). Taking counselling and psychotherapy outside: Destruction or enrichment of the therapeutic frame? *European Journal of Psychotherapy and Counselling*, *12*(4), 345–359.

Menninger, K. (1958). *Theory of psychoanalytic technique*. New York: Basic Books.

Minikin, K. (2021). Relative privilege and the seduction of normativity. *Transactional Analysis Journal*, 51(1). https://doi.org/10.1080/03621537.2020.1853349

Minikin, K., & Rowland, H. (2022). Letter from the coeditors: Systemic oppression: What part do we play? *Transactional Analysis Journal*, *52*(3), 175–177. https://doi.org/10.1080/03621537.2022.2080263

Mullan, J. (2023). *Decolonising therapy*. NY: W.W. Norton & Company.

Obama, M. (2018). *Becoming*. New York: Crown Publishing/Penguin Random House.

Oliver, M. (1983). *The politics of disablement*. London: Palgrave MacMillan.

Oxford English Dictionary (2014). Oxford: OUP.

Shadbolt, C. (2022). The many faces of systemic oppression, power, and privilege: The necessity of self-examination. *Transactional Analysis Journal*, *52*(3), 259–273. https://doi.org/10.1080/03621537.2022.2076411

Thompson, N. (1998). *Promoting equality: Working with diversity and difference*. London: Red Globe Press.

Tudor, K., Green, E., & Brett, E. (2022). Critical Whiteness: A transactional analysis of a systemic oppression. *Transactional Analysis Journal*, *52*(3), 193–208. https://doi.org/10.1080/03621537.2022.2076394

Tudor, K., & Summers, G. (2000). Co-creative transactional analysis. *Transactional Analysis Journal*, *30*(1), 23–40. https://doi.org/10.1177/036215370003000104

Turner, D. (2021). *Intersections of privilege and otherness in counselling and psychotherapy*. London: Routledge.

UKCP. (2017). Standards of Education and Training. https://www.psychotherapy.org.uk/media/03olj3jw/ukcp-adult-standards-of-educationand-training-2017.pdf

Universal Declaration of Human Rights (1948). https://www.un.org/en/about-us/universaldeclaration-of-human-rights

Woodstreetradio. (2020). https://woodstreetradio.radiostream321.com/

Chapter 4

A Transcultural and Intersectional Ego State Model of the Self, 2025

The influence of Transcultural and Intersectional Identity on Self and other

This chapter presents an updated Transcultural and Intersectional Ego State Model that takes into consideration the reality of systemic oppression and the influence of transcultural and intersectional identity on self and other (Crenshaw, 1989). The model considers the intersect and interplay between race, ethnicity, gender, and other cultural selves and takes into account the complexity of cultural experience and narrative. Through inquiry about cultural selves and mapping those onto an ego state model, it is possible to develop more insight into intersectional identity, including how privilege and oppression are manifested in the self and enacted in the world; and to reflect on and locate cultural impasse, unconscious bias, transgenerational oppression, White privilege, othering, racism, power dynamics and systemic enactments in our work. A dialogue with a colleague is offered, and intersectional identities are mapped and discussed.

You are also invited to consider your own transcultural experience and locate your own intersectional identity, thus accounting for power dynamics (using Figure 4.1). So reflecting on – in each unique encounter – who holds the power in the room? (Baskerville, 2022). What is being projected? What parts of the self are being hidden, are seen, or unseen? What parts of the self are being split off, gotten rid of, masked, or adapted? What is allowed and not allowed? How will systemic oppression be manifested in this relationship now? What am I bringing of my ancestors? What am I holding in my body? What is constructed? What is innate?

A developing model

The Transcultural and Intersectional Ego State Model of the Self was first published in an article in the *Transactional Analysis Journal* (Baskerville, 2022). This chapter presents an edited version of the original 2022 article, and an updated 2025 version of the model. I have always seen the model as changing and evolving, as social constructs change and as social, cultural, and political contexts shift. Through my evolving social and political awareness, and further uncovering of unconscious bias, I have updated social constructs in the original model and reassessed my intersectional identity – proving the ever-changing nature of the transcultural and intersectional self, and staying true to my ideas around deconstruction and reconstruction

DOI: 10.4324/9781003509424-4

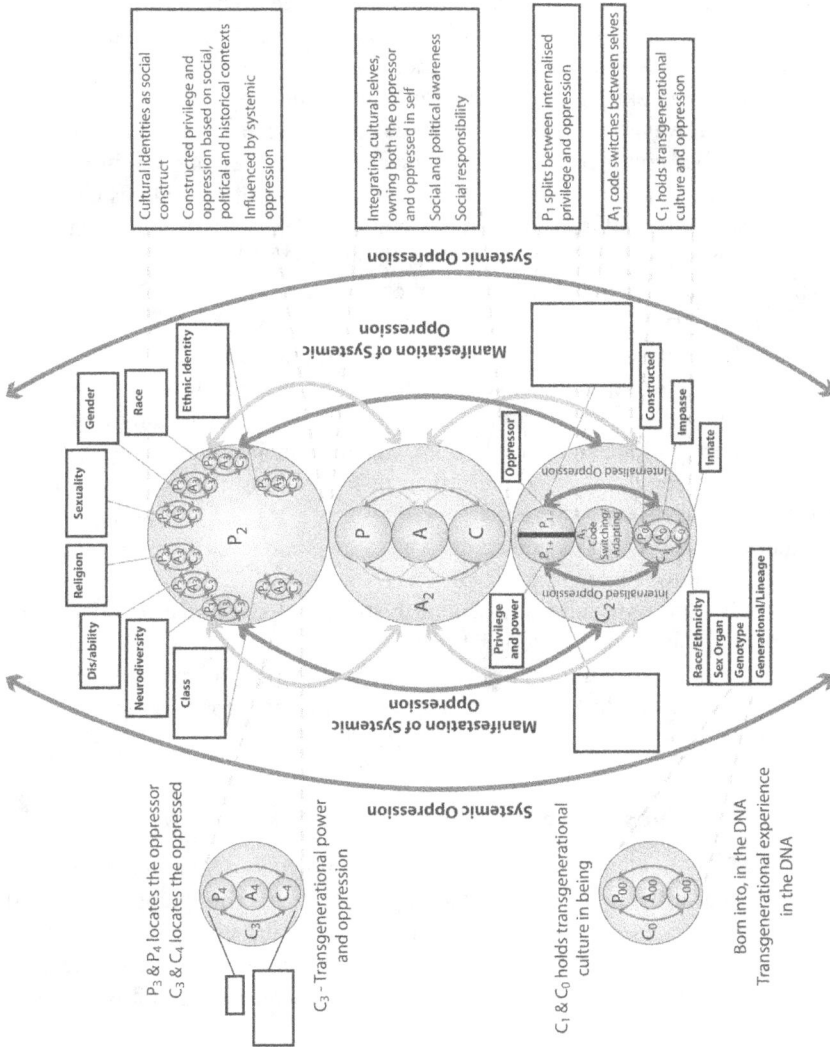

Figure 4.1 Diagnostic model to locate Transcultural and Intersectional Identity (Baskerville, 2025)

of theory through an intersectional lens. (See Appendix 3 for a critique of the 2022 model and some of the considerations behind the 2025 updated model.)

My aim in the model described here is to put intersectionality at the heart of practice and thus invite more awareness and a shared social responsibility for locating the difference between us and identifying the part we each play in systemic oppression. Historically, culture has been defined as the ideas, customs, and social behavior of groups of people and societies with regard to race and origin. Generally, people have been defined by monoculture (a single culture), thereby discounting the complexity of intersectional identity and the intersection of multiple oppression. However, we embody many cultural selves as a result of centuries of migration across continents, changing societies and behaviour, environmental influences, language, and social and political contexts. As the world has changed, cultural experience has addressed themes around gender, sexuality, class, and beyond. Culture presents itself in many forms. Some may be hidden consciously or unconsciously, and some may be favoured more than others.

Indeed, cultural selves may be held in a person's DNA. They may be generational and/or here and now and may well hold contradictions in relation to each other, causing discomfort, impasse, and splitting off aspects of the self. Everyone has a unique cultural narrative derived from one's ancestry and leading on to present-day experience. It is paramount that we consider intersectionality as it brings in the multidimensional nature of the self in relationship to the wider world and lays the foundation for anti-oppressive practice. It is a way of accounting for the cultural narrative in each of us and enables us to own and identify oppression and privilege and the power dynamics between us.

To bring alive the transcultural self and to locate intersectional identity, I am going to share an unscripted dialogue I had some time ago with a colleague with both of us sharing our cultural narratives and engaging in radical openness and non-defended dialogue (Hart, 2017). J has given permission to share our dialogue and for me to write up her intersectional identity.

Cultural narratives of J and V

The context of the dialogue was that J and I were invited to deliver a keynote talk and intersectional training at a psychotherapy conference. The dialogue included each of us sharing some of our transcultural narrative and engaging in dialogue about our differences. The dialogue between us began before we entered the conference presentation room, when our projections were already in full flow.

J: *I feel like I am an imposter. What am I doing here? I feel scared. I am not sure I can meet you in your power. You hold all the power, your Whiteness, you being the director of an institute. It's worse when I see the majority in front of me. I'm not sure I will be able to cathect my power. It just drains out of me.*

V: [I am impacted, I see J as confident, potent, knowledgeable. I am stopped in my tracks. I feel a heaviness. I take a breath. I feel pained. I take responsibility.]

Yes, I am White, I do have power, I am protected in my Whiteness. And I feel scared and like an imposter. Will I use the right words? Will I be as eloquent as you? Can I bring who I am? That's how I feel as soon as I am in a normative group.

J: *Really? But your difference didn't begin at birth. Being born an Indian girl, the oppression starts immediately.*

V: *I was brought up heterosexual, but I am a lesbian. I had to hide that part of me from a young age.*

J: *Really, that early ...*

V: *Yes, and in normative forums I feel scared and then I get angry.*

J: *Really?*

V: *Yes.*

J: *Gosh. But you, you can be angry. I have spent all my life feeling I can't be angry. I see that as privilege. I don't have the privilege of being angry. I am so scared, I am immobilized in fear. Yet you have the power to be angry, you hold it all. I am immobilized in fear. You still have a voice. You have White privilege.*

V: *I do.* [I could feel some competition rise in me. I wanted to shout out my experience of oppression. I'm scared, I'm working class, I'm a lesbian! I experience oppression every day! I know what oppression looks like! I held back. I could hear in J the catastrophic onslaught of her oppression, J's lived experience of being Brown and my White privilege. I felt called to hear J, to be impacted by her, to surrender to my defence and to stay with I am White, I am White privileged, I am a part of White supremacy. And there are parts of me that are oppressed.] *It's the visual. I am White, I can hide my sexuality, I can pretend I'm heterosexual, and sometimes I do, to keep myself safe. But you can't hide your Brownness. I think I go to a place of anger: You think you are better than me. It's a passive-aggressive working class trait I have.*

J: *Yes, but you still can, that is privilege. I see you as this White freedom fighter. You can fight; all I can do is walk in your shadow. You have determination. I don't have that. If I speak up, I'm going to have my legs chopped off. I haven't had the opportunities you've had.*

V: [I felt pain, I felt angry, I felt defensive, I recognised my determination, the fight in me, in my history, in my DNA, in my working class fight. And I am White and privileged, and J feels held back in my shadow.]

At that point, we entered the room where the conference presentation would be given.

We faced a sea of Whiteness with no other differences in sight. I came in, in my Whiteness and felt fear, anger, shame, and responsibility for inviting J in. I held power; I was protected in my Whiteness. I could hide my difference, but J just sat with her Brownness. I knew my privilege. J began to describe her visceral response as she entered the room: she felt her throat constrict and a strangling sensation. We began our dialogue and telling our cultural narratives. I got into my stride protected by my Whiteness and status. I pushed down my discomfort and anger and painfully understood our difference in this White context.

I noticed that there, before the audience, J and I did not take the same risks as we had behind closed doors when we both sat within the wider context of systemic oppression, a microcosm of the world. Instead, we both hid some parts of ourselves and took as many risks as we each felt the context allowed us.

J: *I can hardly speak, my throat is restricted, it's closing up, can I have my voice here?* [J was immediately in touch with the oppression in the room and J's internalised experience.] *All the trauma and the terror, the shame, the confusion and split are in me, in my history. Even though I was born in the United Kingdom, when I think about my cultural narrative there was a lot of trauma. My mum told me about her experience of the partition in India when she was aged 11, which was a really traumatic social, political, religious split for the people in India. My mum was born in Lahore, which was once in India but since partition has been in Pakistan. Her family was uprooted, and she walked all the way from Lahore to the Punjab, miles away. She had to leave everything behind to walk alongside thousands of others to the Indian side, in the north, in Punjab. I cannot comprehend that journey, the loss and terror, the bleakness of it all, the risk to her life, and how vulnerable she was, how displaced those people were, but also the trauma of not knowing when the attack was coming. I remember her saying they would have to set up camps along the way, and she never knew if she was going to be raped or kidnapped or lose her primary family. That was also around the time of colonialism, the British Empire in India. That trauma lives in me today as I claim to be British, born here, and Indian, nervous and ashamed. I hold both the oppressor and the oppressed in my history.*

V: *I am deeply impacted by your story, hearing about the harrowing trauma your mum endured and the ongoing trauma living in you. And your daily experience of terror, shame, split, and confusion in you, British and Indian. You say you are ashamed. We have talked before about the great Whites; I am implicit in this. I am White privileged. I am part of White oppression. I am ashamed and I am responsible now here with you. There is an experience of chronic attack in you, attack in your history and here now with me.*

J: *You know the panic and nervousness in my history is a revering of the great Whites and sort of being deferential to them. When I must stand in my own power, I find it is very hard. I find it hard to stand in my power with you. I feel I can only stand in your shadow. Yet I am middle class now, I work for a large company, I have won prizes for public speaking, yet here now I see you as having all the power.*

V: *Yes, I hear you. White supremacy is in your history and here now.*

J: *It is …* [J visually looks different; she is finding her voice.] *Tell me about your history.*

V: *I am thinking where I go back to. My maternal great-grandparents came over from Ireland to the Midlands in England during the potato famine. They were called 'Cassidy', which is an Irish name. When they arrived in England, they changed their name to 'Cassily' because it was English. They also changed from Catholics to saying they were Methodists. There was always a hostility towards Catholicism in my family, as if we had always been Methodists. We were also English; there was never any mention of being Irish. It's interesting how it plays out in me now.*

J: *Does it cause a tension in you? In terms of the religious aspect?*

V: *There was a confusion in me. I didn't know the story of my ancestors. I never really understood why we were so strongly Methodist and abhorred the Catholics and the Irish. At the same time, I felt a pull to Catholicism and an oppression from the Methodist religion. The older I got, the more strongly I rejected being English. To this day I don't identify as English. I've always identified as Northern, moving away from the Midlands at age three. In my history, migration seems to have killed off what came before. I certainly identify with having to hide parts of myself.*

J: *Yeah, and hiding parts of myself is rooted in my family history because after my mum married, she and my father went to East Africa and were then kicked out. All Indians were told to leave, so she went from Lahore to India to East Africa and finally to the United Kingdom. The challenge of holding on to who we really are is a desire, but I understand the tension of trying to repress or hide who we really are as it doesn't fit into the dominant culture. So, then comes the dilution. I remember walking down Leyton High Street in London, and because I was born here, my first language is English. I'm lucky I can speak my indigenous language, but there's some shame in that too. I remember walking with my mum in her shalwar kameez and just thinking I wish she wasn't wearing that. I feel so much shame about that. Shame makes you want to hide. And I wanted to hide. I wanted to hide my Indianness. I wanted to hide my mum.*

V: *That is so painful, J—the challenge of holding on to who you are, wanting to hide your Indianness, wanting to hide your mum, really highlighting the split in you, British and Indian, the oppression you have endured from the dominant culture and the oppression you have internalised, your deep desire to hide parts, to kill off parts of yourself that are different in order to survive and fit in.*

J: *Yes, I had to reject my Brownness, my Indianness. Tell me more about your history...*

V: *Both my grandparents on my mum's and dad's side were coalminers, which involved a really dark existence. Both suffered chronic health problems from being down in the mines in the wet, damp conditions and bending over all day. Their job was to serve others, and their wellbeing didn't matter. My dad used to tell me that he was a bright lad, and when he was 15, his head teacher came to his house and asked his father if George could carry on at school. His father said, 'No boy of mine is going to get above his station'. So, my dad left school at 15 and went for an interview as a white-collar worker. When he went home and told his father he got the job, his father beat him up with the strong message: revere the middle class, don't become 'them'.*

J: *I can relate to that—the sense of 'Don't Make It' is inherent in Indians. And yet you see there's this constant striving for education because it's a way out of poverty. For girls it's very different. That's what I wanted: I wanted to be the smart Indian. Like your dad, I said to my dad I wanted to go to university. He said girls don't go to university. And the warrior Sikh in me said I don't care what you say, I'm going to university. I did and I kept going and I got my Master's degree, and one day perhaps I'll get my doctorate. But I reflect, what's that really about? My attempt to move away as far as I can from my roots, to go against the Don't Make It injunction. For me, there is a huge amount of shame in East London, being an East Londoner. That's why I haven't been back in 25 years. This is very triggering because it is putting me right back in touch with my shame around me being working class and Indian living in East London. And my life now couldn't be further removed from that, yet my heart belongs in the East. I feel I'm coming home to myself, although there is a way to go.*

V: *Yes, I understand. My experience of displacement started later. When my parents married, they had their honeymoon in Blackpool. I suffered with bronchitis in industrial Stoke on Trent, so they had this profound aspiration to move to Blackpool. In the 1970s, Blackpool was an alive, vibrant, working class seaside town—not that I knew it was a working class town back then. In the early 1980s, people started to go to Benidorm in Spain, and poverty started to unfold alongside the emerging of Thatcher's Britain. It was only when I moved out of Blackpool to the South that I started to feel shame for coming from Blackpool, because for me it had been the ultimate, it was home, I belonged. Then I got in touch with the shame of working class culture because I was outside of it: 'Oh gosh, that's where you're from?' and from my family: 'Who do you think you are?'. So, I didn't belong in either culture. I am thinking about how we, within ourselves, reject part of ourselves. I know that place of shame, different from you, but I know it. And you describe the warrior in you, that goes further back, the Sikh warrior. I have the sense of being a warrior myself: a working class warrior, or maybe the Irish in me, the Celts.*

J: *In a way, it's a gift for us both because we can identify these parts of ourselves: what it's like to be less than and wanting to be more than, what it's like to hold the power and how this impacts the other.*

Later reflections on our dialogue

I was aware of being more defended once we entered the public White forum. I noticed that sharing oppressed parts of ourselves was more comfortable in that context and brought us together; we were allies to each other. Acknowledging the power dynamic between us and our differences was more threatening, stirring, painful, and at times chronically uncomfortable. In these moments, both before and during the public forum, we risked severing our connection, feeling what divided us more than what connected us, inviting defence. However, we were both willing and open to working towards a deeper connection through laying down our defences and courageously accounting for the difference between us.

Considering our different experiences of oppression and privilege, I realised that growing up in a working class White town has enabled me to belong, to feel safe, and to be mirrored in my Whiteness, to be mirrored in the social context. I am OK. Although my sexuality was not mirrored, I could hide that part of myself.

In contrast, J was constantly under threat. She grew up in a deprived, predominantly White area of East London, so she was always minoritised, seen as an immigrant. She was Brown, she experienced racism, she felt the onslaught of shame and had to split off that part of herself in order to survive. And when she could, she left for a middle class lifestyle.

Since our dialogue, J has described getting in touch with rage. Feeling heard, understood, and met by me in our dialogue became the catalyst for her getting in touch with decades of anger towards the 'great Whites'. Our interaction also forced me to surrender, to lay down my defences and accept my Whiteness and power in a way that I had not before. And at the same time, I challenged J to see me not just in my Whiteness but to see that I also experienced oppression in my history, my class, my gender, and my sexuality. J heard me, and our dialogue continues.

The dialogue between us emphasises the need for a relational ego state model that adds depth and complexity to understanding the unconscious manifestation of systemic oppression within social and cultural identity. Seeing the individual within the social context also returns us to our radical social psychiatry roots in transactional analysis and builds on the breadth of voices challenging normativity and marginality today.

Transcultural and intersectional ego state model of the self, 2025

The ego state model described here locates and accounts for the multi-diverse complexity of our transcultural selves in relationship to self, other, and the wider world. Significantly, this model is placed within the context of systemic oppression and accounts for the effects of systemic oppression on the self and what is experienced and what is internalised. The model illustrates the profound impact that social, political, historical, and cultural contexts have on the self. Where we are placed in the world affects how we are seen, the levels of discrimination we experience, and what rights we have. Thus, it shapes the development of the self through conscious and unconscious experience and manifests in the internalisation of oppression and privilege.

The model I am proposing moves away from the notion of monoculture and uses a relational, dynamic lens that shows how multiple cultural selves are developed and constructed by generations before us and continue to be constructed throughout our lifetimes. For example, J described the impact on her of generations before her, the profound influence of the partition of India and Pakistan, the British Empire, her parents immigrating to Britain, and her rejection of her Indian self in order to fit in with the wider world and White supremacy.

In developing this model, I have built on Hargaden and Sills's (2002, p. 99) model of the development of the cultural self; expanded on ideas discussed by Drego (1983), Shivanath and Hiremath (2003), Minikin (2021), and Tudor and Summers (2000); and adapted Berne's (1961) original model of structural ego states, which offers a complex map and a comprehensive, historical lens with which to view the development of the transcultural and intersectional self. To comprehend and to bring more depth to transgenerational aspects of the self, I have added a fourth-order structural model, which I see as including the unconscious aspects of the self passed down through generations in the social, political, and cultural contexts of time. I hypothesise that when culture is passed through generations, it is held in Parent and Child, the conscious and unconscious, in cognition as well as in the DNA and the body/somatic.

This may account for both J and myself experiencing the 'warrior' in our beings: J the Sikh warrior and I the fight of the working class or maybe something of my Celtic history.

In the model I am proposing, Berne's original model of ego states is imagined and drawn with spheres rather than two-dimensional circles (as shown in Figure 4.2), thereby inviting more movement and dynamics between parts of the self and interaction with others and the wider world. Then, in Figures 4.3 and 4.4, the model has been developed to include each individual's intersectional identity by using rings to orbit particular ego states, thus highlighting aspects of culture that are either privileged or oppressed.

Figure 4.2 is presented in stages in order to offer complexity and clarity.

Transcultural and intersectional ego state model of the self, 2025, explained

The ego state model shown in Figure 4.2 is located within the context of systemic oppression, which is represented by the curved outer arrows surrounding the model. These show the two-way interaction and demonstrate the profound, significant influence of systemic oppression on the self. The interplay between privilege and oppression is named as the manifestation of systemic oppression and is located between Parent and Child in all structures, thus recognising the dynamic nature that is again illustrated by curved two-way arrows. The internal manifestation of privilege and oppression is located in the Child (C_2) between P_1 and C_1 to demonstrate the influence of the internalised experience of systemic oppression. *[For a key to understanding and use of ego state abbreviations, see the end of this article.]*

The Parent ego state (P_2)

In this model, P_2 holds 'social constructs' as introjects. These represent our cultural identities now and that of generations before us. We begin with the premise that culture is socially constructed through the shaping of ideas, experiences, and

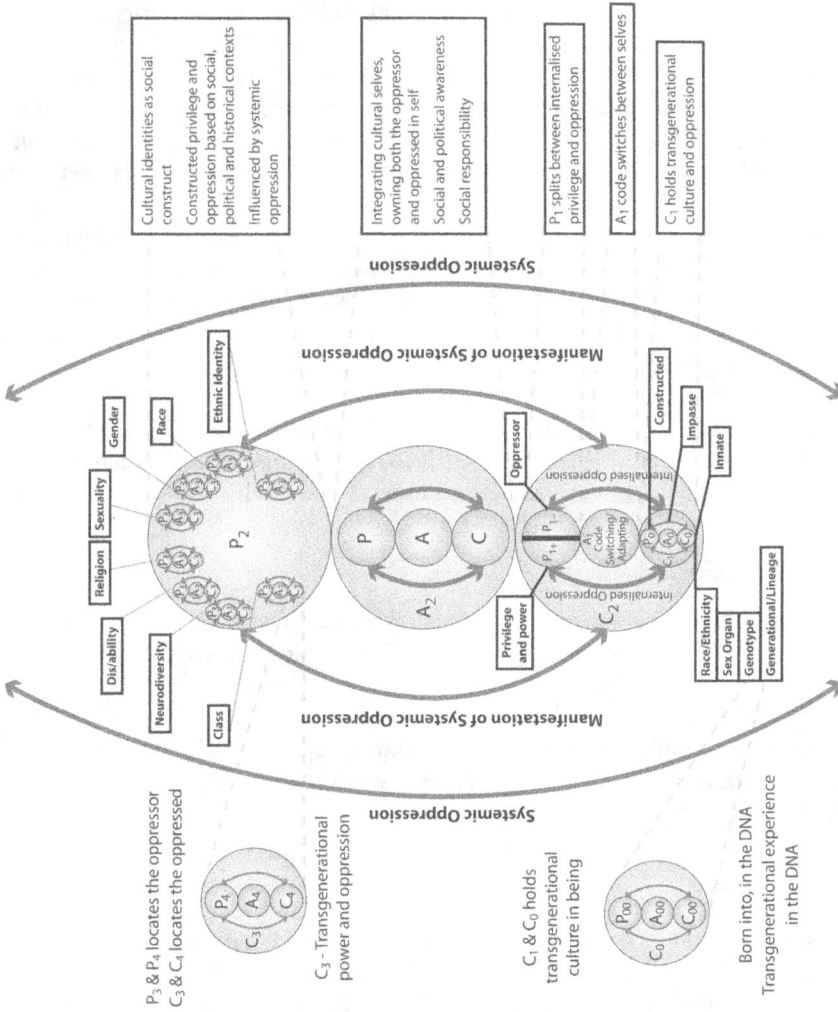

Figure 4.2 Transcultural and Intersectional Ego State Model of the Self, 2025 (Baskerville, 2025)

understandings throughout our lives and the lives of those before us. 'A social construct is something that exists not in objective reality, but as a result of human interaction. It exists because humans agree that it exists' (Bainbridge, 2020, para. 1).

Cultural identities are described as social constructs and housed as introjects in P_2. These include race, ethnicity, gender, class, sexuality, religion, neurodiversity, dis/ability, and so on. Within each cultural identity, privilege and oppression have been socially constructed based on social, political, and historical contexts through time largely based on the power within human and societal relationships. These constructs/introjects – P_3, A_3, and C_3 housed in P_2 – go back generations and were influenced by decades and centuries of systemic oppression. P_3 is identified as holding the privilege and oppressive aspect of the culture, whereas C_3 contains the oppressed aspects of the culture. The arrows demonstrate the interplay between these cultural selves.

These introjects, which have passed down privilege and oppression through generations, remind us of English's (1969) 'hot potato' and were influenced in the case of J and myself by the experience of slavery, the British empire, colonisation, ethnic cleansing, gentrification, and so on. C_3 takes us back historically, putting an additional spotlight on generational experience of cultural selves. Indeed, I see this model as spanning back to P_4, A_4, C_4, and beyond, with P_4 locating the privileged and oppressor and C_4 locating the experience of the oppressed. A_3 and A_4 intuit how to survive in these cultural identities. Indeed, generations before us have found ways to survive, adapt, kill off, and inflate aspects of the self.

The Adult ego state (A_2)

I identify A_2 as holding social and political awareness and knowledge of cultural selves in the here and now within the context of systemic oppression. This involves owning one's intersectional identity by locating and taking responsibility for both the privileged, oppressor, and oppressed parts of the self and the impact of different configurations of multiple privilege and multiple oppression. These, I argue, are owned through a rigorous and ongoing, ever-evolving process of self-awareness and active social responsibility.

The Child ego state (C_2)

C_2 houses the primitive complexity of cultural selves and intersectional identity and shows how systemic oppression is manifested through internalised oppression. P_1, housed in C_2, splits between internalised privilege and oppression, with P_{1+} holding privilege and power and P_{1-} acting out the internalised oppressor. Located in P_1 are the rejected cultural aspects of the self, the unintegrated as described by Hargaden and Sills (2002). A_1, housed in C_2, is the part of self that finds a way to survive by intuiting at a deeply unconscious level how to adapt or code switch cultural selves as a way of protecting the self in normative and oppressive contexts. This reminds me of sinking into despair, driven by fear as I pretend to be a heterosexual again while J does all she can to pump up her privilege and get away from her Brownness. Turner (2021) described this process as follows:

> In order to go through our day to day living we all need to repress or to kill off, [sic] a part of ourselves which is deemed unworthy by society that suggests that we go through life in a constant state of inauthenticity. We perform, we put on a mask, we shuck and jive, we pretend, so we are not too loud, too angry, too gay, too female, too old, or appear disabled to such an extent that we 'frighten' those in front of us into some form of ableist fragility. In order to survive, we become a fantasy of what we think the world needs us to be in order for us to get through our daily existences without fear of attack, vilification, or retribution.
>
> (p. 79)

C_1, housed in C_2, holds the experience of culture and internalised privilege and oppression, bringing a focus to innate versus culturally constructed experience. P_0, housed in C_1, is identified as cultural selves that have been constructed through time. C_0, housed in C_1, is viewed as holding our innate experience, including race/ethnicity, sex organs, genotype, and generational lineage. Within this, C_0 takes us back to transgenerational experience, what has come before us, what is held in our DNA, in the somatic, and in the being of our ancestors (P_{00}, A_{00}, C_{00}).

Klosin et al. (2017) researched genetic instructions in our DNA, thereby bringing to light what is held in the somatic through generations and the discovery that the environment we live in can lead to genetic changes. For example, as a result of a study of roundworms, researchers discovered that environmental genetic changes can be passed down for 14 generations, which supports the idea that as humans we hold experience, trauma, privilege, and oppression in our somatic experience. Thus, P_0 versus C_0 can continue internalised oppression through generations. What has been constructed in P_0 and what is innate in C_0 can potentially cause an impasse and can be challenging to differentiate.

A diagnostic transcultural and intersectional ego state model of the self

I now offer a development of the model to locate intersectional identity by using rings to orbit ego states, thereby identifying the parts of the self that are privileged as well as the oppressor and the parts of the self that are oppressed. This ego state model can be used as a diagnostic model to locate an individual's unique intersectional identity and to account for multiple cultural selves.

In Figure 4.3, I have added two-way arrows between Parent (P_2) and Adult (A_2) and Child (C_2) and Adult (A_2). These demonstrate the need for continued awareness of cultural selves and intersectional identity in the Adult (A_2), for example, Adult awareness of the cultural constructs/introjects we hold in the Parent and where these are placed within systemic oppression as well as Adult awareness of how privilege and oppression have been internalised in the Child. Within the Adult (A_2),

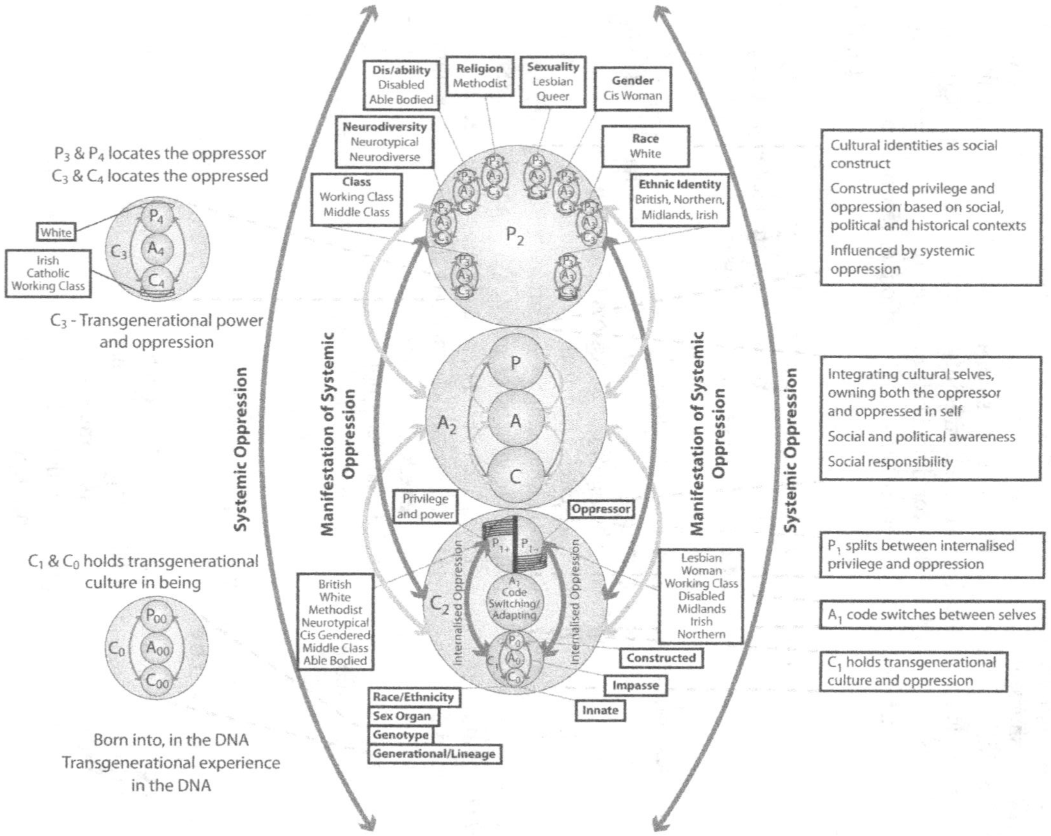

Cultural identities as social construct

Constructed privilege and oppression based on social, political and historical contexts

Influenced by systemic oppression

Integrating cultural selves, owning both the oppressor and oppressed in self

Social and political awareness

Social responsibility

P_1 splits between internalised privilege and oppression

A_1 code switches between selves

C_1 holds transgenerational culture and oppression

Systemic Oppression

Manifestation of Systemic Oppression

Gender
Cis Woman

Race
White

Ethnic Identity
British, Northern, Midlands, Irish

Sexuality
Lesbian
Queer

Religion
Methodist

P_2

Disability
Disabled
Able Bodied

Neurodiversity
Neurotypical
Neurodiverse

Class
Working Class
Middle Class

P   A   C

A_2

Lesbian
Woman
Working Class
Disabled
Midlands
Irish
Northern

Constructed

Impasse

Innate

Oppressor

Internalised Oppression

P_{1+} P_{1-}

A_1
Code
switching/
adapting

P_2

Internalised Oppression

C_2

Privilege
and power

British
White
Methodist
Neurotypical
Cis Gendered
Middle Class
Able Bodied

Race/Ethnicity
Sex Organ
Genotype
Generational/Lineage

Systemic Oppression

Manifestation of Systemic Oppression

P_3 & P_4 locates the oppressor
C_3 & C_4 locates the oppressed

P_4 A_4 C_4

C_3

White

Irish
Catholic
Working Class

C_3 - Transgenerational power and oppression

C_1 & C_0 holds transgenerational culture in being

P_{00} A_{00} C_{00}

C_0

Born into, in the DNA

Transgenerational experience in the DNA

Figure 4.3 Diagnostic model to locate Transcultural and Intersectional Identity – V (Baskerville, 2025)

I have placed the dynamic PAC model to illustrate the ongoing, lifelong process of accounting for the difference and the reality that as long as we are alive, we will continue to move in and out of awareness around themes of discrimination.

In presenting this diagnostic model, I have used rings to orbit ego states in order to locate privilege and oppression within each social construct of culture. 'To orbit' can be described as a curved path around a celestial body, which I have adapted as the self. Or we may define 'orbit' as the sphere of power or influence of a person (*Dictionary.com*, n.d.). To describe it another way, we might imagine cultural selves being housed within a juke box, as stacks of records, some historical, some current, each one playing in different times and contexts, keeping some well hidden at the bottom of the stack and often managing multiple tunes playing at the same time, with some being more current, more popular, liked or disliked, or even gotten rid of.

To bring this model alive, I will describe what I perceive to be my intersectional identity (Figure 4.3) and then how J perceives hers (Figure 4.4). I do not see either of these as static but as an evolving process as we uncover unconscious bias.

Starting with P_2, I begin by identifying my class cultural constructs. My middle class culture privileged and the oppressor orbits P_3, while my working class culture oppressed orbits C_3 and C_4. I have identified my neuro identity as neurotypical culture as privileged and the oppressor orbiting P_3, while my emerging neurodiversity oppressed orbits C_3. I have identified my dis/ability culture as able-bodied as privileged and the oppressor orbiting P_3, and my developing disability as oppressed orbiting C_3. I have identified my religion as Methodist orbiting P_3 as privileged and the oppressor while naming my generational Catholic culture as orbiting C_4 as oppressed. I have identified my sexuality as Queer and lesbian both orbiting C_3 as oppressed. I have identified my gender as cis gender woman, cis gender orbiting P_3 as privileged and oppressor, alongside woman orbiting C_3 oppressed. My race is constructed as White and orbits P_3 privileged and the oppressor as well as generationally White orbits P_4 privileged and the oppressor. My ethnic identity British orbits P_3 privileged and the oppressor, Northern orbits C_3 oppressed. Midlands orbits C_3 oppressed. My ancestral Irish culture orbits C_3 and C_4, oppressed.

Furthermore, C_2 locates the manifestation of my internalised experience of privilege and oppression. P_{1+} represents internalised privilege and power and P_{1-} the internalised oppression, experienced as the oppressor. In this my privileged identities are British, White, Methodist, neurotypical, cisgender, and middle class and able-bodied orbiting P_{1+}, while my lesbian, woman, working class, disabled, Midlands, Irish, and Northern orbit P_{1-} internalised oppressor. These are experienced in C_1 as either privileged or oppressed and may create an impasse between what is constructed P_0 and what is innate C_0. Indeed these ego states could overlap highlighting that identities have been derived by generations before us.

Beginning with P_2, within class, J has identified her middle class culture as privileged and the oppressor, which orbits P_3; while her working class culture as oppressed orbits C_3. She has identified her neurodiversity as neurotypical,

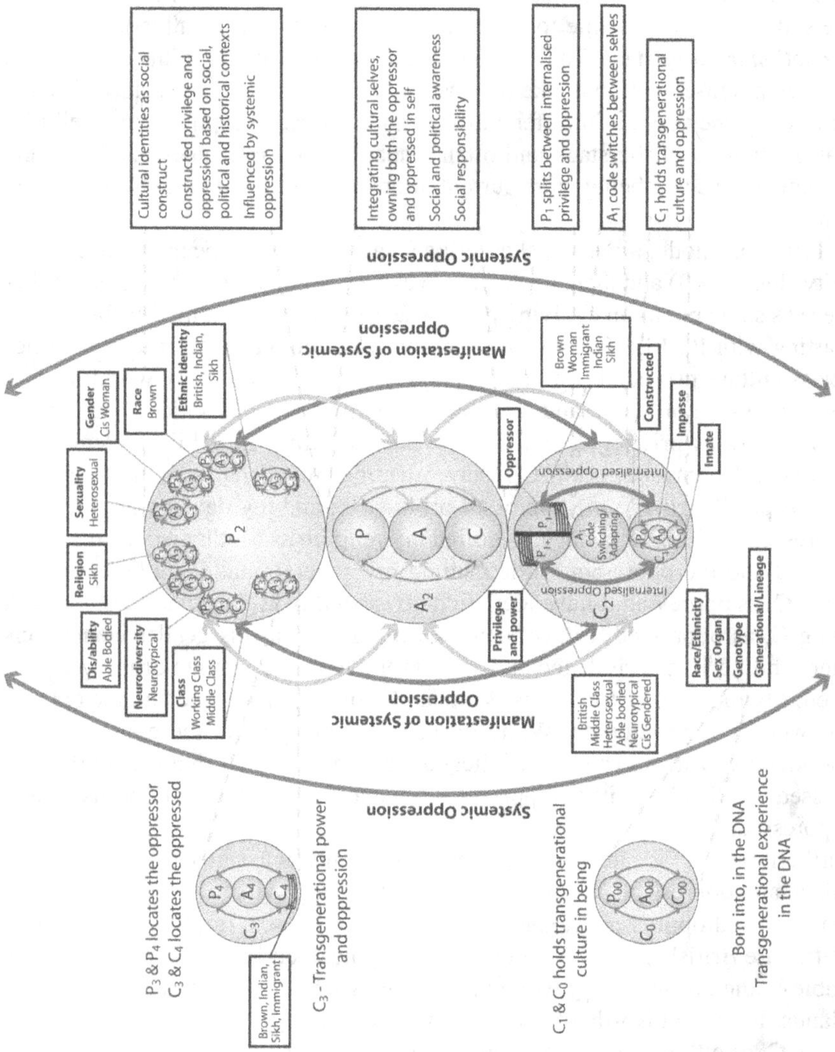

Figure 4.4 Diagnostic model to locate Transcultural and Intersectional identity – J (Baskerville, 2025)

orbiting P_3 constructed as privileged and the oppressor; and her disability status as able-bodied orbiting P_3 constructed as privileged and the oppressor. J has identified her religion as Sikh orbiting C_3 as oppressed, while identifying her generational Indian and Sikh culture as orbiting C_4 as oppressed. She has identified her sexuality as heterosexual orbiting P_3 as privileged and the oppressor. Her gender is cis woman constructed as privileged and oppressor, and woman orbits C_3 oppressed. J identifies her race as Brown which orbits C_3 and C_4 as oppressed, while she identifies her ethnicity as British as privileged and the oppressor orbiting P_3. Her Indian, Sikh ethnicity she identifies as oppressed orbiting C_3 and C_4, alongside her immigrant transgenerational history as oppressed orbiting C_4.

J identifies her British, middle class, heterosexual, able-bodied, neurotypical and cis gendered selves as orbiting P_{1+} representing internalised privilege and power. On the other hand, her Brown, woman, immigrant history, Indian, and Sikh identities orbit P_{1-} representing internalised oppressor. These all influence her experience of privilege and oppression in C_1 and may create an impasse or overlap between what is constructed P_0 and what is innate C_0.

When reflecting on the dialogue between J and myself and locating our intersectional identities, it is evident that J experiences multiple oppression and discrimination as a Brown, woman, Indian, Sikh with an immigrant generational experience and working class history alongside holding privilege in being British, heterosexual, able-bodied, neurotypical, middle class, and cis gendered. These social categories are shaped by the way they overlap. For example, although both J and I are British, we present different configurations of overlapping cultural selves and bring varying levels of discrimination, for example, White British versus British Brown Indian. I experience more privilege because I am protected by the systemic dynamics of White supremacy alongside the parts of me that are oppressed, such as my Irish roots, my working class history, being a woman, and my lesbian identity.

Through dialogue, J and I have found connection in our experience of oppression and at the same time have accounted for our difference and the power dynamic between us.

Conclusion

Jorge Gutierrez (cited in Romero, 2018) said: 'I always feel that I am at the edge of two borders.... It feels like I am fighting two different struggles. Whenever I come across LGBT folk that don't support immigrant rights, I feel marginalised and oppressed by my own community. Equally, when I am around people belonging to the immigrant community, I am saddened that some don't support equal rights for LGBT people' (p. 115). In each encounter we may be met in some identities and oppressed in others, as illustrated in my dialogue with J. This is reminiscent of Black, lesbian, mother, warrior, and poet Audre Lorde (1997), who wrote that she was defined as 'other' in every group of which she was a part. This is the lived experience of intersectionality, the discourse between different cultural groups and selves, as evident in today's tension between the Trans-exclusionary radical feminists and the Trans community, for example.

So, what does this mean for the therapeutic relationship? We need in some way to surrender to the reality of systemic oppression and the fact that relationships are not equal. We need to ask, how will this play out in this relationship? Who holds the power? What parts of me are welcome here? What parts do I need suppress, split off in this relationship?

J and I found a deeper connection through our honest exploration, by daring to dialogue about our differences and challenging perceptions in ourselves and each other, recognising defences and working through shame and disturbance. Our ancestors sat between us, in solidarity and in deep conflict, inviting us to bear the unbearable and to radically and genuinely see each other.

The embodiment of social responsibility and social and political awareness invites us to deeply acknowledge who holds the power in the room and to consider the oppressor and oppressed in each therapeutic encounter. Doing so allows us to become aware of internalised oppression, cultural impasse, and enactment, and enables themes of generational trauma to emerge and White privilege to be accounted for. This sets the scene for significant, courageous, and difficult conversations about difference and othering and paves the way for social change, anti-oppressive practice, and transformation. As Crenshaw (2019) said: 'The core task of any intersectional approach is not just scratching the surface but specifically tackling social injustices at their very roots' (p. 1).

> Not everything that is faced can be changed, but nothing can be changed until it is faced.
>
> (Baldwin, 1962, 1972)

Key for ego state abbreviations

Overview of ego states

- P_2: Introjects of parents and parent figures
- A_2: Integrates healthy aspects of the Parent and Child
- C_2: Behaviours, thoughts, and feelings replayed from childhood, including trauma, script, and real self

Parent ego state (P_2)

Parent Introjects in P_2 are divided into three sections:

- P_3: Parent in the original parent figure

- A_3: Adult in the original parent figure
- C_3: Child in the original parent figure

In the transcultural and intersectional ego state model, P_4, A_4, and C_4 have been located in C_3 to take us back generationally to the internalised social construct of privileged and oppressed in our cultural histories.

Child ego state (C_2)

- P_1: The child's primitive response and understanding of the original parent. Unintegrated P_{1+} and P_{1-} creates a split between positive and negative experience.
- A_1: Adult in the Child – 'The Little Professor'. The Adult in the Child intuits how to survive in the world.
- C_1: Child in the Child – 'the somatic Child'. What is held in the body unconsciously.

C_1 – Child in the Child

P_0, A_0, and C_0 located in C_1 are the unconscious somatic experience, what is in the DNA, the being, the core of our relational, emotional, and psychological needs (the real self).

- P_{00}, A_{00}, and C_{00} take us further back generationally.

References

Bainbridge, C. (2020). *Why social constructs are created*. Verywellmind. Retrieved July 20, 2021. https://www.verywellmind.com/definition-of-social-construct-1448922

Baldwin, J. (1962). Quote from *New York Times,* January 14, 1962.

Baldwin, J. (1972). *No name in the street*. (Penguin Modern Classics, 2024). London: Penguin Random House.

Baskerville, V. (2022). A transcultural and intersectional ego state model of the self: The influence of transcultural and intersectional identity on self and other. *Transactional Analysis Journal*, *52*(32), 1–16. http://doi.org/10.1080/03621537.2022.2076398

Berne, E. (1961). *Transactional analysis in psychotherapy. A systematic individual and social psychiatry*. New York: Grove Press.

Crenshaw, K. (1989). 'Demarginalizing the intersection of race and sex: A black feminist critique of antidiscrimination doctrine, feminist theory and antiracist politics'. *University of Chicago Legal Forum*, Issue 1, Article 8. https://scholarship.law.columbia.edu/faculty_scholarship/3007

Crenshaw, K. (2019). 'Reach everyone on the planet …': Kimberlé Crenshaw and intersectionality (Gunda Werner Institute in the Heinrich Böll Foundation and the Centre for Intersectional Justice, Eds.). https://eu.boell.org/en/2019/04/28/reach-everyone-planet-kimberle-crenshaw-and-intersectionality

Dictionary.com. (n.d.). Retrieved July 20, 2021 from https://www.dictionary.com/browse/orbit

Drego, P. (1983). The cultural parent. *Transactional Analysis Journal*, *13*(4), 224–227. https://doi.org/10.1177/036215378301300404

English, F. (1969). Episcript and the "hot potato" game. *Transactional Analysis Bulletin*, *8*(32), 77–82.

Hargaden, H., & Sills, C. (2002). *Transactional analysis: A relational perspective*. East Sussex: Brunner-Routledge.

Hart, A. (2017). From multicultural competence to radical openness: A psychoanalytic engagement of otherness. *The American Psychoanalyst*, *51*(1), 12–13, 26–27. https://apsa.org/wp-content/uploads/apsaa-publications/vol51no1-TOC/html/vol51no1_09.xhtml

Klosin, A., Casas, E., Hidalgo-Carcedo, C., Vavouri, T., & Lehner, B. (2017). Transgenerational transmission of environmental information in *c. elegans*. *Science*, *356*(6335), 320–323. https://pubmed.ncbi.nlm.nih.gov/28428426

Lorde, A. (1997). *The cancer journals*. San Francisco: Aunt Lute Books.

Minikin, K. (2021). Relative privilege and the seduction of normativity. *Transactional Analysis Journal*, *51*(1), 35–48. https://doi.org/10.1080/03621537.2020.1853349

Romero, M. (2018). *Introducing intersectionality*. Cambridge: Polity Press.

Shivanath, S., & Hiremath, M. (2003). 'The psychodynamics of race and culture'. In C. Sills & H. Hargaden (Eds.), *Ego states* (Key concepts in transactional analysis: Contemporary views) (pp. 169–184). Worcestershire: Worth Publishing.

Tudor, K., & Summers, G. (2000). Co-creative transactional analysis. *Transactional Analysis Journal*, *30*(1), 23–40. https://doi.org/10.1177/036215370003000104

Turner, D. (2021). *Intersections of privilege and otherness in counselling and psychotherapy*. London: Routledge.

Chapter 5

Deconstructing and reconstructing the curriculum through an intersectional lens

Historically, counselling and psychotherapy, and indeed transactional analysis have been influenced by western/northern hemisphere concepts and ideology. Thus, largely offering a White, individualistic, heteronormative, neurotypical, middle class, and binary lens to theory, practice, and curriculums.

This chapter offers a model to deconstruct and reconstruct, and begin to decolonise our theories and curriculums, aiming to facilitate the reconstruction of theories through an intersectional lens. A key transactional analysis theory will be presented, bringing the ideas of deconstruction and reconstruction alive in practice.

What is deconstruction?

Deconstruction is about breaking something down into parts in order to better understand its meaning, to 'reduce something to its constituent parts in order to reinterpret it' (OED, 2012); 'the analysis of something (as language or literature) by the separation and individual examination of its basic elements' (The Merriam-Webster Dictionary, 2022); 'in popular usage the term [deconstruction] has come to mean a critical dismantling of tradition and traditional modes of thought' (Encyclopedia Britannica, 2025).

> We are all mediators and translators
>
> Jacques Derrida (DK, 2024, p. 314).

In philosophy, the term 'deconstruction' was coined by the French philosopher Jacques Derrida in the late 1960s. He criticised philosophers of the Western tradition for assuming fixed reference points for truth; he used the word deconstruction to describe the process of exposing this illusion. 'Using the example of written texts Derrida argued that since the meanings of words always depend on the meanings of other words, it is impossible to have a complete understanding of them' (DK, 2024, p. 73).

Deconstruction was a way 'of reading texts to bring these hidden paradoxes and contradictions into the open … bringing into question the relationship between language, thought and even ethics' (DK, 2024, p. 314). In short, Derrida considered

DOI: 10.4324/9781003509424-5

not just what is said in the text but what is not said – dismantling language to see what lies beneath the surface (Norris, 2002).

In developing the idea of deconstruction of theory through an intersectional lens, literary concepts and ideas are applicable. Texts cannot represent reality and theory does not fully capture lived experience, as each concept produces a variety of meanings and understandings.

Deconstruction and social constructs

Our theories, influenced by the social, cultural, political, and intersectional identities of the authors of their time arguably bring a lens of systemic oppression, whether this be through the intersects of race, gender, sexuality, and so on. According to Subramaniam (2010), social constructionism is a 'theory of knowledge that holds that characteristics typically thought to be immutable and solely biological – such as gender, race, class, ability, and sexuality – are products of human definition and interpretation shaped by cultural and historical contexts. As such, social constructionism highlights the ways in which cultural categories – like "men", "women", "Black", "White" – are concepts created, changed, and reproduced through historical processes within institutions and culture'.

Deconstruction challenges such social constructs, serving to analyse the contents of one's belief system, described as 'a concept that exists not in objective reality, but as a result of human interaction. It exists because humans agree that it exists' (Bainbridge, 2020).

Deconstruction and binary oppositions

A central idea of deconstruction is that texts/ideas are made up of a series of binary oppositions – e.g., black and white, male and female, presence and absence. The pairs of binaries are assumed to be objective and stable but the process of deconstruction reveals them to be otherwise, i.e., subjective and unstable. A binary consists of two concepts that are presented as being at odds with each other, arguably contributing to themes of discrimination and polarisation.

Queer theory (Chandler & Munday, 2011) and the Trans movement further challenge the binary aspects of social construction at the root of systemic oppression. Queer theory is a way of thinking that dismantles traditional assumptions about gender and sexual identities – the field emerged from sexuality studies and women's studies. Queer theorists analyse gender and sexuality as socially and culturally constructed concepts. Arguably, the idea of gender as binary is a Western concept that was forced upon native cultures around the world through colonisation. Certainly, many eastern and indigenous cultures pre-colonisation brought a gender fluid lens.

Hines (2022) states: 'Gender systems in the west have largely followed a binary model, in which male and female are understood to be the only gender categories, with women and men seen fundamentally different. A consideration of gender systems across the globe shows that this has not been the case elsewhere' (p.78).

Just a few examples of this include the Hijra community that is a significant part of culture in India, and legally recognised as a third gender, along with deities and mythology defying the gender binary. In Pakistan, Hijra people who are Trans or intersex were traditionally well respected. While North American 'two spirited' members of the Zuni community were held in high regard by Native Americans and were believed to have greater spiritual gifts. The Travesti in Latin America, people understood to be both men and women, have been considered as the third sex; along with the Muxe in Mexico pre-Spanish colonisation, and the gender diverse Kathoey people in Thailand (Hines, 2022). 'Gender diversity has also been documented in China, Iran, Indonesia, Japan, Nepal, South Korea and Vietnam. And in Indonesia which has the largest population of Muslims, Waria people, who were assigned male at birth … live openly as women' (Hines, 2022, p. 80).

Thus, the process of deconstruction of our theories serves to challenge binaries, exclusion, and power dynamics, as well as the lack of representation of Black and minoritised groups and cultural and social perceptions.

Colonisation of the curriculum

One of the most significant problems relating to the curriculum in transactional analysis and psychotherapy training is the lack of representation and lived experience of Black and minoritised groups. This is commonly referred to as the colonisation of the curriculum. Colonisation of the curriculum has offered, through a dominant culture, one view. Its normative monocultural lens has arguably excluded many students of psychotherapy and transactional analysis (Ahmed et al., 2023). Decolonising the curriculum means creating safe spaces for all transcultural difference, inviting dialogue, while considering use of resources on how to include and envision all intersectional identities and knowledge systems in the theories and the curriculum. It challenges what is being taught and how it frames transactional analysis and the wider world.

White dominance in western psychotherapy theory offers only one lens to understand the self – the self that is seen through the White gaze (Morrison, 1998), whatever the ethnic and race identity of the other. Decolonising is integral to an inclusive curriculum and seeks to both recognise and address the legacies of disadvantage, injustice, and racism that have arisen from historic global White supremacy and systemic oppression. Deconstructing our theories is one way of addressing this.

Deconstructing our models

The model outlined here serves to deconstruct the theory or indeed decontaminate and deconfuse the theory simultaneously through intellectual critique and evolving social and political awareness, an examination of unconscious bias, and intersectional positioning. Intersectionality offers a more complex map considering all the differing transcultural aspects and intersects of self-experience within the context of systemic oppression. Let us be clear, this is not to dismiss our original theories but to gain a depth understanding of their context and to bring them into contemporary thinking.

The idea of deconstructing and reconstructing the curriculum is informed by social constructivism, decolonisation, intersectionality, and Queer theory; evolving ideas of social activism as a way of informing contemporary theory; and moving away from the constraints and the limitations of one lens holding power and authority. It draws on marginalised voices, fringe thinking, podcasts, dialogue, and interviews.

When deconstructing a theoretical model, I invite consideration of the cultural, social, political, and historical contexts of the author at the time of writing. This gives insight into the construction of each theoretical concept. I ask who was the author? What are their cultural contexts and intersectional identities? Thus, considering their part in systemic oppression, the complexities of multiple privilege and multiple oppression.

I consider what was going on in the world at the time of writing socially and politically? What were the social norms? I consider the political contexts at the time of writing and the political positioning of the author. I then consider historical contexts of the author both generationally and ancestrally.

In each of these critical questions I seek to establish what informs the theoretical constructs, whether they are influenced by individualistic culture, collective culture, normative or marginalised culture, whether they offer a colonised lens, including heteronormative, White, and binary gendered.

In critiquing the theory, I consider who is excluded, whose voices are amplified, who has been marginalised, where does the power sit? What aspects have been split off, gotten rid of? (Baskerville, 2022; Turner, 2021). Where is the bias in this? Who is it representing? Whose lived experience? How has this theory been socially constructed? What is the binary?

We deconstruct something to be able to describe or show exactly how a past event happened – in this respect deconstructing theory is to see how past theory was constructed through the lived experience of its author. Thus, considering theory as held in its time, offering a case for the need to reconstruct as societies change, but also challenging how history was logged and through whose lens.

What is reconstruction?

The action of reconstructing can be described as the act or process of rebuilding, repairing, or restoring something: to fix up, modernise, overhaul, reassemble, rebuild, recreate, re-establish, or regenerate. To reiterate, this is absolutely not to dismiss our original theories but to reassemble to gain a depth understanding of their context and to bring them into contemporary thinking.

Linguistic reconstruction is a procedure for inferring an unattested ancestral state of a language on the evidence of data that are available from a later period. Thus, considering language and theory as held in its time, offering a case for the need to reconstruct as societies change and reorganising it to be more representative and inclusive in the present.

Reconstructing our models

When considering reconstruction of core theory, I begin by asking: Is this theory translatable transculturally? What may be lost in translation? Is this theory and are these concepts translatable across the breadth of intersectional lived experience and social, cultural, and political contexts? For example, the 'I'm OK, you're OK', is an individualistic concept embedded in western language (Baskerville, 2021). I consider how we may translate this formative existential idea through collective, indigenous, and polygamous cultures. The important question is: how do we bring *multiple* intersectional lenses and frames of reference to this theory/concept/diagram?

I consider the following questions (see Figure 5.1).

How may we reconstruct the theory through an intersectional lens? How may we account for power dynamics? How may we account for difference? How may we consider representation? How may we account for lived experience presently, historically, and ancestrally?

In this, I also consider a meta perspective of the critique and parallel process. What does the person or persons who critique bring? What intersectional lens are they bringing to this theory? What unconscious bias may be present? What parallel process may be enacted? And which defences do you need to lay down?

Case study: Deconstruction and reconstruction of symbiosis theory with an intersectional lens

For the purpose of bringing alive the idea of deconstruction and reconstruction of theory through an intersectional lens, and in order to make theory more representative I will use the model (see Figure 5.1), to demonstrate critiquing the original theory of 'symbiosis' (Schiff & Schiff, 1971). While remembering it as a social construct of its time, now transported into the present, I have chosen this particular theoretical concept – symbiosis – following discussion in my community around differing intersectional configurations.

All cultural contexts will have experience of symbiosis and differing frames of reference around what is health. I am not disputing it as a concept that offers insight into the early relationship between infant and carer/carers; or the manifestation of the second order symbiosis into adulthood. However, many will feel excluded by the construction of the language and the organisation of the diagram as binary, gendered, and heteronormative, along with the lack of attention paid to systemic power dynamics, highlighting the absence of different cultural and social experience.

Deconstruction and reconstruction of theory through an intersectional lens

Baskerville, 2025

Deconstruction through an intersectional lens

- Who was the author?
- What were their cultural and social contexts and intersectional identities at the time of writing? Consider historical contexts of the author both generationally and ancestrally.
- What was going on in the world at the time of writing politically?
- What was going on in the world at the time of writing socially? What were social norms?
- How did the author position themselves?
- What lens does the theory bring? Whose voices are amplified? Where does power sit?
- Who has been marginalised? What aspects have been split off, gotten rid of?
- Where is the unconscious bias in this?
- Who is it representing? Whose lived experience?
- What part of systemic oppression is being played out in this theory?

Reconstruction through an intersectional lens

- How may we reconstruct the theory through an intersectional lens?
- How may we account for power dynamics?
- How may we account for difference?
- How may we consider representation?
- How may we account for lived experience presently, historically and ancestrally?

Meta perspective of the critique and parallel process

- What lived experience does the person/s critiquing bring?
- What intersectional lens are they bringing to this theory?
- What unconscious bias may be present?

Figure 5.1 Deconstruction and reconstruction model

This case study does not aim to critique or comment on the ethical practice of Jacqui and Aaron Schiff, it aims to offer some ways of thinking around deconstructing and reconstructing the symbiosis theoretical model/diagram, in order to account for intersectional difference and lived experience.

A case example from a TA East London psychotherapy training group

The group is made up of 20 colleagues – including 18 students and 2 educators. In the room there is a breadth of intersectional lived experience, for example, configurations of Trans, non-binary, non-monogamous, polygamous, Queer, lesbian, heterosexual, birth mothers, mothers who have had children through donor insemination, cis men, cis women, Black, White, dual heritage, of Caribbean descent, of African descent, Spanish, Italian, Latino, indigenous, German, native British, British citizen, Scottish, English, Irish, Polish, English as a second language, multilingual, Autistic, ADHD, neurodivergent, neurotypical, Ukrainian asylum seeker, middle class, working class.

I introduce the original theoretical concept of symbiosis through definitions and explanation. I am aware of both its extraordinary insight into relationship and its limitations in this diverse cultural context and in our consulting rooms.

In considering all lived experience I begin by naming the model as being framed within a White, heteronormative, binary gendered and individualistic lens.

I invite the deconstruction of the theory by inviting in all intersectional experiences in the room. Deconstruction begins by researching the social, cultural, political, and historical context and intersectional identity of the author/s at the time of writing. This sets the scene in understanding the lens of the theory and concept.

Students work together in small groups researching the author and critiquing theory across different cultural contexts within themselves and with each other. In the whole group we invite in all intersectional voices. Together we deconstruct the theory and reconstruct through an intersectional lens. Moving away from the 'normative gaze' to an intersectional lens.

The following gives an example of this active process each time we meet original core theory.

Introduction

Schiff and Schiff (1971), originally presented the concept of symbiosis in their article 'Passivity'. They stated: 'Symbiosis is a normal condition of the oral stage in the development of a child. It is experienced by both the mother and the child as a merging or sharing of their needs'. They added that the structure of a symbiosis involves two individuals using only those ego states that together combine to form one total personality.

Schiff and Schiff (1971) stated that pathology is likely to result from disturbances in the symbiotic relationship or in the differentiation of the child from the mother. It is also likely to occur in instances where parenting is inadequate to prepare the child to function as an independent person who can solve problems in the world.

Subsequently, Schiff and Cathexis Institute (1975) clarified this definition by stating: 'A symbiosis occurs when two or more individuals behave as though between them, they form a whole personality. This relationship is characterised structurally by neither individual cathecting a full complement of ego states'.

The diagram showing symbiosis has evolved through various forms.

In their 1971 article, 'Passivity', the Schiffs depict it only by using dotted lines and solid boundaries for the ego state circles. In *Cathexis Reader* (1975), they add arrows running between the active ego states in the two parties. The version of the diagram commonly used in current literature, with an envelope drawn round the active ego states, made its first published appearance in the article 'Normal Dependency and Symbiosis' by Woollams and Huige (1977); this was then cited in Schiff (1977), 'Personality Development and Symbiosis'.

Deconstruction

Who were the authors?

Jacqui Schiff and Aaron Wolfe Schiff

What were their cultural and social contexts and intersectional identities at the time of writing? Consider historical contexts of the authors both generationally and ancestrally.

Jacqui Schiff –	White, Jewish, American, parented by young mother, primarily raised by grandmothers, authoritarian stepfather – 'you can do what you want', cis woman, western ideology, heterosexual relationship, married to Moe Schiff, Jewish, who was a psychiatric social worker, mother (lost multiple pregnancies, had three children), psychiatric social worker, second generation transactional analyst, founder of Cathexis School (Gheorghe et al., 2019).
Aaron Wolfe Schiff –	White American, heterosexual, cis man was reparented and later legally adopted son of Jacqui Schiff, taking her last name; had come for treatment for 'psychiatric problems' seven years earlier. Later graduated from Virginia with a degree in psychology, briefly worked as a therapist, advanced member of ITAA. Consultant at the Cathexis Institute. Married and had a child.

What was going on in the world (USA) at the time of writing politically?

It was after the Vietnam war, and there was a rising of the anti-war movement. The 1970s continued radical ideas of the 1960s. There were advances in the African American civil rights and the women's movement, homosexuality was decriminalised, and the Gay liberation movement flourished. The Cold War between the capitalist West and the communist East was ongoing. Apartheid continued in South Africa. There was racial segregation in some American states.

What was going on in the world (USA) at the time of writing socially? What were the social norms?

It was a time of restlessness and a questioning of traditional authority, a time of new age, rebirthing, and pop psychology. Privileged Americans turned away from the problems of society looking for spiritual fulfilment, through exercise, psychotherapy, health food, and alternative religions, following the teachings of self-anointed prophets and spiritual gurus. There was a binary between those challenging traditionalism and those drawing on fundamental Christian values.

How did the authors position themselves?

Jacqui Schiff –   transactional analyst, psychotherapist, radical, pioneer, expert, authoritarian, guru; we must also account for her Jewish identity and lineage of marginalisation.

Aaron Wolfe Schiff –   *client/patient, adopted child/adult, took on Schiff's surname, therapist, Cathexis consultant.*

What lens does the theory of symbiosis bring? Whose voices are amplified? Where does the power sit?

Individualistic, White, western, heteronormative, nuclear family, binary gendered, 'normative culture'. Focus on parenting from Parent and Adult ego state, inviting regression in the other, thus holding power. It does not account for intersectional power dynamics, patriarchal structures, colonisation, and systemic oppression, meaning a person who is marginalised may systemically be positioned in Child and may have to soothe those holding power in order to exist safely in the world.

Who has been marginalised? What aspects have been split off, gotten rid of?

Collective culture, people of colour, non-traditional families, LGBTQIA + and Queer families – Gender Sex Relationship Diversity (GSRD).

Where is the unconscious bias in this?

Mother as the primary caregiver, one primary parent, cis gendered parents. Construct of mother as heteronormative, wife, cared for by husband. Influence of White western lens on what is 'normal' dependency and what is 'healthy' versus 'unhealthy'.

Who is it representing? Whose lived experience?

Cis gendered mothers from an individualistic White heteronormative socially constructed lens.

What part of systemic oppression is being played out in this theory?

Schiff positions the theory from a normative position, thus offering one cultural experience while others will be marginalised. The power sits in the individualistic and heteronormative experience. The power sits in one person holding the power and the other giving up their power, thus from a place of privilege versus oppression.

   For the purpose of illustration, I have drawn on the critical musings in all training year groups I have taught from TA 101 to year 4. I own that I bring my lived experience to these musings. Once these reflections are considered in group training settings, bringing the lived experience of all group members, we then reflect on reconstructing the theory with an intersectional lens.

Reconstruction

How may we reconstruct the theory of symbiosis through an intersectional lens?

Regarding the first order symbiosis and the idea of healthy early attachment and symbiosis, we may consider the social construct of mother/caregiver and parent/parents. Drawing on social contexts, including lived Queer experience, lived Black, non-binary and Trans contexts, lived class experience, and so on, accounting for the complexity and intersection of these identities within each individual, moving away from colonisation, the influence of patriarchy, heteronormativity, capitalism, imperialism, and dominant 'normative' culture *per se*. We will consider lived experience in our multi-diverse transcultural communities, collective culture, indigenous cultures that have come before and the evolving of Queer families. In this we may or may not consider the second order symbiosis as pathological, thus a culturally sensitive lens is paramount, in attending to a breadth of contexts and differences around individualistic and collective culture's attachment styles, values, and ideas around interdependence.

How may we account for power dynamics?

Reflecting on 'pathological symbiosis' between two adults (a symbiosis is said to occur when two or more individuals behave as though between them, they form a single person), it is important to account for systemic oppression and the binary of societal identities. For example, oppressive structures like White supremacy, binary gendered, neurotypicality, arguably sit in Parent, while marginalised identities sit in Child; in a relational dynamic that serves to diminish the 'others' experience. While second order symbiosis could account for the systemic lived experience of those who are marginalised having to placate those in power (code switch). For example, the Palestinian student who talked about not being allowed to exist in the world, or the Latino student, who described experiencing racism when they came to Europe. Or the Queer student who tells their story of code switching to acting heterosexual, so that they are safe from homophobia (Figure 5.2).

How may we account for difference? How may we consider representation? How may we account for lived experience presently, historically, and ancestrally?

Accounting for different lived experience is paramount, intersectionality puts a spotlight on all the unique cultural and social configurations we each inhabit presently, historically, and ancestrally. Thus, accounting for the social construct of primary parent through history from gender fluidity to gender binary and the idea that a cis gendered woman equates to mother. We may develop the first order symbiosis (Figure 5.3) and the second order symbiosis (Figure 5.4) concept and

Privileged   Oppressed

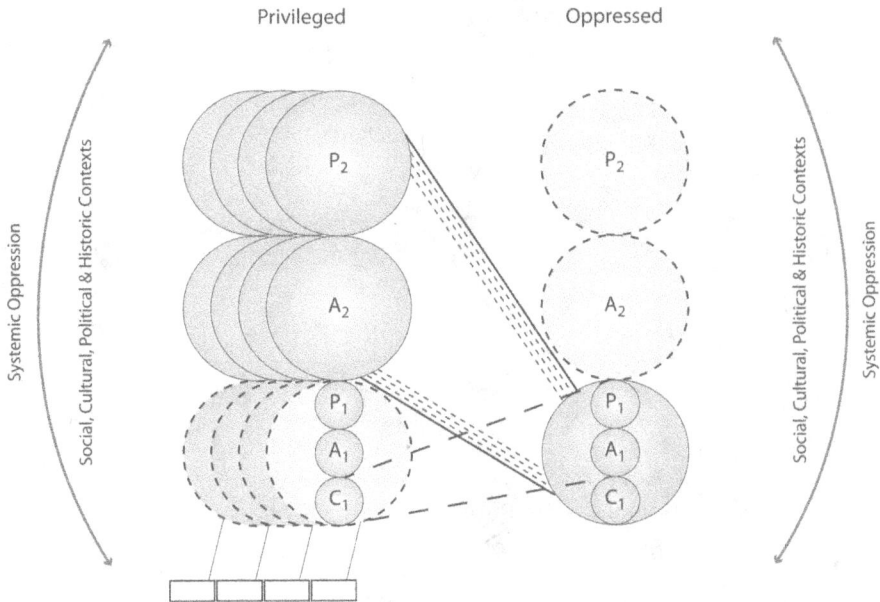

Figure 5.2 Systemic second order symbiosis diagram (Baskerville, 2025)

diagram to include all the configurations of primary parents/caregivers, considering ethnicity, heritage, and gender, and indeed all the complexities of intersectional identities. Thus including collective culture, families and communities that raise a child, multiple primary carers including aunts, uncles, grandparents, older siblings, accounting for multiple mothers; including polygamous families, surrogacy mothers, birth and non-birth mothers, adoptive mothers, single cis mothers and queer mothers, the DNA of egg donating mothers, two mothers in a same sex relationship, Trans men who are birth mothers, Trans women who are mothers, two fathers as primary parents, fathers who identify as the construct of mother and so on. The model and diagram needs to open up frame of reference by adapting to all these configurations and many more. Indeed, an infant/child may be in symbiosis with multiple parents in collective, polygamous, and Queer cultural contexts and communities. To this end, the inclusive first order and second order symbiosis diagrams (Figures 5.3 and 5.4) enable the practitioner and client/s to consider multiple symbiosis and relational attachments through an intersectional lens.

Furthermore, the second order symbiosis diagram has been further developed by being placed within systemic oppression, thereby accounting for social, cultural, political, and historical contexts, highlighting systemic enactment and power differentials of privileged identities located in Parent and marginalised identities located in Child.

Primary Caregiver/s   Infant

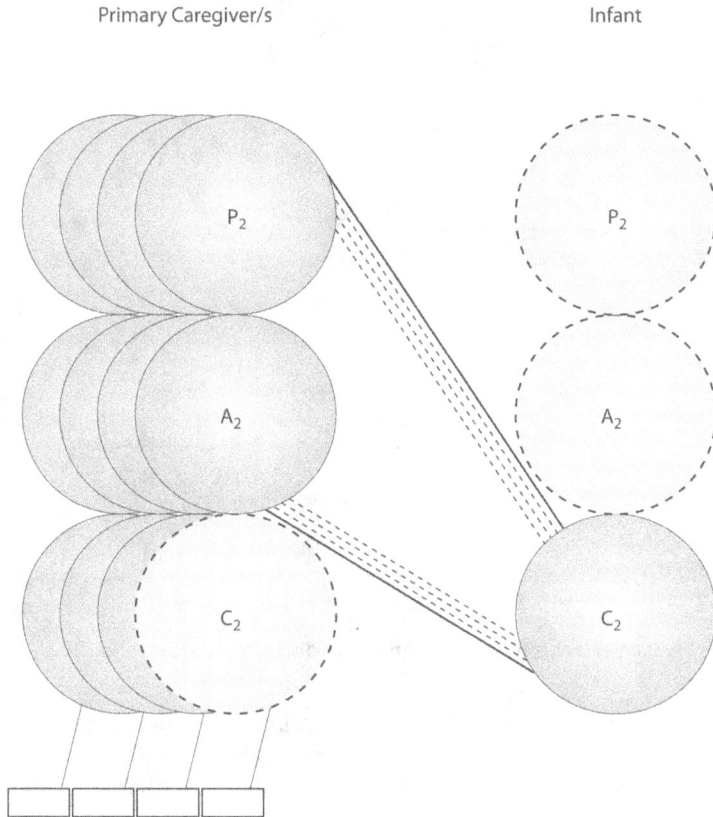

Figure 5.3 Inclusive first order symbiosis diagram (Baskerville, 2025)

Meta perspective considerations

Moreover, in the deconstruction and reconstruction, and decolonisation of theory we may consider what unconscious bias/prejudices sit in the shadow of the author?

What is not being said here, or erased? (Vaid-Menon, 2022). What part of systemic oppression is being played out in this theory? And indeed, what was not in social conscious awareness at the time of writing?

For example, the founder of transactional analysis, Eric Berne/Bernstein, a man and radical pioneer of his time, brought his lived experience of internalised oppression and the manifestation of internalised power and privilege. Berne arguably shortened his name to fit into northern hemisphere/USA culture. Alongside killing off other parts of himself, his Polish and Russian ancestry, his leftist history and political identity (Baskerville, 2022; Turner, 2021) all serving to fit into the western construct of 'normative psychotherapy' described by Hart (2017) as 'a strange exclusive profession'. Thus, in the group process we consider a meta perspective

Primary Caregiver/s   Infant

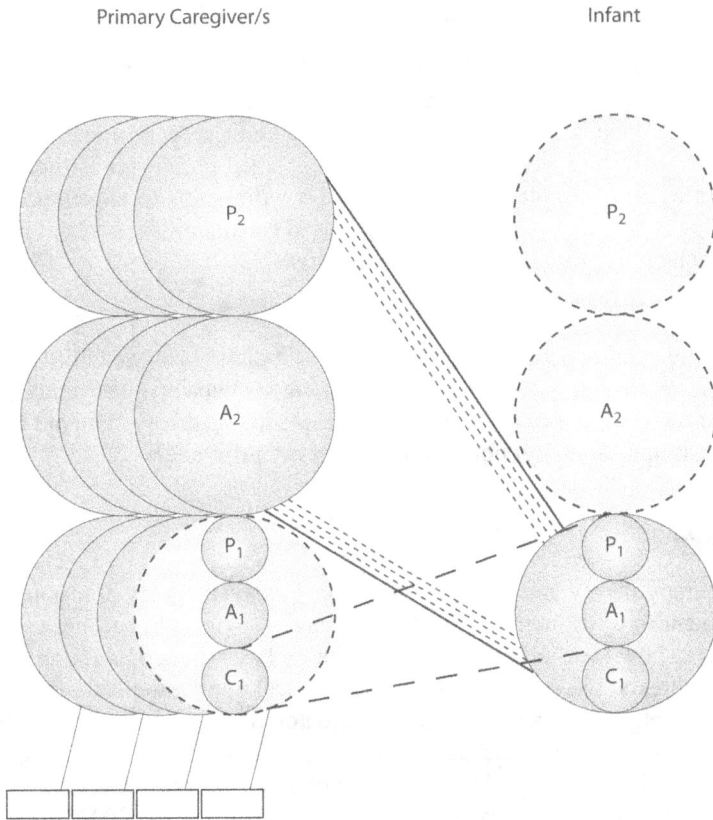

Figure 5.4 Inclusive second order symbiosis diagram (Baskerville, 2025)

of the critique and parallel process, reflecting on what lens we may each bring to the critique.

What lived experience does the person/persons who critique bring?

Who is holding the power, where does privilege and oppression sit? What may be enacted? Here each person accounts for their lived experience and reflects on who may be holding the power in the room and what may be enacted systemically.

What intersectional lens are they bringing to this theory?

Considering lived experience of intersectionality in the room – who is represented? Here I invite intersectional awareness of the critique of the critique, are all voices being heard here?

What unconscious bias may be present?

Here we consider whose voices are being heard, who are we including? Who are we excluding? What is lost in translation and what new meanings are emerging? There will be unconscious bias and students and educators will pick this up with each other, some will feel heard and others excluded in the reconstruction. Challenging this takes courage and curiosity and a willingness to engage in radically open dialogue (Hart, 2017), and a willingness to consider if the concept is translatable or even relevant in differing cultural contexts.

What parallel process may be enacted and which defences do we need to lay down?

For example what parts of myself may I be defending? Is my inability to own my Whiteness or indeed my White fragility blocking my capacity to account for power dynamics and the absence of marginalised voices in this theory? Or am I highlighting my marginalisation but not accounting for my privilege?

Summary

Psychotherapy theory and indeed transactional analysis theory are rooted in their time, influenced by the authors' lived experience, a social construct not a truth. This is evident in how ideas around diagnostic theory have changed through social and political contexts. Diagnosis has mirrored political oppression and human pathology and has later been identified as discriminatory.

I ask, is it our task as transactional analysts and psychotherapists to go against the tide, to challenge theoretical constructs? Indeed, over the years, many authors – Aldridge and Stilman (2024), Barrow and Marshall (2020, 2023), Dhananjaya (2022), Filipache (2022), Jusik (2022), Marshall (2023), Minikin (2018, 2021, 2024), Oates and Moores (2024), Pandya (2024), Rowland and Cornell (2021), Shadbolt (2004, 2022), Shivanath and Hiremath (2003), Tudor (2024), Tudor et al. (2022) amongst others – have pioneered and evolved critical analysis of normative theory, which of course is not fixed and will become dated. Each time we meet theory, I invite the reflection: Does this theory serve us transculturally? Who is it representing? This chapter offers a model of deconstructing and reconstructing of theory with an intersectional lens; it offers a frame to continually, actively, and rigorously challenge theoretical concepts as constructs influenced by the author and social, cultural, political, and historical contexts.

As psychotherapists, we state that theory is only relevant when it comes alive in self. However, many marginalised groups have not felt represented in our theories. This is borne out in every session at TA East.

References

Ahmed, N., Baskerville, V., Neish, G., & Nelson, V. (2023). UKCP research project final report: Inclusivity and exclusivity in training – The trainees' experience. *The Transactional*

Analyst, *13*(1), Winter 2022/23 4–12. https://www.dropbox.com/s/j4m2i6mlutcyot5/the%20Transactional%20Analyst%2013%281%29Winter%2022_23.pdf?dl=0

Aldridge, B., & Stilman, R. (2024). Unmasking neurodiversity: Revisiting the relationship between core self and sense of self to examine common neurodivergent script decisions. *Transactional Analysis Journal*, *54*(1), 47–62. https://doi.org/10.1080/03621537.2024.2286576

Bainbridge, C. (2020). *Why social constructs are created*. Verywellmind. Retrieved July 20, 2021. https://www.verywellmind.com/definition-of-socialconstruct-1448922

Barrow, G., & Marshall, H. (2020). Launching eco-TA: A movement of our time. *The Transactional Analyst*, *10*(2), Spring.

Barrow, G., & Marshall, H. (2023). Revisiting ecological transactional analysis: Emerging perspectives. *Transactional Analysis Journal*, *53*(1), 7–20. https://doi.org/10.1080/03621537.2023.2152528

Baskerville, V. (2021). Evolving an inclusive training. *The Transactional Analyst*, *11*(4), 5–9. https://www.dropbox.com/s/y7yhww52wmxkxko/Transactional%20Analyst%2011%284%29%20Autumn%202021.pdf?dl=0

Baskerville, V. (2022). A transcultural and intersectional ego state model of the self: The influence of transcultural and intersectional identity on self and other. *Transactional Analysis Journal*, *52*(32), 1–16. http://doi.org/10.1080/03621537.2022.2076398

Chandler, D., & Munday, R. (2011). Queer theory. *A dictionary of media and communication*. Oxford: Oxford University Press.

Dhananjaya, D. (2022). We are the oppressor and the oppressed: The interplay between intrapsychic, interpersonal, and societal intersectionality. *Transactional Analysis Journal*, *52*(3), 244–258. https://doi.org/10.1080/03621537.2022.2082031

DK (2024). *The philosophy book*. London: Dorling Kindersley.

Encyclopedia Britannica (2025). 'Deconstruction' https://www.britannica.com/topic/deconstruction (accessed 5/2/25).

Filipache, I. (2022). Shattered dignity and unsymbolized past: Facing the legacy of a totalitarian system. *Transactional Analysis Journal*, *52*(3), 178–192. https://doi.org/10.1080/03621537.2022.2076416

Gheorghe, N., Brunke, M., Deaconu, D., Gheorghe, A., & Ionas, L. (2019). All my parents: Professional transgenerational trauma in the TA community. *Transactional Analysis Journal*, *49*(4), 263–278. https://doi.org/10.1080/03621537.2019.1649847

Hart, A. (2017). From multicultural competence to radical openness: A psychoanalytic engagement of otherness. *The American Psychoanalyst*, *51*(1), 12–13, 26–27. https://apsa.org/wp-content/uploads/apsaa-publications/vol51no1-TOC/html/vol51no1_09.xhtml

Hines, S. (2022). *Is gender fluid?: A primer for the 21st century*. London: Thames & Hudson Ltd.

Jusik, P. (2022). Systemic oppression and cultural diversity: Putting flesh on the bones of intercultural competence. *Transactional Analysis Journal*, *52*(3), 209–227. https://doi.org/10.1080/03621537.2022.2076981

Marshall, H. (2023). A place for the ecological third: Eco-TA in therapeutic practice. *Transactional Analysis Journal*, *53*(1), 93–108. https://doi.org/10.1080/03621537.2023.2152567

Minikin, K. (2018). Radical relational psychiatry: Toward a democracy of mind and people. *Transactional Analysis Journal*, *48*(2), 111–125. https://doi.org/10.1080/03621537.2018.1429287

Minikin, K. (2021). Relative privilege and the seduction of normativity. *Transactional Analysis Journal*, *51*(1), 35–48. https://doi.org/10.1080/03621537.2020.1853349

Minikin, K. (2024). The personal and the political. *Transactional Analysis Journal*, *54*(2), 126–135. https://doi.org/10.1080/03621537.2024.2323870

Morrison, T. (1998). 'Toni Morrison Beautifully Answers an "Illegitimate" Question on Race' (Jan. 19, 1998) | Charlie Rose https://www.youtube.com/watch?v=-Kgq3F8wbYA

Norris, C. (2002). *Deconstruction: Theory and practice* (3rd ed.). Abingdon: Routledge.

Oates, S., & Moores, J. (2024). What is psychological and what is neurological? A political and phenomenological exploration of neurodivergent identity and encounters with third-ness. *Transactional Analysis Journal*, *54*(1), 63–77. https://doi.org/10.1080/03621537.2023.2286575

OED (2012). *Oxford English Dictionary entry: 'Deconstruct'*. Oxford: Oxford University Press.

Pandya, A. (2024). System imago: A new perspective on leadership and power. *Transactional Analysis Journal*, *54*(3), 216–230. https://doi.org/10.1080/03621537.2024.2359287

Rowland, H., & Cornell, W. F. (2021). Gender identity, queer theory, and working with the sociopolitical in counseling and psychotherapy: Why there is no such thing as neutral. *Transactional Analysis Journal*, *51*(1), 19–34. https://doi.org/10.1080/03621537.2020.1853347

Schiff, A. W., & Schiff, L. J. (1971). Passivity. *Transactional Analysis Bulletin*, *1*(1), 71–78. https://doi.org/10.1177/036215377100100114

Schiff, J., & Cathexis Institute (1975). *Cathexis reader: Transactional analysis treatment of psychosis*. New York: Harper & Row.

Schiff, S. (1977). Personality development and symbiosis. *Transactional Analysis Bulletin*, *7*(4), 310–316. https://doi.org/10.1177/036215377700700407

Shadbolt, C. (2004). Homophobia and gay affirmative transactional analysis. *Transactional Analysis Journal*, *34*(2), 113–125 https://doi.org/10.1177/036215370403400204

Shadbolt, C. (2022). The many faces of systemic oppression, power, and privilege: The ne-cessity of self-examination. *Transactional Analysis Journal*, *52*(3), 259–273. https://doi.org/10.1080/03621537.2022.2076411

Shivanath, S., & Hiremath, M. (2003). The psychodynamics of race and culture. In Sills, C. & Hargaden, H. (Eds.), *Ego states (key concepts in transactional analysis: Contemporary views* (pp. 169–184). Worcester: Worth Publishing.

Subramaniam (2010). Cited in chapter: *'Gender and sexism'*. https://pressbooks.umn.edu/interculturaldialogues/chapter/chapter-7-gender-and-sexism/

The Merriam-Webster Dictionary (2022). 'Deconstruction'. Dallas, US: Merriam-Webster.

Tudor, K. (2024). *Transactional analysis proper and improper: Selected and new papers*. Abingdon: Routledge.

Tudor, K., Green, E., & Brett, E. (2022). Critical whiteness: A transactional analysis of a systemic oppression. *Transactional Analysis Journal*, *52*(3), 193–208. https://doi.org/10.1080/03621537.2022.2076394

Turner, D. (2021). *Intersections of privilege and otherness in counselling and psychother-apy*. Abingdon: Routledge.

Vaid-Menon, A. (2022). Alok: The urgent need for compassion. Man Enough. https://youtu.be/Tq3C9R8HNUQ

Woollams, S. J., & Huige, K. A. (1977). Normal dependency and symbiosis. *Transactional Analysis Journal*, *7*(3), 217–220. https://doi.org/10.1177/036215377700700303

All theory and practice placed within systemic oppression through an intersectional lens

Introduction

In this chapter, I am proposing that all theory is viewed through an intersectional lens placed within systemic oppression, in order to offer a multi-dimensional view of the development of self within social, cultural, political, and historical contexts. Thus, accounting for intersectional identity and systemic positioning, presently, historically, and ancestrally.

Berne's 'original' theory of transactional analysis sits within its time and like all theory, is informed by the lived intersectional experience of the author and the social and political contexts of the time. While transactional analysis has continued to evolve over the decades and many writers have accounted for the systemic, a normative lens has continued to be prevalent, furthering a one-dimensional and binary approach to core theoretical ideas, models, and diagrams.

The aim is to deconstruct and reconstruct transactional analysis's philosophical ideas, theory and models through an intersectional lens, with the expectation that practitioners will hold systemic oppression in mind when making hypotheses of clients' lived experience and way of being in the world, along with themes of power and intersectional dynamics (systemic enactments).

The TA philosophy 'All people are OK' is called into question here. 'Okness' for many has meant adaptation, assimilation, and conversion.

Theories now need to account for systemic oppression making space for a breadth of lived experience and family/community configurations. Furthering the idea that the self is constructed generations before us and is influenced and shaped by systemic oppression, and supporting the idea and research that generational wounds (oppressions) and indeed transcultural experiences may live in our genes.

'On the simplest level, the concept of intergenerational trauma acknowledges that exposure to extremely adverse events impacts individuals to such a great extent that their offspring find themselves grappling with their parents' post-traumatic state. A more recent and provocative claim is that the experience of trauma – or more accurately the effect of that experience – is "passed" somehow from one generation to the next through non-genomic, possibly epigenetic mechanisms affecting DNA function or gene transcription' (Yehuda and Lehrner, 2018, p. 243).

DOI: 10.4324/9781003509424-6

Hence, development of TA philosophy, theory and models through an intersectional lens intends to consider the layers of the self, from the individual's lineage and DNA, to family and the social, cultural, political, and historical context, to the impact of systemic oppression.

TA philosophy through an intersectional lens

All people are OK

While this philosophical existential position is one that we would all hope to strive for, marginalised peoples and marginalised parts of self have not been afforded OKness in systemic positioning. This awareness exposes systemic racism and other systemic oppressions, and the idea that 'all people are OK' can risk the masking of inequalities.

Connection and OKness can be experienced through the acknowledgement and acceptance that equality does not exist, forging a willingness to keep raising our awareness and doing the work on ourselves around systemic racism and oppression, however that shows up in us, and the parts we play. Offering a willingness to profoundly open up and accept the other, in whatever human configuration/intersectional identity they show up in – ultimately equates to 'all people are OK'.

Everyone has the capacity to think

Again, this is an optimistic position inviting autonomy and redecision in the individual. The idea that everyone has the 'capacity' to think is truly liberating, yet we are finding ourselves increasingly influenced by social media algorithms, living in echo chambers which can profoundly influence thinking patterns and beliefs. In particular, young people are being influenced by TikTok, and it is challenging to distinguish what is truth and what is fake. Societies as a whole are being swayed by those who hold power or those pushing against it, and political splits are growing.

Moreover, a surge in individualism and individual thinking, fuelled by capitalism has brought further alienation and marginalisation. Alongside, there are 'normative' expectations around how to think, or what is the correct way to think. Thinking certainly shows up differently along the spectrum of intersectional difference, and more recently there is increasing awareness around neurodiverse ways of thinking and the understanding that there is more than one way.

Ultimately having the capacity to think in transactional analysis intends to invite a person to re-decide their own destiny – viewed within systemic oppression this is problematic as many are not given this privilege, and are not responsible for the systemic positioning they find themselves in. Awareness of this is crucial when considering 'everyone has the capacity to think' and yet do they have the right to exist and to thrive?

The idea of 'everyone' has the 'capacity' to think, could bring a collective lens focusing on the 'we' and bringing shared social responsibility and highlighting the need for humanity.

'Representing oneself as part of a collective mind strengthens relational bonds and increases cooperation, especially when it functions as both the origin and target of a representation' (Shteynberg et al., 2023). This would involve thinking together as a 'we': a collective including all intersectional minds deemed as equally important, each making significant contribution for the collective good, for all peoples and living things.

All people can change

This is in part an optimistic and inspirational philosophy yet many do not have the privilege to change. Certainly, psychotherapy is only accessible to the few; other fields are more equitable and far-reaching, for example psycho-education through education, counselling, and organisational settings. Yet support for the individual to change is still scarce and in many ways puts over-responsibility on the individual.

Systems and contexts need to change to facilitate change for people – diagnosing the environment and the context alongside the individual. We also need to consider motivation for change, asking who is driving this? How do we account for systemic oppression? Is this change for example influenced by the White gaze? (Morrison, 1998), the male gaze? (Mulvey, 1975), or the cis gaze? Is this then another form of oppression? A form of colonisation?

All people are OK, all people can think, and all people can change needs to assert that all intersectional identities and all lived experience are as valid as the other. Alongside an awareness that we are humanly interconnected and have healthy dependency on the other/others and the more-than-human (Abram, 1996) and our planet – eco systemic (Barrow & Marshall, 2023). Trees provide an example of such vital interdependency and interconnectedness:

> Research has hinted that these connections—known as mycorrhizal networks—can extend between trees, letting one tree transfer resources below ground to another. Some scientists even argue that trees are cooperating, with older trees passing resources to seedlings and nurturing them as a parent might.
>
> (Pappas, 2023, p. 12)

Ego states – Structural and systemic analysis

Structural and systemic analysis

Ego states, or indeed structural analysis, are core to the theory of transactional analysis and are the bread and butter of every transactional analyst across all fields. Structural analysis facilitates a detailed understanding of ourselves and our clients/organisations/institutions stories, presently, historically, and ancestrally. Placing ego states within systemic oppression brings an intersectional lens and demonstrates that the individual is not separate from and is profoundly influenced by the systems in which they reside (see Figure 6.1).

Developing more layers of structural ego states accounts for our generational lineage and the impact of transgenerational trauma. Therefore, congruent with the Transcultural and Intersectional Ego State Model, 2025 (see Chapter 4), I have proposed a third, and fourth order structural model accounting for lineage in analysing the (intersectional) self.

I invite consideration of the content of ego states through culturally sensitive enquiry, considering each individual/group's transcultural narrative, through exploration of stored memories as totalities (Federn, 1926) of intersectional experience. Reflecting on where we may locate each intersectional identity: asking which intersectional identities, parental messages, informed by supremacies, do you introject into Parent, P_2? What social, cultural, political, and historical sense of these do you make in Adult, A_2? How do you internalise these in Child, C_2? Thus, accounting for the impact of internalised oppression/oppressor P_{1-} and internalised privilege P_{1+} on C_1, and the impasse between innate and socially constructed/script self.

Ego state diagnosis or ego state hypothesis

Berne (1961) stated that there are four requirements in diagnosing or hypothesising an ego state: behavioural, social, historical and phenomenological. The following have been adapted in accounting for systemic oppression.

Behaviour with cultural sensitivity

Here the practitioner reflects on behaviour through a culturally sensitive intersectional lens, ensuring not to jump to conclusions from different cultural and social awareness or unconscious bias.

Social and systemic enactment

Here the practitioner reflects on the social transaction and the ego state a client may be inviting them into or to transact from. Here the practitioner not only needs to consider which ego state they might be inviting the client into, but also what could be a systemic enactment. Here the practitioner needs to be mindful of their intersectional identity and what is being manifested in this relational dynamic, accounting for power differentials.

History and lineage

Here the practitioner enquires about transgenerational history/lineage of the client/clients, alongside family and childhood – and is simultaneously aware of their own lineage that will influence frame of reference – being mindful of what

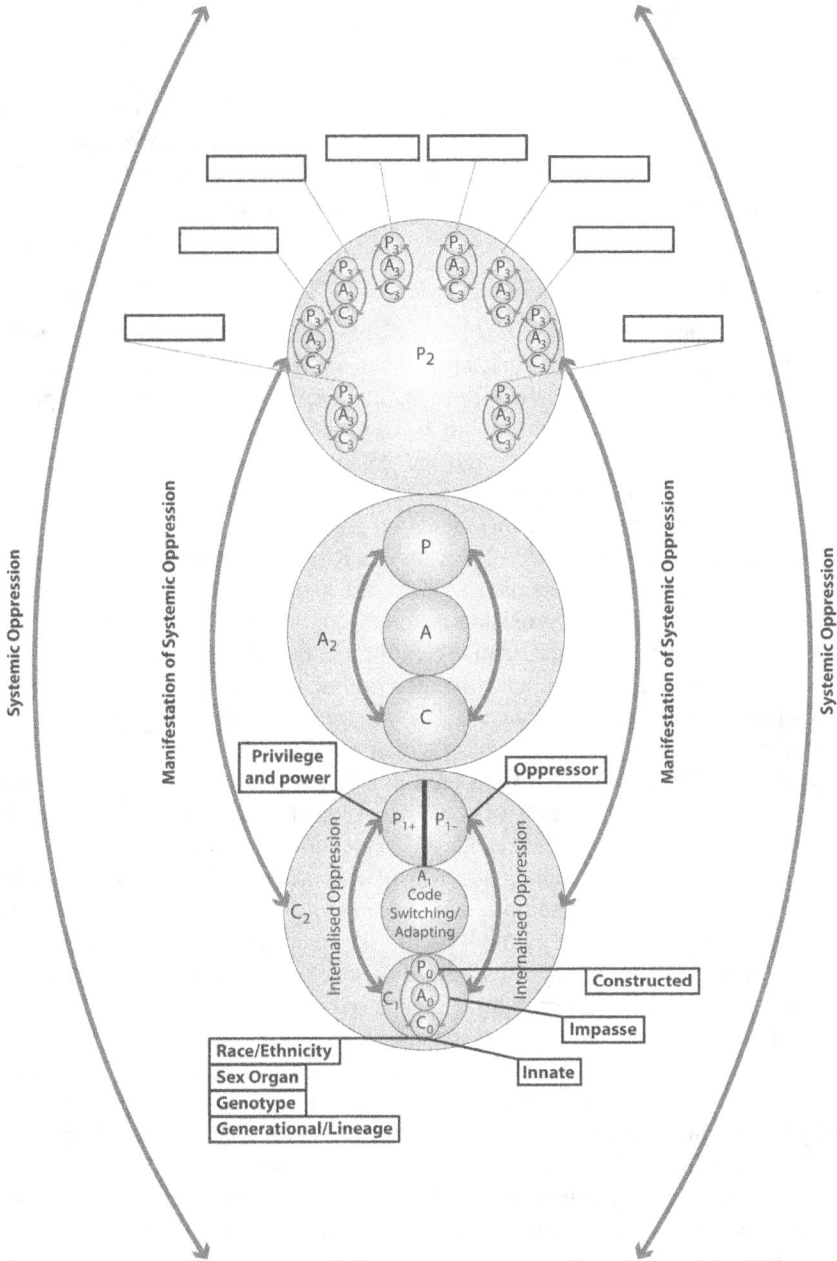

Figure 6.1 Structural and systemic ego state model (Baskerville, 2025)

may be held in DNA, lineage of both privileged and marginalised historical experiences.

Phenomenological and transgenerational trauma

Here the client is in touch with past experiences and events re-experiencing them in the now, in touch with their feelings back then, and undoubtedly wounds of our ancestors, transported through transgenerational trauma. Again cultural sensitivity is needed and cultural, social, and political awareness of the context/s.

Life and systemic positions

Life positions (Berne, 1962) have been described as beliefs about self and others, decided in childhood and based on experiences and conscious and unconscious messages received. Viewing life positions within the context of systemic oppression considers the social, cultural, political, and historical influences on the individual's decision-making process – and indeed injunctions enforced and carried through DNA for generations.

Marginalisation brings a strong message: you are not OK – resulting in 'I am not OK, you are OK'. Racism which is prevalent across the western/northern hemisphere has not afforded Black people a sense of OKness for centuries. Trans people continue to fight for their very existence across continents. Disabled people are expected to stay out of sight across many cultural contexts. While caste, religion, class, sexuality, gender, skin colour, tribe, geographic location, language, neurodiversity all serve to inform the sense of self in relation to systemic oppression.

However, individuals will have multiple intersectional identities, and some will experience multiple messages of 'you are not OK', while others will experience multiple messages of privilege, 'you are OK'. And, of course, many may switch between life positions across the breadth of intersectional identities.

We could call this code switching as a way of managing the original life position prescribed systemically. For example, a White, neurodivergent, non-binary person can be OK in their Whiteness, yet not OK in their neurodiversity, or their gender. However, the White person may use their privilege to mask or code switch to protect themselves by taming their marginalised parts. However, a person of colour cannot hide their constructed race and society's position on it.

Marginalised people are seen as less than by systems of supremacy: you are not OK, you are a woman; you are not OK, you are Trans; you are not OK, you are Black; you are not OK, you are neurodivergent; you are not OK, you are… resulting in the internalised life position – I am not OK, you are OK.

I propose that the individual will have a primary life position, informed by and intersecting with their systemic life position and multiple surviving positions (code switching). Ultimately, life positions framed within systemic oppression offer a deeper understanding of our clients/students/organisations 'decisions' reinforced by discrimination, through an intersectional lens, and invite a cultural sensitivity around each person's/persons'/organisation's unique journey, story, and lineage.

Fundamentally, the I'm OK, you're OK is an existential desire, a yearning, a longing, experienced in moments between us, where both/all account for the power between us.

Inherently, the I'm OK, you're OK will only be truly achieved when there is liberation and autonomy afforded to all humans and the more-than-human on the planet – 'I am here, you are here – "we are" interconnected'.

Life script and systemic script

Life script defined by Berne (1972), states that by the age of seven a child has decided and formed their life script, based on conscious and unconscious messages from parents and parent figures. 'An unconscious life plan, made in childhood, reinforced by the parents, justified by subsequent events and culminating in a chosen alternative' (p. 445).

While Woollams and Brown (1978) describe script as 'a personal life plan which an individual decides upon at an early age in reaction to her interpretation of both external and internal events' (p. 151).

Widdowson (2024) challenges this: 'This view of script as a static, ossified phenomenon is not consistent with what we now understand from recent developments in both developmental theory and also from our understanding of adult learning theory. Viewing script as static does not account for the sometimes radical rescripting that occurs in people who have experienced a severe and overwhelming trauma in adult life' (p. 344).

He goes on to cite other TA authors who have opened up thinking about life script focusing on changes in script during the developmental stages of childhood and adulthood, considering influences outside the family and the idea of life script being a cyclic plan that we meet and update throughout life (Cornell, 1988; Erskine, 1980).

When considering an intersectional and systemic lens, I propose a further definition of life script:

Life and systemic script, an unconscious life plan, beginning in the bodies of our ancestors, passed through generations, reinforced by parents, parental figures and the social, cultural and political contexts we reside in, culminating in a sense of self informed by intersectional identity and systemic oppression, changed and updated by significant events through our lifetime.

Ultimately bringing the idea that messages are unconsciously gathered from descendants spanning generations, offering a more complex map in understanding the ancestral influences on life script and the impact of transgenerational trauma, intersectional identity, and the ever-evolving interplay of oppression and privilege.

Script and systemic system

The script system originally described as a self-reinforcing, distorted system of thinking, feeling, and behaviour is based on a system creating and reinforcing beliefs about self, others, and the world. These script beliefs, formed by around the age of seven years old, are based on the child's primitive understanding of caregivers' messages and interpretation of others and the world around them.

Authentic feelings are suppressed in favour of script beliefs created for survival. Beliefs are twinned with emotions, physical manifestations, and fantasies, alongside life events that serve to reinforce core beliefs.

Viewing the model within systemic oppression would account for feelings and needs that have been repressed through transcultural and transgenerational lineage, influenced by social, cultural, political, and historical contexts spanning generations.

For example, girls and women living in patriarchal structures, along a continuum may well hold beliefs that men are more important, more powerful, more capable, wise, etc. These social constructs are not truths but the systemic story which profoundly influences the early and ongoing development of the self both cognitively and phenomenologically.

Within the script and systemic system (see Figure 6.2), I have developed the script displays to include enquiry around the somatic and dreams – opening up and accounting for unconscious ancestral phenomena – and I have added systemic experiences and transgenerational trauma as influencing and reinforcing script and systemic beliefs.

The script and systemic matrix

The script matrix (Steiner, 1966; Woollams & Brown, 1978) serves to lay out the development of script by citing messages received from caregivers consciously and unconsciously. The diagram is a two-person model, based on binary gender and is usually deemed as heteronormative, with a nuclear family lens, labelled mother and father, daughter, and son. This immediately alienates those whose lived experience sits outside this norm, including collective cultures, Queer and Trans identities, polygamous dynamics, and differing family configurations.

I propose the model is updated to allow for more than two caregiver influences, accounting for all configurations of family influences, including collective families where grandmother or aunty are significant caregivers, or polygamous families where there can be three or four parents, similarly with Queer families, adopted or fostered children and children born through surrogacy, egg donation and sperm donation (see Figure 6.3).

It is important that the script matrix diagram provides space for one, two, and multiple caregiver/parental influences.

Again, the model implies that the self is solely influenced by parents and does not account for transgenerational influences and contexts, including the profound

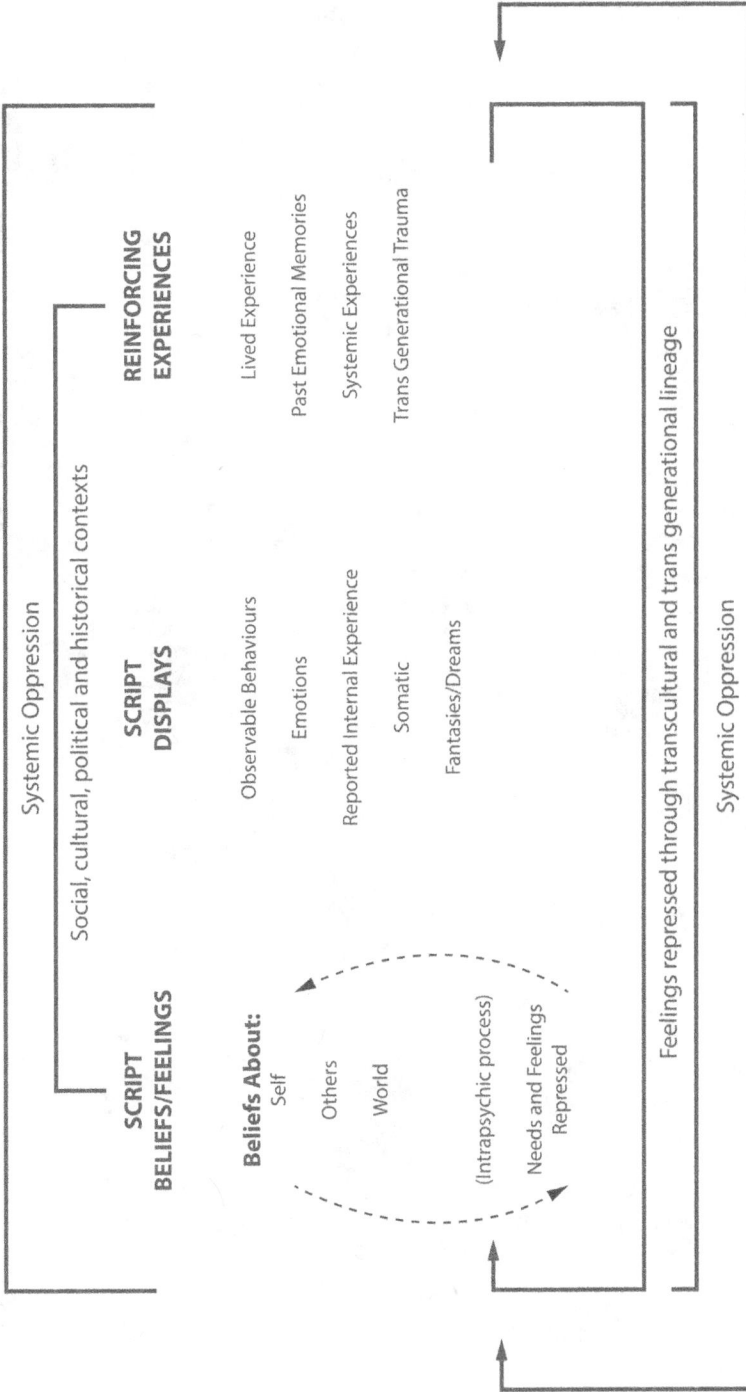

Figure 6.2 Script and systemic system (Baskerville 2025; adapted from Erskine & Zalcman, 1979)

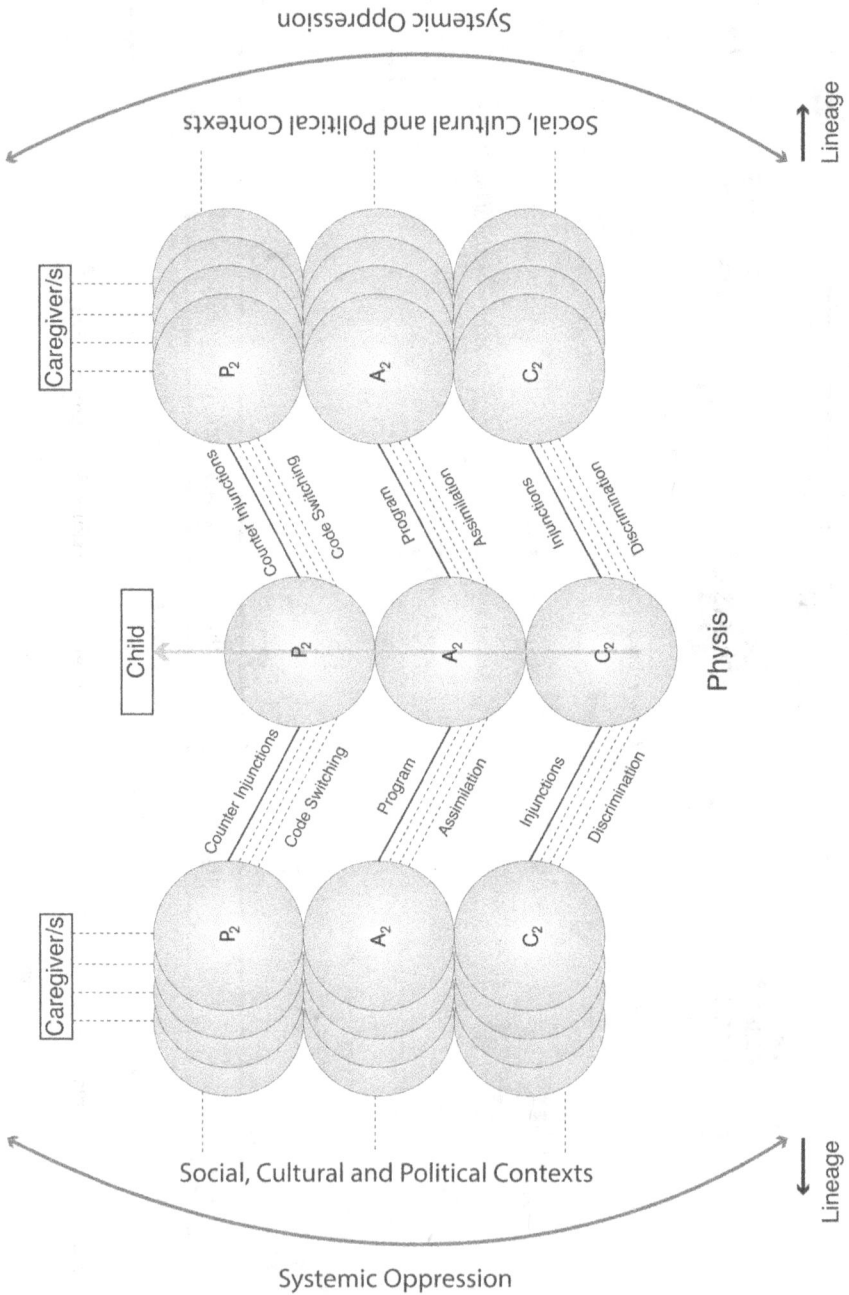

Figure 6.3 Script and systemic matrix (Baskerville 2025; adapted from Steiner, 1966; Woollams & Brown 1978)

influence of systemic oppression on the development of the self. I propose that the script matrix is placed within systemic oppression, accounting for the influence of systemic lived experience in the formation of script passed down through generations (of intersectional dynamics).

Injunctions (discrimination), counterinjunctions (code switching), program (assimilation)

Injunctions are constructed through social, cultural, and political contexts transgenerationally. For example, racism, homophobia, transphobia, classism, ableism, and all forms of oppression construct otherness and create a Don't be you or Don't exist injunction, passed on from generations of systemic racism and oppression. This aligns with ideas and research around transgenerational trauma, epigenetics, and 14 generations held in the body (Klosin et al., 2017).

A person of colour born into a 'Don't be you' or 'Don't exist' injunction created by systemic racism did not take on this message but was given it.

Counterinjunctions can be aligned with ideas around code switching: I can survive in this family/social and cultural norms, systemic oppression, if I am not too gay, too Black, too disabled, or indeed knowing my place as girl, as a Muslim person, as a working class person. (Turner, 2021, 2023)

Knowing your place within supremacies, within the countries and systems we reside in may result in 'Don't be you' incited by racism – prompting 'please others' to placate and stay safe, or 'be strong' to suppress need and not make demands, or 'be perfect' out of fear or 'hurry up' to catch up. Or indeed to keep privileged selves intact by living up to the expectations as a White cis woman 'being perfect', or 'being strong' as a White cis man.

Programming can be considered as this is how to survive in this family, context, systemic oppression. For example, from our parent/parents/family/carers who have learnt to assimilate in a culture from a place of fear and a desire to belong. When in the UK, speak English, wear western clothes, etc. All these can be considered within systemic oppression and the influence of colonisation.

Intersectional identities within systemic oppression will shift between multiple social and cultural injunctions, permissions, and programs, and each family will interpret messages from previous generations and reconfigure them. These all need to be considered when reflecting on the development of script, and hypothesis and diagnosis need to consider the systemic influences, rather than focus solely on the individual.

To this end, I have updated the script matrix (Steiner, 1966; Woollams & Brown, 1978) to the 'script and systemic matrix', and revised the diagram to include: discrimination alongside injunctions; assimilation alongside program; and code switching alongside counterinjunction. I have allowed for different configurations of caregiver/s and to consider these dynamics within the systemic – influenced by social, cultural, and political contexts and lineage. I have highlighted Physis (Berne, 1968, 1972) within the Child, aiming to further emphasise the human innate drive to survive, and ultimately 'given the right conditions, the capacity to thrive'.

Transactional analysis proper and systemic dynamics

Transactional analysis proper is a theory of communication. Placed within systemic oppression we can bring light to power dynamics and systemic enactment between those in privileged positions and those in marginalised positions.

Complementary transaction and systemic dynamics

The complementary transaction is when the ego state addressed is the one that responds, offering a flow of stimulus and response which could go on indefinitely, between Parent and Child, Parent and Parent, Child and Child.

The complementary transaction viewed through the systemic could be that people afforded systemic power primarily function from Parent (P_2) and those marginalised are expected to reside in Child (C_2). (However, marginalised individuals may take up an inflated position (P_{1+}) to defend against the wrath of power, to protect self.)

Parent and Parent could represent power and collusion, and Child and Child could mean shared oppression systemically.

Crossed transaction and systemic dynamics

It is noted that individuals switch between privilege and marginalisation. A person afforded White privilege (P) may switch positions when hiding an aspect of their marginalised intersectional identity (C) leading us to the idea of crossed transactions.

A crossed transaction occurs when one person switches ego states and the vectors cross. Systemically this may occur when a person with less power drops into Child, in relation to the person with more power in Parent, or when a person in Parent owns their power and switches to Adult.

The crossed transaction usually means communication has come to a stop, or this could be the moment of a switch in the 'Game', or a code switch systemically, or indeed inviting Adult in order to intervene in a Game or systemic enactment.

Ulterior transaction and systemic dynamics

An ulterior transaction occurs when at the social level a message is given and at the psychological level a different message is given and received.

When considering the ulterior or psychological transaction through the lens of systemic racism and oppression we may reflect on unconscious bias as an ulterior transaction or even a microaggression. For example, at the social level of transacting A–A 'Where are you from?' with the ulterior/psychological transaction P–C 'You are not from here'.

Empathic transaction and cultural sensitivity

The empathic transaction is when the respondent is able to respond empathically to the stimuli/person. Here the practitioner will be transacting from A_2 while offering in a psychological message from A_2 to the C_2 of the respondent. At the social level I may be owning my Whiteness and systemic power and at the psychological level communicating I am willing to take the journey and connecting by laying down my defence and hearing the other's narrative.

Games or survivorship and systemic enactment

Games are a series of ulterior transactions resulting in a 'Game' where both parties switch and receive their script payoff. Games begin with a discount of self, other or the situation. Arguably, marginalised selves are victims of systems that have decided that some identities are not worthy of equality and equity, which sit within the context of discounting reality.

Games further the idea of systemic enactments and pay off reinforcing the status quo. They may also be a way of code switching, in order to survive in the family and wider systemic contexts.

We could also argue that these positions are 'authentic' responses when viewed through systemic oppression. In hypothesising Game positions it is important to offer a culturally sensitive and intersectional lens.

For example, in a therapy group a member is presenting in their 'please others' driver. With cultural sensitivity I consider the systemic context, this is a person who has experienced multiple marginalisation, Black, cis woman, Queer, working class. Through being in relationship and hearing her ancestral, historical, and present story, this person has survived by pleasing others, by placating, soothing the privileged other. I will sensitively name this as a systemic position, a counterinjunction and an authentic response, a way of code switching, a survivorship rather than an invitation into a Game.

Drama triangle or code switching and systemic triangle

The Drama Triangle (Karpman, 1968), drawn as a triangle offers three positions as ways of being/surviving in the world: Persecutor – P, Rescuer – R, and Victim – V. Clarkson added Bystander as a potential fourth Game position (Clarkson, 1987, 1993).

Games positions serve to keep the individual's script reinforced and maintained.

These roles are interwoven by life positions: Persecutor – I am OK, you're not OK; Rescuer – I am OK, you're not OK; Victim – I am not OK, you are OK. Again serving to keep beliefs in place to keep running life script.

Berne originally separated Drama Triangle positions from 'real' experiences of persecutor, rescuers, and victims.

However, Game positions seen within the context of systemic oppression bring a different lens to the individual's experience and the complexity between inauthentic positioning and 'authentic' systemic positioning.

Reflecting on systemic enactment we may consider the Persecutor position representing systemic power and the enactment of racism and oppression. While the Rescuer position may again represent systemic power and the enactment of the White saviour, for example. And then the Victim position representing all forms of marginalisation.

To this end, I have reconsidered the Drama Triangle, updating it as the 'code switching and systemic triangle', viewing the original drama triangle as the code switching triangle, within and influenced by systemic oppression. The outer triangle represents systemic positions, which are both authentic and socially constructed by generational lineage. It is authentic to state that Black, Brown and non-White people experience racism and are therefore marginalised, and yet this is a social construct, and there is no objective reality beyond systemic racism and oppression.

And it is authentic to state that White people are elevated and afforded privilege through social construction, and this has been reinforced through generations of White supremacy resulting in being the systemic oppressor or saviour.

In this diagram I propose that the systemic triangle influences the code switching triangle – for example, a person who is marginalised may take up the Victim position congruent with their systemic life position, or may code switch by becoming the Rescuer and take care of others, or indeed become the Persecutor, enacting the internalised oppressor (see Figure 6.4).

Again, a hypothesis requires careful examination of the complexity of intersectional identity and the influence of transgenerational trauma and lineage, as well as accounting for multiple marginalised and privileged selves, which will take up different positions informed by social, cultural and political contexts.

Physis and autonomy through an intersectional lens

Physis, a Greek word, is described as an innate drive towards health, the organismic self, a creative force of nature (Berne, 1968). This motivation towards growth can be seen in all living things. And it is the task of the transactional analyst to sit alongside and to nurture and enable this in our clients and organisations. Ultimately, inviting autonomy 'manifested by the release or recovery of three capacities: awareness, spontaneity and intimacy' (Berne, 1964, p. 158).

In the world right now we are watching the systematic withdrawal of rights and freedom for many people, across continents, from the stripping of DEI (diversity, equity and inclusion), to ethnic cleansing and genocide. Yet people continue to fight for freedom, to stand up and say: 'I matter', 'they matter', 'we matter' – demonstrating a deep desire for autonomy and liberation.

And it seems that autonomy is limited to those who fit social norms within systemic oppression. Yet, the innate drive of physis is unstoppable: just as the plant coming through the crack of the pavement survives and grows towards the light, so do marginalised communities, individuals, and parts of self, continue to strive to thrive.

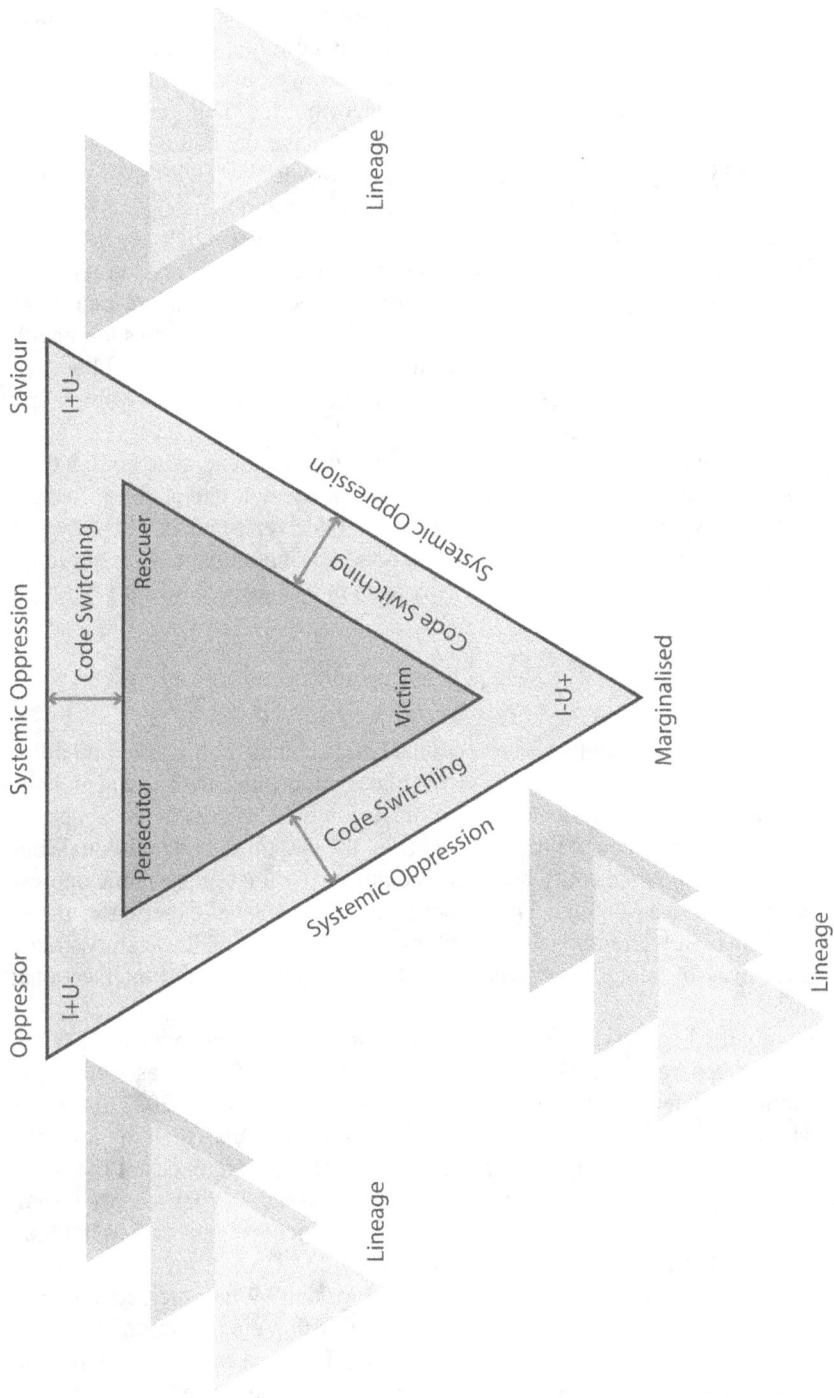

Figure 6.4 Code switching and systemic triangle (Baskerville 2025, adapted from Karpman, 1968)

Yet the strive for autonomy is limited and limiting for marginalised selves particularly as these have been, or are, bound by social, cultural, and political changing contexts. Autonomy is both informed by, and allowed or not within systemic oppression. For example, a Trans person may be aware that their gender does not align with their sex assigned at birth, and they may have the courage to take the authentic journey congruent with their real self. However, the law of their country does not recognise transgender and at worse deems it unlawful.

Actualisation and autonomy are more complex – however much an individual may strive for intimacy, spontaneity, and awareness, systemic oppression will cast a shadow. We have watched intimate moments between the Palestine people as they have fought for their survival and buried their dead. We have seen spontaneity in creatively finding ways to survive and thrive, and yet autonomy and liberation are not in the hands of the Palestinian people, or in the hands of the women and children of Sudan and the women of Afghanistan.

And in consulting rooms, we will meet practitioners and clients who hold in their bodies systemic trauma and generational trauma that has not, and is not, affording them autonomy; we will meet those who are innately driven towards a healthy self that cannot thrive in our current world. It is our task to sit alongside, with humility, enabling intimacy and the autonomy to speak truth in this space, towards liberation for all peoples.

Summary

Transactional analysis through an intersectional lens accounts for the profound influence of systemic oppression across all aspects of our philosophy, theory, and models.

The social, cultural, historical, and political contexts we reside in shape us personally – we cannot separate the personal from the systemic. The individual cannot be viewed as a separate entity but is interconnected by lineage, systemic oppression, and the more-than-human. This is not to discard personal experience, rather to view the personal within the system and to consider the individual's story, frame of reference, way of being in the world as informed by context and intersectional positioning.

For example, when making a hypothesis it is important to account for a wider lens, spanning generations and across political and social contexts, as well as the transcultural and intersectional identity of the client (Baskerville, 2022). And for the psychotherapist/TA practitioner to own and consider that their hypothesis/ diagnosis of each client is subjective, asking: what frame of reference am I viewing from? What intersectional identities am I viewing through? What are my social, cultural and political beliefs? Am I reflecting on my unconscious bias? What may I be projecting onto the client? What understanding do I have of my intersectional positioning and my internalised privilege and oppression? What intersectional dynamics are in the room? How am I making sense of this client's injunctions and counterinjunctions through an intersectional lens? Is this a systemic injunction/ discrimination and are the counterinjunctions a way of them staying safe within oppressed identities by code switching? Am I challenging script from a normative lens and risking missing the client, and even entering the realm of deception, thus alienating my client? (Minikin, 2024).

These intersectional ideas aim to guide practitioners in being culturally sensitive when making hypotheses about clients, educational settings, and organisations, while being mindful of pathologising through unconscious bias and enabling each person's unique journey towards autonomy and liberation.

> Malcom X is a distinct shape in a very pivotal period of my life. I stand here now – Black, Lesbian, Feminist – an inheritor of Malcolm and in his tradition, doing my work, and the ghost of his voice through my mouth asks each one of you here tonight: Are you doing yours?
>
> Audre Lorde (1982, 1984)

References

Abram, D. (1996). *The spell of the sensuous: Perception and language in a more-thanhuman world*. London: Penguin Random House.

Barrow, G., & Marshall, H. (2023). Revisiting ecological transactional analysis: Emerging perspectives. *Transactional Analysis Journal, 53*(1), 7–20. https://doi.org/10.1080/0362 1537.2023.2152528

Baskerville, V. (2022). A transcultural and intersectional ego state model of the self: The influence of transcultural and intersectional identity on self and other. *Transactional Analysis Journal, 52*(32), 1–16. http://doi.org/10.1080/03621537.2022.2076398

Berne, E. (1961). Transactional analysis in psychotherapy. *A systematic individual and social psychiatry*. New York: Grove Press.

Berne, E. (1962, 1976). Classification of positions. *Transactional Analysis Bulletin, 1*(3), 23.

Berne, E. (1964). *Games people play*. New York: Grove Press.

Berne, E. (1968). *A layman's guide to psychiatry and psychoanalysis* (3rd ed). New York: Simon & Schuster. (Original work published 1947 as 'The Mind in Action').

Berne, E. (1972). *What do you say after you say hello?* New York: Grove Press.

Clarkson, P. (1987). The bystander role. *Transactional Analysis Journal, 17*(3), 82–87. https://doi.org/10.1177/036215378701700305

Clarkson, P. (1993). Bystander games. *Transactional Analysis Journal, 23*(3), 158–172. https://doi.org/10.1177/036215379302300307

Cornell, W. F. (1988). Life script theory: A critical review from a developmental perspective. *Transactional Analysis Journal, 18*(4), 270–282. https://doi.org/10.1177/036215378801800402

Erskine, R. G. (1980). Script cure: Behavioral, intrapsychic and physiological. *Transactional Analysis Journal, 10*(2), 102–106. https://doi.org/10.1177/036215378001000205

Erskine, R. G. & Zalcman, M (1979). The racket system. *Transactional Analysis Journal, 9*(1), 51–59. https://doi.org/10.1177/036215377900900112

Federn, P. (1926). Some variations in ego-feeling. *International Journal of Psychoanalysis, 7*, 434–444.

Karpman, S. (1968). Fairy tales and script drama analysis. *Transactional Analysis Bulletin, 7*(26), 39–43.

Klosin, A., Casas, E., Hidalgo-Carcedo, C., Vavouri, T., & Lehner, B. (2017). Transgenerational transmission of environmental information in *C. elegans*. *Science, 356*(6335), 320.

Lorde, A. (1982). Learning from the '60s', Malcolm X Weekend, Harvard University. https://www.blackpast.org/african-american-history/1982-audre-lorde-learning-60s/

Lorde, A. (1984). *Sister outsider*. UK: Penguin Random House.

Minikin, K. (2024). *Radical-relational perspectives in transactional analysis psychotherapy: Oppression, alienation, reclamation*. London: Routledge.

Morrison, T. (1998). 'Toni Morrison beautifully answers an "illegitimate" question on race' (Jan. 19, 1998) | Charlie Rose. https://www.youtube.com/watch?v=-Kgq3F8wbYA

Mulvey, L. (1975). Visual pleasure and narrative cinema. *Screen, 16*, 6–18.

Pappas, S. (2023). A tangled web. *Scientific American Magazine, 328*(5),12. https://doi.org/10.1038/scientificamerican0523-12

Shteynberg, G., Hirsh, J. B., Wolf, W., Bargh, J. A., Boothby, E. J., Colman, A. M., Echterhoff, G., & Rossignac-Milon, M. (2023). Theory of collective mind. *Trends in Cognitive Sciences, 27*(11), 1019–1031. https://doi.org/10.1016/j.tics.2023.06.009

Steiner, C. (1966). Script and counterscript. *Transactional Analysis Bulletin, 5*(18), 133–5.

Turner, D. (2021). *Intersections of privilege and otherness in counselling and psychotherapy*. London: Routledge.

Turner, D. (2023). *The psychology of supremacy: Imperium*. London: Routledge.

Widdowson, M. (2024). *Transactional analysis: 100 key points and techniques*. London: Routledge.

Woollams, S., & Brown, M. (1978). *Transactional analysis*. Huron Valley: Huron Valley Institute Press.

Yehuda, R., & Lehrner, A. (2018). Intergenerational transmission of trauma effects: Putative role of epigenetic mechanisms. *World Psychiatry, 17*(3), 243–257. https://doi.org/10.1002/wps.20568

Chapter 7

Relational TA with an intersectional lens

Systemic enactment and working with the shadow of the collective soul

> We need to be clear that there is no such thing as giving up one's privilege to be "outside" the system. One is always in the system. The only question is whether one is part of the system in a way that challenges or strengthens the status quo. Privilege is not something I take and which therefore have the option of not taking. It is something that society gives me, and unless I change the institutions which give it to me, they will continue to give it, and I will continue to have it, however noble and equalitarian my intentions.
>
> (Brod, 1989)

There is also no such thing as giving up one's marginalisation to be outside the system. Therefore, we have a responsibility as privileged and marginalised psychotherapists/transactional analysts to do the work.

> To say: no person, trying to take responsibility for her or his identity, should have to be so alone. There must be those among whom we can sit down and weep, and still be counted as warriors.... I think you thought there was no such place for you, and perhaps there was none then, and perhaps there is none now; but we will have to make it, we who want an end to suffering, who want to change the laws of history, if we are not to give ourselves away.
>
> (Adrienne Rich, 1984)

This chapter explores and undertakes a re-examination and extension of relational ideas of transference and countertransference through the implications of intersectional theory and practice. It considers systemic enactment in the consulting room when oppressions and supremacies are not accounted for. There will be a focus on Hargaden and Sills' (2002) transferential domains and transformational transference, reframed as 'transformational awakening', when therapist and client together explore the shadow of their collective soul, thus moving from the I to the We.

I have been a relational transactional analyst since early 2000, and trained from the mid-90s at the Metanoia Institute with Helena Hargaden and Charlotte Sills

DOI: 10.4324/9781003509424-7

at a time when 'the relational turn' in transactional analysis was beginning to be worked out.

I was placed in a Queer East London volunteer counselling agency, which called for a deeper understanding of working with clients' multi-diverse lived experience. Set against the AIDS epidemic and anti Queer laws, transactional analysis of the time fell short of making sense of complex lived experiences and processes in the consulting room and lacked a therapeutic frame and holding for the practitioner.

The shadow of escape hatch closure (shutting down ways of being that were considered to be unsafe through a normative lens), ideas around protection, and 'enough Adult' did not account for lived intersectional difference and systemic trauma. Marginalised groups were often pathologised and deemed to need protection, rather than there being space to make sense of intrapsychic processes and interpersonal dynamics within social, cultural, and political contexts.

In 2002, Hargaden and Sills published *Transactional Analysis: A Relational Perspective* which profoundly transformed the way transactional analysts were thinking about the therapeutic relationship. They wanted to move away from cognitive insight in transactional analysis and build on, and open up, Berne's ideas around the unconscious, making explicit the psychodynamic aspect of transactional analysis within a humanistic philosophical frame.

Hargaden and Sills pioneered a significant shift in the emphasis of transactional analysis, delineated by a move away from cognitive insight, as the vehicle of psychological change, to the importance of unconscious relational interactions as a means of growth, transformation, and change. Offering the idea that deconfusion alongside decontamination takes place from the beginning of the therapeutic relationship was in itself revolutionary, and moved away from the idea that the psychotherapy journey is linear.

Hargaden and Sills (2002) underlined the importance of culture, developing two diagrams that account for the development and significance of culture on the self and the therapeutic relationship. They attended to themes of racism and Whiteness and called for interconnectedness and hope of reconciliation.

Twenty years later there is now more of a focus on the impact of the systemic on the self. The International Association of Relational Transactional Analysis stated: 'The importance of context has become more significant where relational practitioners recognise and account for the fact that personal experiences are embedded in political situations, contexts, and realities and acknowledge these as possible sources or causes of psychological difficulties. In reality, this is likely to involve the therapist in consciousness raising, or "demystification" (Steiner et al., 1975); challenging standard definitions of, for example, identity and mental illness' (IARTA, 2025).

In 2022, Minikin and Rowland co-edited a themed issue of the *Transactional Analysis Journal* on 'Systemic oppression, the part we play', where intersectionality was cited as central to the development of the self and relational dynamics (Baskerville, 2022; Dhananjaya, 2022; Jusik, 2022; Minikin and Rowland, 2022).

In addition, Minikin (2024) has brought the radical back to the centre of relational transactional analysis, drawing on Wycoff's ideas of Oppression + Deception = Alienation. Thus giving further prominence to the idea that 'people's troubles have their source not within them but in their alienated relationships, in their exploitation, in polluted environments, in war, and in the profit motive' (Steiner et al., 1975, pp. 3–4). The radical relationship lens calls for all relationships to be viewed as intersectional relationships: where both the psychotherapist/ practitioner and the client/clients have awareness around their interlocking intersectional identities, both consciously and unconsciously informing their subjective selves, their intersubjective relating, and the systemic enactments between them.

Practitioners thereby attend to the influence of systemic oppression enacted in the relationship as central to the liberation and awakening of both parties. Attending to: back then – our ancestors; here now – our identities and stories; and out there – the social, cultural, and political contexts that sit between us (Chinnock, 2011; Jacobs, 1988; Menninger, 1958). Accounting for these means reflecting on marginalisation and privilege, unconscious bias, the individual lens versus the collective lens, and the place of accountability for equity.

Practitioners who do not attend to power and systemic oppression, risk deception leading to alienation of clients' marginalised identities (Minikin, 2024). By this, I mean the practitioner risks colluding with the delusion of normative systems. For example, the cis psychotherapist/practitioner who is systemically the oppressor (Baskerville, 2022) in not owning this 'deception', can lead to alienation of Trans/ non-binary clients (Steiner et al., 1975).

And, likewise, how do we account for the multiply marginalised psychotherapist who holds less power systemically than the client? Or the psychotherapist who holds on to oppressed intersectional identities, but does not own their privileged selves, which could also serve to alienate the client. Or the risk of those enduring oppression becoming the oppressor, defending and consequently retaliating and conforming to the expectation of their oppressor (Turner, 2023).

Hargaden and Sills (2002) state that the therapist has to be willing to go to the depths of the soul with their clients, and that therapists can only facilitate their clients as far as they have gone themselves. From an intersectional perspective, practitioners are called to examine the part they play in upholding systemic oppression and how this may be enacted within the therapeutic relationship. In this, I consider the transferential relationship and what is projected by both the client and psychotherapist simultaneously, both dancing between the personal and the systemic in relation to self and each other.

Clarkson (2003) described two types of countertransference: reactive and proactive. Reactive countertransference: 'Describes those responses of the psychotherapist which are elicited by or induced in the psychoanalyst by the patient, and which specifically resembles the intrapsychic object relations patterns of the patient's historical or fantasised past' (p. 90).

While proactive countertransference: 'Is the term... reserved for those issues, feelings, atmospheres, dreams, fantasies, projections, fears and desires introduced into the psychotherapy or the psychoanalysis by the psychotherapist himself or herself' (p. 91).

However, as Hargaden and Sills (2002) state: 'It is almost impossible to separate transference from countertransference for how can you tell the dancer from the dance? And yet we attempt some distinction for the reason that the therapist's role requires that she be more conscious than the patient and use her "self in the service of the patient"... therefore she must have some detachment' (p. 61).

'The capacity to work relationally', according to Cornell and Hargaden (2005), 'emerges out of an evolving sense of self developed through an exploration of, and engagement with one's own unconscious life and those of our clients' (p. 244). It is of paramount importance then, that the psychotherapist/practitioner considers their systemic positions, otherwise they risk projecting their unconscious bias onto the client through the lens of privilege and marginalisation.

It is crucial, therefore, that unconscious norms in psychotherapy are examined: what am I, the practitioner, projecting in terms of race, in terms of gender, in terms of patriarchy? In what way am I holding power or losing power? Indeed, what is projected onto the face of the Black client by the White practitioner or *vice versa*, projected onto the White client by the Black practitioner? How do other identities intersect? Moreover, which identities are perceived to be 'good objects' or 'bad objects?' within systemic oppression, reframed as the normative versus othering? Who decides?

Here two-person psychology (Stark, 2000), comes to the fore; the importance of supervision and personal psychotherapy; and awareness of cultural bias in the profession and consulting room. The therapist fully moves into the therapeutic relationship and is as much part of the therapeutic field as the client. Carefully considered self disclosure of unconscious material by the therapist must happen for this approach to be used. Therapy is seen to 'cure' not by insight but by the interaction between the client and the therapist. Both can be transformed by the therapeutic encounter.

The idea of disclosure is an interesting one and to disclose or not is frequently reflected on in the training room and in the supervision relationship. Disclosure can be akin to walking on a tightrope, carefully stepping through unknown territory, sometimes holding on for years, waiting, anticipating, will this serve the client? Whose need is this disclosure serving?

Yet disclosure is always present in the room particularly with regard to unconscious intersectional dynamics. I recently had a dialogue with a White student who stated she does not make disclosure, yet her visible race, accent, neurotypical thinking, demeanour, choice of hair style, clothes, and shoes, all created a social and cultural frame of reference and intersectional identity – all clearly disclosing. In this, disclosure is a misdemeanour; however, this example colludes with the idea that normative culture does not have a culture.

Yet Black, Brown, non-White, dual heritage psychotherapists are under no illusion around visual disclosure and their lack of privilege in choosing when to disclose around themes of marginalisation and difference.

Each client will interpret disclosure in the room differently, projecting onto the psychotherapist what they need, invite, and do not want.

Projection has been seen as a psychological 'defence mechanism in which some aspect of the self that is unacceptable to the person is attributed to someone else' (Tilney, 1998, p. 95) and can be seen as the transfer of intersectional parts of self (objects) onto the face of the psychotherapist.

Projection can also be described as projecting the face of a significant other, parent, or parent figure onto the other. Systemically, we will project social ideas and constructs onto the face of the psychotherapist, projecting what is internalised by the social, cultural, and political contexts.

Yet the psychotherapist will also project onto the client unwanted intersectional parts, seeing intolerable parts of self identity in the client. The task of the psychotherapist is to engage in their own intersectional therapeutic journey in parallel, to consider: what it is that the client is splitting off here with me, and what am I splitting off? How are we together upholding supremacies in this room? Am I, the practitioner, hiding behind the transference? What is being repeated and what is needed? (Stern, 1994). Thus considering it necessary to move into the real relationship – in order to work through systemic enactments – through the process of radically open and non-defended dialogue (Hart, 2017). (See case study, Asif, below.)

Viewing transference through an intersectional lens sheds light on systemic dynamics and the interplay between privilege and oppression intrapsychically and interpersonally.

Introjective transference through an intersectional lens

Introjective transference is described as the 'longed for' relationship (Hargaden & Sills, 2002), highlighting the need to idealise – the idealising transference; the need to be like others – the twinship transference; and the need to be mirrored, the mirroring transference (Kohut, 1971).

The client longs to be seen, understood, heard, accepted, taken care of, protected, attuned to, and walked alongside. Yet which intersectional identities are being understood, heard, and accepted?; and, which are not acceptable here?

Reflecting on the relationship and systemic positioning there is much to consider. Whom/what is the client longing for? Which intersectional identities is the client seeking to twin with, be mirrored by? What does it mean if a client of colour is seeking a mirror in their White psychotherapist? Could the idealising transference, entering into a symbiosis, be an enactment of White supremacy, where Whiteness is constructed through racism, as holding more power, and in colonial terms, more knowledge?

Here the psychotherapist/practitioner has a responsibility to reflect on their intersectional positioning and the power they hold and in what way they may be inviting systemic conformity and oppression.

The need to idealise invites in the therapist a protective Parent, who is bigger than the internalised Parent of the client. How may we consider this through race, gender, class, caste, ableism, neurodiversity? How may we consider the potential harm caused in idealising those who systemically hold more power – the idealisation afforded to Whiteness, to cis men, to the middle and upper classes, to a higher caste, to the able-bodied, to the neurotypical?

Indeed, are we upholding privilege in this? Do the marginalised selves long to 'be seen' by the privileged other, thus, enacting internalised systemic oppression?

Considering supremacies in the room is paramount: what part of the system is the client idealising?; twinning with?; being mirrored by? (Turner, 2023). Who have I become for this client and indeed who has the client become for me? In what way am I examining my internalised bias and privilege, creating otherness?

Projective transference through an intersectional lens

Hargaden and Sills (2002) developed Moiso's (1985) ideas when considering the projective transference describing projection of Parent ego states (P_2) and projection of Child ego states (P_1).

The P_2 transference is presented as the reenactment of actual rackets and Games played with parents as they were perceived and recorded by the client (and the psychotherapist). An intersectional extension of this brings systemic enactment as central to the formation of original survivorship (Games) and code switching.

P_1 transference (P_{1+} and P_{1-}) is presented as projections of good objects or bad objects owing to immature P_1 functioning. An intersectional lens highlights that we live in a world of binaries and splits, and social constructs dictate what is deemed to be good or bad, and that the idea of 'immature P_1 functioning' can be symptomatic of inequalities in societies.

In the Transcultural and Intersectional Ego State Model of the Self (2022/25) systemic intersectional identities introjected into P_2 are constructed as privileged (P_3) or oppressed (C_3). Housed in C_2, P_1 internalises these binaries of good object (P_{1+}) and bad object (P_{1-}). P_{1+} represents privilege and power and P_{1-} represents oppression and acting out the internalised oppressor.

Here I consider the individual and collective systemic enactment, and what is being projected, repeated, and reinforced in terms of privilege and oppression? For example, when reflecting on race, a client visibly sees race and systemically projects a frame of reference (P_2 Transference – Moiso, 1985), of holding or not holding power (P_3/C_3). Simultaneously, the client may unconsciously project P_{1+} good object/privilege or indeed P_{1-} bad object/marginalised (P_1 Transference – Moiso, 1985) depending on the intersectional identities of both the client and the psychotherapist.

Systemic enactment is in full flow and it is the task of the psychotherapist to reflect on where their intersects collide with their clients, asking: do I risk reinforcing the status quo of systemic racism and oppression?; am I reflecting on the client and myself functioning within the system?; where is the unconscious bias in this relationship, with sameness and difference?; what is being perceived as normative and where is the risk of othering?

So how do we work with these systemic projections?

Case study: Asif (pseudonym)

Asif is a British Muslim of South Asian origin. He was in an arranged marriage from aged 19, and after 20 years he wanted to leave his wife, yet he knew, by doing that, he would have to divorce his cultural heritage and collective culture. And, while he would fall into the arms of his mistresses, his wife and daughter would fall prey to the demonisation and ostracisation of failed wives and families. And his son may well follow in the footsteps of his father, reinforcing his elevated position as the youngest boy in the family.

Asif projected onto me White, English, middle class, heterosexual, cis woman. And simultaneously, I projected onto Asif, South Asian, patriarchal, Muslim, heterosexual, cis man. As a lesbian, I naively thought I sat outside heteronormativity, yet Asif projected onto me what he needed: protection by my Whiteness, heteronormativity, and 'western values' – perhaps seeking permission for his infidelity.

His projection of English and middle class stirred me, as I did not identify as either. Yet I was steeped in a middle class profession. And I was a cis woman, and a woman immersed in northern hemisphere privilege.

Simultaneously, I responded to his large tall frame, to his righteousness and entitlement, even providing a parking space for his large car, agreeing a lower fee with a man with family wealth. I fell prey to patriarchy, I knew my place as a woman, yet he idealised me, or did he? Maybe he thought as a 'White western woman' I would protect him with my Whiteness, giving permission to leave his wife, colluding with the infidelities of western/northern hemisphere culture, and 'get him out'.

I also saw, and mirrored, the boy who longed to be seen, by gently entering into his world: a little boy whose mother had been afforded little power and sat in the shadow of her unfaithful husband. I noticed our intersectional positions and who we had become for each other.

I considered the systemic enactment. I shifted between I am White (privileged and idealised) and I am a woman (oppressed and devalued). While Asif shifted between I am a cis man (privileged and idealised within both cultures) and I am South Asian (oppressed and devalued) within the complexity of growing up in both British and South Asian cultures.

Turner (2023) offers a model to reflect on conscious and unconscious supremacy in the consulting room: 'The psychology of supremacy recognises that it is social constructs of identity which therefore lead us to believe that one is better than another. Supremacy is therefore not a universal idea. It is a socially constructed one that influences all our psychologies' (p. 38).

Turner identifies patriarchal, White, capitalist, and religious supremacy and how they intersect in upholding power systems. He offers a diagram illustrating how conscious and unconscious supremacies manifest in self and the relationship dynamic. When reflecting on White supremacy he cites the conscious and unconscious acts of upholding these, stating conscious racism is supported by unconscious White sympathy, white-splaining, tokenism, tone policing, microaggressions, silencing, and so on.

However, he does not see White supremacy as acting alone. 'The idea that supremacy is just about Whiteness is hugely flawed and reductionistic and does not recognise that when there are socially constructed ideas of identity, these social constructions come with them a hierarchy of who is better or worse than the other.

Authors from de Beauvoir to Judith Butler have explored this narrative *ad infinitum* – the hierarchical nature of social constructs – and it is an area of concern for our trainings as counsellors and psychotherapists that we struggle to see these things play themselves out, not just in the world but in our courses, among our students, within our teaching faculties and within our client cases and therapy rooms' (Turner, 2023, p. 53).

In this, an intersectional lens is paramount. In further reflecting on my therapeutic relationship with Asif, a number of supremacies were enacted: White, patriarchal, heteronormative, and capitalist. Some were brought into consciousness in the therapeutic relationship, and others were for me to wrestle with in supervision and in personal therapy.

Transformational transference (awakening)

Transformational transference – awakening – is where the client and therapist get locked in past feelings, ancestral wounding, oppressions, and power dynamics through projective identification. Enactments bring ethical dilemmas and the potential for healing of ruptures. Shadbolt (2012), in her article 'The place of failure and rupture in psychotherapy' was instrumental in highlighting relational phenomenon which can impact negatively on the therapeutic dyad. Unprocessed systemic enactment can certainly cause harm (Ahmed et al., 2022).

Shadbolt stated that both failure and rupture are attempts at communication and an opportunity for change, resolution, and transformation. She stated that we are wounded in relationship and will most likely be healed in relationship. Our task in holding an intersectional emphasis is to work through ruptures and systemic enactments in order to heal.

For example, I felt oppressed by Asif's assumption that I was heterosexual – heteronormativity creates otherness – yet I was an object he needed, a White, heterosexual, western, cis woman, who he deemed would give him permission to leave his arranged marriage. My experience of patriarchy in the room meant that he projected onto me woman (P_{1-}) yet simultaneously he projected White, middle class, heterosexual (P_{1+}).

Simultaneously, I projected onto Asif, P_{1+}, a man who holds power through patriarchal, capitalist, and heteronormative supremacy. I also experienced anger towards him and rage cathected in C_1, in response to internalised oppression/oppressor (P_{1-}). And, later I became aware of my P_{1-} projection – race enactment.

I considered which intersectional faces were needed and killed off in this relationship; and which intersectional processes I needed to work through. I reflected on my part in the enactment, my fear of Asif, and my passivity and conformity within patriarchy. My anger grew and the day came when I said to Asif that he could no longer use my parking space, and his fee was going up.

This opened up dialogue. I explained to Asif that I felt scared of him and I was angry. I said I was no longer bowing to his call. Asif, within the intimacy of our relationship was able to own his part in the enactment, his power and entitlement, and the impact he had on women within his patriarchal and collective culture. He began to get in touch with his power and understood his wife's fear and became concerned for his daughter's and son's future. He began to empathise with his wife and his mother, and challenged his father's infidelity. He also had to process Whiteness as the false protector? As the oppressor? And the idea of White women being less moral.

I asked myself, why him, why me, what are 'we' working through together here? Asif and I were in the realm of two-person psychology, where the emphasis became the importance of our real relationship (Stark, 2000). Asif and I related to each other as real people and moved into intimacy making sense of what had happened between us personally and systemically. We had to both be willing to go to the edge of our comfort zone, both accounting for who we are and the part we play within systemic oppression. I had to own the coloniser in my Whiteness and British identity and honour Asif's lineage of colonisation. A different relationship emerged, I had to give up to Asif, showing my vulnerability, my not knowing, and my willingness to re-learn.

I felt shame as I had believed he had come to me, chosen me, as being able and willing to understand his lived experience of South Asian and Muslim heritage. Yet I asked myself, how can I possibly? I knew what it was like to be othered, yet I do not know what it is like to be of South Asian heritage in the UK and experience racism. I had to own that my positioning was racist, painful to own, yet I am White and part of the structure that creates racism. I reflected on my unconscious white-splaining and maybe tokenism. I projected onto Asif, P_{1-}, created by my internalised privilege and White supremacy P_{1+}. While simultaneously experiencing the onslaught of oppression as a cis woman, experiencing sexism, misogyny, and homophobia, created by Asif's internalised cis man and heterosexual privilege P_{1+}, where he projected P_{1-} onto me.

Asif began to see me and became aware of his systemic positioning, his role in being the oppressor (patriarchy, heteronormativity, and capitalism) as well as his marginalised selves, he took back his disowned feelings, owning his power and powerlessness. And I took back mine and owned my power and powerlessness. We found self in each other and together formed a whole. Intersectional intersubjective engagement facilitates two adults in the room really taking account of who each other are. Both being willing to enter into courageous dialogue resulting in transformation for both the client and psychotherapist.

Here I offer an extension of the Transcultural and Intersectional Ego State Model of the Self (2022/2025), illustrating the relational complexity of intersectional dynamics and systemic enactment, informed by Moiso (1985) and Hargaden and Sills (2002), and demonstrating the projective transference of both the client and psychotherapist. Thus accounting for the fact that all intersectional identities – seen through systemic oppression – are social constructs and not truths, and therefore transferential: locating 'the intersection' of the 'enacted systemic oppression' in the relationship; accounting for the part we both play in the enactment; and what internalised marginalised and privileged parts we project onto the face of the other. Thus working through projective identification, via the vehicle of radically open and non-defended dialogue, brings connection, transformation, and awakening (Hart, 2017).

This relational model brings together two sets of individual transcultural and intersectional ego states (see Chapter 4). Accounting for how we experience 'the other' in terms of their intersectional identities located within privilege or marginalisation, framed by systemic oppression (P_2 introjected intersectional identities – P_3 privileged/C_3 oppressed); and how these intersect with our own intersectional identity (P_2 introjected intersectional identities – P_3 privileged/C_3 oppressed), and impact on internalised privilege (P_{1+}) and internalised oppression, creating an internalised oppressor (P_{1-}), resulting in systemic enactment.

For example, I experience 'the other' in a privileged identity, I unconsciously project P_{1+} as I have experienced them as holding power within systemic oppression. Simultaneously, the other may unconsciously project onto me marginalisation, demonstrating that privilege creates otherness (Turner, 2021), therefore, projecting onto me P_{1-}.

Both reinforcing internalised privilege or oppression in this enactment, for example informed by: 'in here' – between us; 'out there' – system oppression; and, 'back then' – the influence of our ancestry and lineage systemically.

The two diagrams (Figures 7.1 and 7.2) illustrate Patriarchal enactment and Race enactment between Asif and I.

In the Patriachial enactment Asif projected onto me cis woman, systemically oppressed (P_{1-}), reinforced by his internalised privilege/patriarchy (P_{1+}). Simultaneously, I projected onto Asif cis man, systemically privileged (P_{1+}), reinforced by my internalised oppressor/misogyny (P_{1-}) (see Figure 7.1).

In the Race enactment Asif projected onto me White, systemically privileged (P_{1+}), reinforced by his internalised oppressor/racism (P_{1-}). Simultaneously, I projected onto Asif, Brown, systemically oppressed (P_{1-}), reinforced by my internalised privilege/White supremacy (P_{1+}) (see Figure 7.2).

It is important to note that there will be many enactments happening simultaneously. These diagrams serve to give examples of two types of enactment explained in the case study.

It is the task of the psychotherapist, transactional analyst to 'be awake' to these systemic enactments. An intersectional lens brings awareness of multiple enactments happening simultaneously, some coming to the fore and others in the background. Our challenge is to become curious about these enactments.

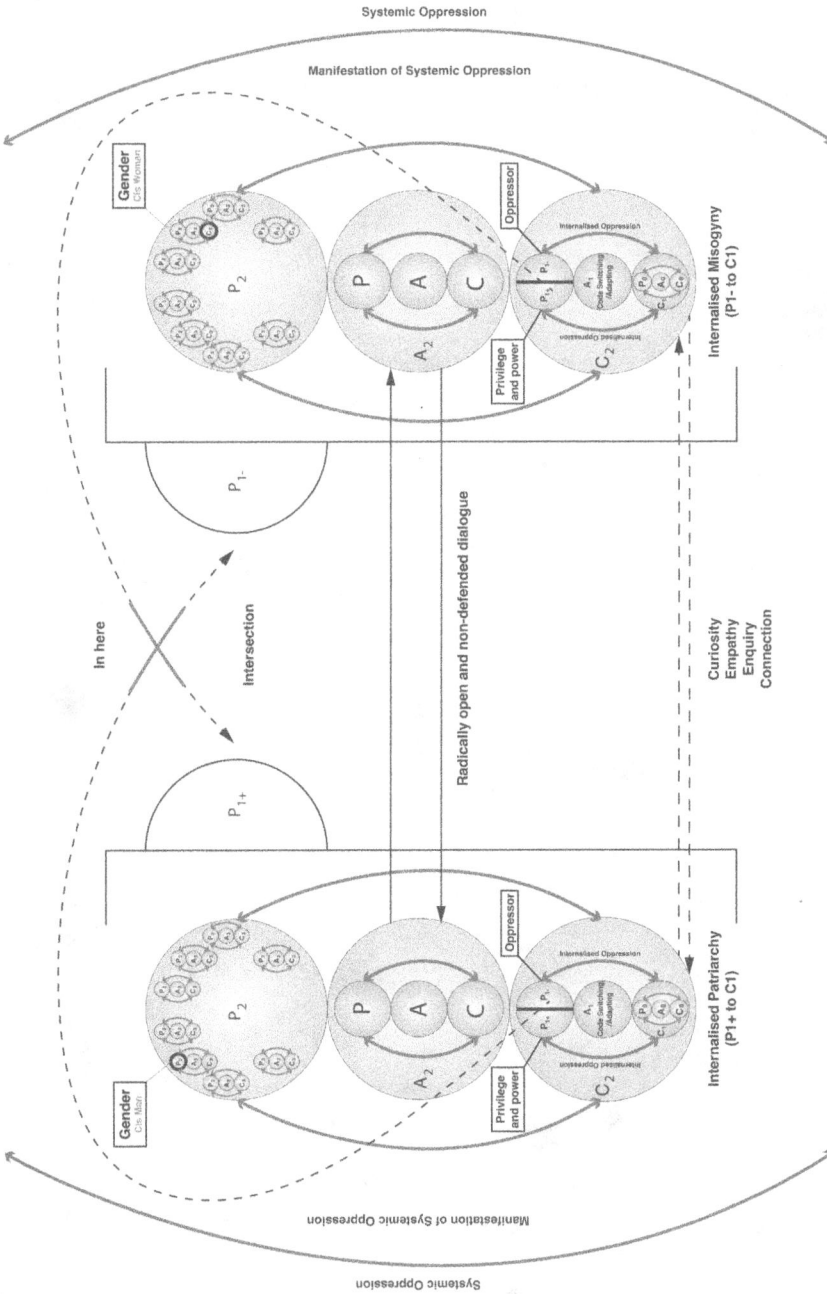

Figure 7.1 Projected privilege and oppression – Patriarchal enactment (Baskerville, 2025)

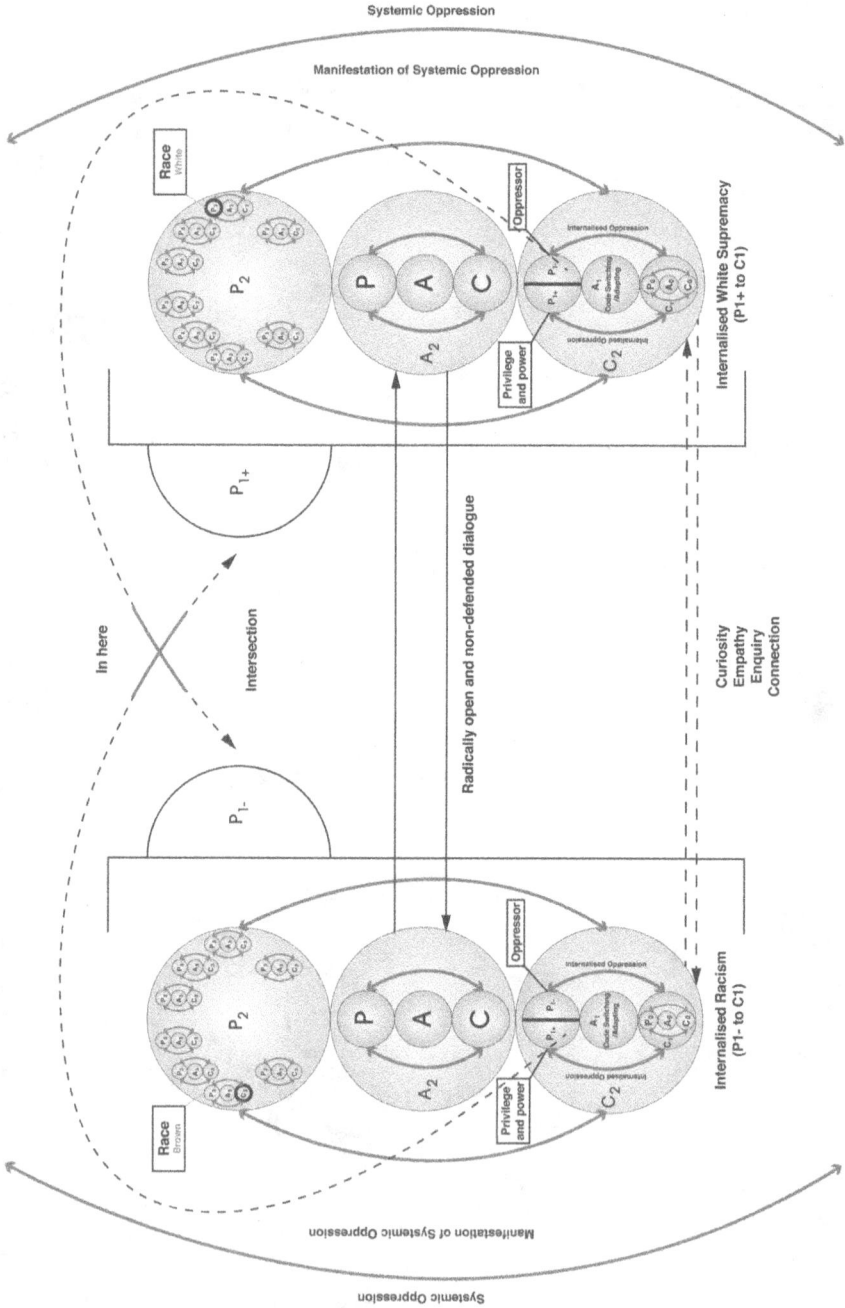

Figure 7.2 Projected privilege and oppression – Race enactment (Baskerville, 2025)

Conclusion

The act of transformational awakening can be seen as liberation – the setting free of someone or something. The act of psychotherapy aims to release these capacities. In the world right now there is a resounding call for liberation across oppressed communities.

Psychotherapy and relational transactional analysis have largely focused on the individual's liberation (and in many ways the further liberation of those with privilege). More than any other time – or maybe it just feels this way in the push and pull of oppression and liberation – it is time to move to a collective lens, where transformation and liberation are about a 'we' culture, a social responsibility for ourselves, each other, and our planet.

Relational therapy serves to heal through the interaction between the client and the therapist. In this, intersectional dynamics need to be accounted for, otherwise we risk colluding with and reinforcing supremacies, rather than challenging them. The shadow of supremacy across the collective soul is in the room with us – individually and systemically interwoven – it is the task of intersectional relational transactional analysts to take the intersubjective journey in challenging and changing systems within us and between us.

Mullan (2023) writes on decolonising therapy 'from historical trauma to healing the collective soul wound' (Chapter 5). She urges psychotherapists to know our ancestral history and to sensitively enquire about our clients'. She says: 'We must get messy... gritty; we must be willing to learn from people whom our education system has conditioned to overlook' (p. 170).

She continues: 'It is my belief that we cannot dismantle, smash, decolonize anything without unlearning – without understanding our role, our kin's role, how we have been conditioned, where we continue to participate in the socialization of others, and where our wounded parts lie' (p. 170).

Mullan speaks to White supremacy as a loss for White people, trading humanity for comfort, being tricked into believing they are supreme, simply because they are White, and that to give this up would threaten survival. She addresses historical trauma, defined as an ethnic group traumatised over an extended period of time resulting in the soul wound. She cites Eduardo Duran (mixed-race Opelousas/Coushatta descendant) 'as the first to utilise the term soul wound to highlight "spiritual injury, soul sickness, soul wounding, and ancestral hurt" in *Healing the Soul Wound*' (p. 174).

Relational psychotherapists/practitioners bringing an intersectional perspective are called to examine the shadow of our collective soul with our clients and our personal psychotherapists in the consulting room, only then will we begin to move towards collective healing and collective liberation through collective consciousness.

We must keep taking the journey, challenging systems, challenging ourselves, doing the work on ourselves through a social, cultural, political lens, knowing our lineage, unlearning, deconstructing, questioning, inviting in all intersectional voices, and being informed by younger generations and non-therapist voices. We also need to advocate for greater access to intersectional relational transactional analysis psychotherapy in groups.

Some will say that an intersectional lens risks moving away from the personal and the interpersonal. And yet the personal contains and reflects, the systemic. Here the relational psychotherapist/transactional analyst has a responsibility to hold the frame of the systemic in their work. To wonder, to muse, to be interested in the power dynamic, to be interested in their intersections, and how they intersect with the client. To wonder in the supervision dyad about what it means when two White bodies are musing about a Black bodied person. To wonder about the gaze (White, Black, male, cis) on this client? To consider if there is unconscious bias in my frame of reference, or racism, transphobia, classism, etc. There probably is, so we must keep examining our motivation, owning the unbearable, feeling the collective pain, going to our shadow, learning, changing, and accounting.

Our collective soul is calling, we must heal together. Only then will we experience a transformational awakening.

Until we are all free, we are none of us free.

(Lazarus, 1883 – Jewish, American poet)

References

Ahmed, N., Baskerville, V., Neish, G., & Nelson, V. (2023). UKCP research project final report: Inclusivity and exclusivity in training – The trainees' experience. *The Transactional Analyst, 13*(1), Winter 2022/23 4–12. https://www.dropbox.com/s/j4m2i6mlutcyot5/the%20Transactional%20Analyst%2013%281%29Winter%2022_23.pdf?dl=0

Baskerville, V. (2022). A transcultural and intersectional ego state model of the self: The influence of transcultural and intersectional identity on self and other. *Transactional Analysis Journal, 52*(32), 1–16. http://doi.org/10.1080/03621537.2022.2076398

Brod, H. (1989), Work clothes and leisure suits: The class basis and bias of the men's movement. In M. S. Kimmel & M. Messier (Eds.), *Men's lives* (p. 280). New York: Macmillan.

Chinnock, K. (2011). Relational transactional analysis supervision. *Transactional Analysis Journal, 41*(4), 336–350. https://doi.org/10.1177/036215371104100410

Clarkson, P. (2003). *The therapeutic relationship.* (1992, 1st ed.). London: Wiley.

Cornell, W., & Hargaden, H. (2005). *From transactions to relations: The emergence of a relational tradition in transactional analysis.* Chadlington, Oxfordshire: Haddon Press.

Dhananjaya, D. (2022). We are the oppressor and the oppressed: The interplay between intrapsychic, interpersonal, and societal intersectionality. *Transactional Analysis Journal, 52*(3), 244–258. https://doi.org/10.1080/03621537.2022.2082031

Hargaden, H., & Sills, C. (2002). *Transactional analysis: A relational perspective.* London: Brunner-Routledge.

Hart, A. (2017). From multicultural competence to radical openness: A psychoanalytic engagement of otherness. *The American Psychoanalyst, 51*(1), 12–13, 26–27. https://apsa.org/wp-content/uploads/apsaa-publications/vol51no1-TOC/html/vol51no1_09.xhtml

IARTA (2025). Steering Group. https://www.relationalta.com

Jacobs, M. (1988). *Psychodynamic counselling in action.* London: Sage.

Jusik, P. (2022). Systemic oppression and cultural diversity: Putting flesh on the bones of intercultural competence. *Transactional Analysis Journal, 52*(3), 209–227. https://doi.org/10.1080/03621537.2022.2076981

Kohut, H. (1971). *The analysis of the self.* New York: International Universities Press.

Lazarus, E. (1883). A quote from Epistle to the Hebrews. https://jwa.org/media/quote-from-epistle-to-hebrews

Menninger, K. (1958). *Theory of psychoanalytic technique*. New York: Basic Books.

Minikin, K. (2024). *Radical-relational perspectives in transactional analysis psychotherapy: Oppression, alienation, reclamation*. London: Routledge.

Minikin, K., & Rowland, H. (2022). Letter from the coeditors: Systemic oppression: What part do we play? *Transactional Analysis Journal, 52*(3), 175–177. https://doi.org/10.1080/03621537.2022.2080263

Moiso, C. (1985). Ego states and transference. *Transactional Analysis Journal, 15*(3), 194–201. https://doi.org/10.1177/036215378501500302

Mullan, J. (2023). *Decolonizing therapy*. New York: W.W. Norton & Co.

Rich, A. (1984). *Sources*. Woodside, CA: Heyeck Press.

Shadbolt, C. (2012). The place of failure and rupture in psychotherapy. *Transactional Analysis Journal, 42*(1), 5–16. https://doi.org/10.1177/036215371204200102

Stark, M. (2000). *Modes of therapeutic action*. Northvale: Jason Aronson.

Steiner, C., Wyckoff, H., Marcus, J., Lariviere, P., Goldstine, D., & Schwebel, R.; Members of the Radical Psychiatry Center (1975). *Readings in radical psychiatry*. New York: Grove Press.

Stern, S. (1994). Needed relationships and repeated relationships: An integrated relational perspective. *Psychoanalytic Dialogues, 4*(3), 317–345. https://doi.org/10.1080/10481889409539020

Tilney, T. (1998). *Dictionary of transactional analysis*. London: Whurr Publishers.

Turner, D. (2021). *Intersections of privilege and otherness in counselling and psychotherapy*. London: Routledge.

Turner, D. (2023). *The psychology of supremacy: Imperium*. London: Routledge.

Chapter 8

Doing the intersectional work

Daring to have radically open and non-defended dialogue

The heart of the matter is learning how to become increasingly undefended around matters of diversity and otherness such that you can be open: open to the other person who will be, in some significant ways, most certainly different from you. A psychoanalytic sensibility suggests to us that genuine openness can only emerge in the context of an unscripted dialogue, one that involves making contact with and participating in an exchange that will, necessarily, threaten the dialogic participants' understandings, identities and perceptions.

(Hart, 2017, p. 2)

Introduction

Radically open and non-defended dialogue (Hart, 2017) is at the heart of embodied intersectional practice and decolonisation. Working on self, personally and professionally, is in the veins of the transactional analyst. In relational psychotherapy intersubjective conscious and unconscious awareness in the practitioner, in relation to the client, is central to the therapeutic process. Attending to social, cultural, historical, and political contexts and dialoguing around difference in the therapeutic dyad, education room and organisational settings is still at an early stage of development. It can be said that there has been a developmental arrest for many, many decades, an impasse and fear in having dialogue and conversations around themes of race and difference.

I would almost go as far to say that authentic dialogue around the 'difference between us' has been seen and experienced as an existential threat, risking the severing of connection. Often, seemingly wanting to dialogue, but not really daring to engage far below the surface of talking about difference.

The real existential threat 'is not engaging in these dialogues' (Ellis, 2021), reminding me of Lorde 1984 – 'I have come to believe over and over again that what is most important to me must be spoken, made verbal and shared, even at the risk of having it bruised or misunderstood' (p. 29) – 'my silence has not protected me. Your silence will not protect you' (p. 30).

Not engaging in these dialogues risks further exclusion and unconscious bias and racism in our therapeutic, education, and organisational spaces, and, in this,

DOI: 10.4324/9781003509424-8

mirroring our world. Fraught with catastrophic polarisation across cultural and political ideologies, our world is experiencing an upsurge in wars, genocides, racism, systemic oppression, and climate crisis. Consequently, there is an urgency to attend to intersectional identities and differences in our consulting rooms, education rooms, and organisations.

The landscape and the call for social, cultural, political, and historical awareness

As I write I visualise groups that I have facilitated at TA East – a microcosm of the world. Each group multi-diverse, each individual with a unique transcultural story, told through truth and bias, presently, historically, and ancestrally. I feel the ancestors in the room. The room is crowded with people and the journeyings of peoples that came before. They are with us consciously and unconsciously.

Mullan (2023) urges practitioners to inform themselves around the history of how difference has been created. I think this is the starting point in becoming aware socially, culturally, and politically in order to engage in radically open and non-defended dialogue, where psychotherapists, counsellors, educators, and organisational transactional analysts research their history and lineage through world history.

To reach beyond what we have been told personally and systemically, to find truth and integrity in our histories – informing our present – is essential. Indeed, many who have been racially marginalised have actively researched their histories, searching to belong, challenging so-called truths by calling on indigenous knowledge and wisdom from lived experience, rather than from the lens of the colonisers. In multi-privileged identities, students and practitioners have often known little of their history, their cultural heritage, and their here and now social and cultural context. Highlighting that all too often, privileged identities do not see their difference, as it is mirrored in all aspects of daily life and in the psychotherapy profession and transactional analysis community.

To engage in radical openness from a place of 'not knowing' our transcultural narrative through lineage, risks rupture, maintaining 'us and them', a binary, a systemic enactment causing polarisation and resulting in systemic payoff. It is for each of us to do the work ourselves, the aim being to learn with each other through dialogue.

Awareness of our transcultural self (Baskerville, 2022/2025) invites a deeper and informed understanding of our intersectional identities: who I am with you here now, along with the lineage of my cultural and social identities, constructed through time highlighting intersections of privilege and oppression. For example, lineage informed by generations being told there is a correct way to exist in the world, the lineage of neuronormativity, the lineage of Queerness, the lineage of race, and so on, are all shaped and fuelled by supremacist structures and colonisation. Reminding me again of Mullan's (2023) ideas of White supremacy as a delusion, not a truth, an invention, a construct; and of Turner (2023), who writes extensively about constructed truth; and ideas of 'White psychosis' are coming into consciousness shedding light on society's perception of race and racism (Andrews, 2024).

The binary of the coloniser and colonised is problematic: for some people with multi-marginalised identities there is a clear distinction, yet for many there is the experience of being both. Researching our histories requires us to delve into the nuanced experiences of the colonised and coloniser within our lived experience and lineage, so as to account for the colonisation of our minds, bodies, spiritual selves, and connection to our lands and peoples.

In truth, we have all been colonised to some degree through neurotypical norms, through individualism, through religion, through ableism, through heteronormativity, through class, the gender binary, and so on. These all serve to keep the hierarchy in place, through 'western standards' and capitalistic structures.

Alok Vaid-Menon (2020) writes about the gender binary and how White supremacy conceptualised 'sex' to justify racism, arguing that the greater the differentiation between males and females within a race, the higher up in racial hierarchy that race would be. Arguably this binary is recreated across all differences, Black and White, disabled and able-bodied, and so on.

In groups, there is inevitably an 'us and them', the us and them sits within us, reinforced by the system and internalised privilege and oppression. Yet in so-called predominately privileged groups, all White for example, there is a risk in not attending to difference and othering. With sameness can come the delusion of safety, yet, underneath, differences are hidden and some individuals may not feel safe. In every group in every relationship there is a complexity of intersectional difference that sits beyond what is seen, at first sight.

In essence the act of radical openness requires taking the action of getting to know our intersectional selves, bringing curiosity, responsibility, accountability, and compassion for the journeying, and lived experience of self and other.

However, this is just the beginning. Radical change through the vehicle of radically open and non-defended dialogue is an intersubjective process and a commitment to changing my frame of reference, here now with you. Am I really ready and able, and willing, to hear this person's story? Can I bear to hear my part in it? Can I embrace uncertainty and vulnerability?

The foundation for engaging in radical openness begins with a willingness to be in relationship with the other, who is different from self, which in essence is everyone. Turning the idea of 'working with difference' on its head, every relationship brings a multitude of intersectional differences, seen, elevated, unseen, hidden, and killed off (Turner, 2021).

The challenge

This 'willingness' was illustrated in my dialogue with J in 2022 (republished in Chapter 4) when J challenged me that my being angry – going into a White monocultural group (because my difference wasn't seen and I didn't feel safe) – was saturated in privilege. She stated: 'I can not be angry, I will have my legs cut off', I was stunned, stopped in my tracks, I really wasn't expecting this, I understood my privilege. I was called to own my Whiteness and the power I hold. In this, I had to surrender to my defences, move out of my White fragility (Diangelo, 2018; Eddo-Lodge, 2017) – which I see as another layer of White privilege – and profoundly own my part in White supremacy.

Offering my raw dialogue with J in a peer-reviewed journal was quite unconventional – an anonymous peer reviewer asked if the dialogue belonged in the journal and suggested I may be uncomfortable with academia. In part this was insightful, and I also wondered if the reviewer was uncomfortable with the rawness of the dialogue. We have often hidden as practitioners behind our professional roles and identity, yet radical openness and non-defended dialogue calls for something different. 'In order to open up speech between ourselves, our colleagues and also our clients and supervisees about the ways that we are different (particularly when such differences intersect with socially charged, historically laden forms of difference, that involve prejudice and "othering", like race and sexual orientation), we must prepare ourselves for – and even seek – difficult, threatening, unsettling, awkward and shame inducing conversations' (Hart, 2017, p. 2).

The invitation to dialogue around race and difference often provokes fear in individuals and palpable terror can manifest in group spaces. In student process groups I often observe individuals going into themselves, silence sits heavy in the air, introspective, frozen in some way, perhaps emotionally distancing – each member imagining and anticipating how this group process may play out. Maybe not wanting to be the first to put their head above the parapet; or not wanting to speak out as they may hold more power systemically; or not wanting to for fear of attack; or maybe feeling 'my voice will not be heard' here. Defensiveness and preconception have immediately been triggered, based on frame of reference and lived experience, and to give up to this is both a risk and a challenge.

Hart (2017) talks about self protection, and the universal belief that the other is the problem, people are the problem, rather than the systems we are living in. He cites German philosopher Gadamer, who talked about ideas of fore knowledge or preknowing: the idea of already knowing the other's position, in relation to me. There is a sense of this in these groups, each is entering the situation already knowing, projecting both internalised privileged and marginalised parts onto the other. In many different forums I hear, White people are like this, Black people think that, Trans people are ..., there is a fore knowledge a preconception (Totten & Neely, 2021).

Fore knowledge can be a defence against risking openness – not having to be forced to reconsider my position, knowing in advance about the other. Hart would go as far to say that this is prejudice, a way of staying safe and a way of upholding systems (Totten & Neely, 2021).

There can also be a misconception that radically open spaces are spaces to say whatever you wish, similar to a charged political debate, to get something off your chest, something held for a long time maybe. Yet these are often unprocessed prejudices, unowned bias, and subjective experiences of present and ancestral trauma, where the privileged part of self holds on to power or the oppressed part of self becomes the oppressor, enabling a surge of the unconscious, a purging of the unspeakable.

And at the same time radically open and non-defended dialogue is the very act 'of speaking the unspeakable truth', which involves making sense of these enactments, while taking risks, that are unscripted. Engaging slowly, enabling self 'to get gritty, get messy, giving up to uncertainty' (Mullan, 2023, p. 170) where this will, 'necessarily threaten the dialogic participants' understandings, identities and perceptions' (Hart, 2017, p. 2).

Setting the scene for radical openness and non-defended dialogue

Radical openness and non-defended dialogue are an embodied experience, a dismantling of defence, an opening up of self with other, a letting in, a deep hearing, a noticing, an experiencing, a call to myself and to you, a giving up to something, an opportunity to not assume understanding, a not-knowing leading towards a deeper knowing. This is an act of deconstruction and decolonisation through heartfelt journeying.

An owning of 'what is', set up long before us, set against each other, us and them; can we bear to hear, to feel confused, derailed, shamed, unseen, exposed; can we bear to be witness to the violence, the rage, the alienation, the grief and the longing? Yet only then, can we truly connect and meet the difference between us, disable defence, and own the intersections of privilege and marginalisation.

Hart describes the process of radically open and non-defended dialogue as the action of a psychoanalytic sensibility, where genuine openness emerges through unscripted dialogue, a giving up of 'mastery-based relating'. Inviting a responsiveness, through the vehicle of unconscious and conscious relating, through curiosity, sensitivity, attunement, and empathy in relationship, accounting for each other. We will both make mistakes, and we will both need to keep taking our personal work to our therapy.

Radical openness is a process that takes time to live into, alongside the individual engaging in their self-reflective transgenerational intersectional work. There is something about 'intentionality' that is important here, being deliberate and purposeful, preparing oneself for the opening up of mind and heart to a different experience, giving up presumptions, and centering curiosity. Mutuality is paramount, where participants in the relationship/group have given consent to engaging in a process that is unscripted, walking unknown territory. In essence, both/all parties have agreed to walk the rocky and potential threatening terrain together. Intentionality with consent, is a process of contracting for a difficult, raw dialogue about difference. Checking out with the other, are they willing to engage in this dialogue? Purposely slowing the process down to notice who is in the room with us ancestrally, within systems, which supremacies sit between us? Yet this is not an intellectual engagement, it is being in contact with the unknown in our DNA and the emerging of our intersectional consciousness, the intersections between us, the creator of our biases.

I am curious with you and you are curious with me. Who are we for each other, what happens for me with you? What is in the relational field between us?

Hart (2017) suggests we recognise the central role of curiosity as an antidote to cultural ignorance and insensitivity and we cultivate such curiosity in ourselves and in others.

Attending to cultural ignorance and insensitivity requires courage. According to Hart: 'The psychoanalytic process shows us it is those moments in which things break down, when speaking comes to a halt, that we experience some of the most difficult, yet most important, moments of all. As we become aware of our uneasiness, there is the opportunity to look at what goes wrong between us, how it happens, and what it tells us about our experience of difference' (p. 5).

Dialoguing about dialoguing

In 2024, student and colleague Alexis (she/her) invited me to engage in a live dialogue on Instagram, for her series titled 'Difficult Conversations'. Here, I offer a snapshot of our unscripted dialogue on difficult conversations in psychotherapy, including race and privilege; reflecting on the importance of deconstructing assumptions and challenging privilege, while holding space to explore different experiences. Both of us explored our journeying in understanding race and intersectionality in psychotherapy training, and the importance of self reflection and a movement towards inclusivity in the field.

We talked of the importance of humility and openness in teaching and learning, that the facilitator sees themselves as a facilitator and a student, acknowledging the need for continuous growth. Together we discussed the importance of intersectionality and emphasis on lived experience and multiple identities. Naming radical openness and non-defended dialogue as central to authentic connection. Alongside acknowledging and educating ourselves around systemic racism and White supremacy. We talked about our race difference (Alexis, dual heritage; and I, White), the intersection of colonised and coloniser, and my discomfort in being a White director with the potential harm caused to people of colour in the profession.

Alexis:	*I don't know if you heard the intro, but I was just saying, just the fact that I'm a student at your institution and we're having a conversation live, is kind of radical in itself. I think there's not often that those two kind of meet like this.*
Victoria:	*Yes, and I was also thinking, the fact that we're doing a live on Instagram is all about the process of deconstructing it, isn't it, really?*
Alexis:	*Yeah, exactly. This series is called difficult conversations – what difficult conversations are you having that you are willing to share publicly?*

Victoria: Thank you. In some ways, I was thinking what difficult conversations am I not having? I think that race and many differences have been kept out of the consulting room. Those difficult conversations haven't happened. I think for me, as time goes on, I think it's more difficult not to have the difficult conversation. When there is an 'elephant in the room'. When there's obviously something going on, a microaggression, or there's power being held by people who have lots of privilege and, and they're not willing to go there. I think that is really difficult.

Now, post the killing of George Floyd, as Ellis (2021) said in his writing, it's more difficult not to. Not having the conversation is excruciating. So the difficult conversations, I guess, are me owning my Whiteness and also really finding a way to challenge people who don't even know their privilege.

Alexis: Yeah, exactly. That's really interesting. I like that, that's challenged my thinking about race and how, since George Floyd, actually not having a conversation is more difficult. Now, I'm going to sit with that for a bit, I think.

One of the things that people have been contacting me about when I mentioned that I'm going to be talking to you, somebody messaged me and said they're training to be a psychotherapist, and they would often get comments by their tutor, you would be really suited to TA East because of the questions that they were asking, which I found really interesting and quite dismissive of their own responsibility, in terms of what work they're doing to dismantle and deconstruct the status quo in terms of psychotherapy training. You talk about intersectional lens, and looking at what we're studying through an intersectional lens, are you able to elaborate on that, about what that actually means?

Victoria: I think first, Alexis, just to pick up on what you've just said, people who are multiply marginalised being sent to TA East, that's wonderful for us, yet there's something about it becoming another split off experience.

The point is how do we have the dialogue amongst all intersectional differences? It's a journey, we're never going to arrive, we need to keep having the difficult conversations again and again. In a few months' time, I will be aware of something else that I'm not aware of now, and that's keeping doing the work, keeping being uncomfortable, keeping being disturbed and interrupted and stirred and shook up and pained and troubled.

Alexis: That's it, isn't it really, and when you were talking, it kind of reminded me of something I read recently about, about the best teachers are the ones who actively are learning as well as teaching. What I'm trying to say is, is that we teach things that we don't know, we can learn alongside our students. It humbles us and it means that we're, we are open to continuing to do the work, and I think that's what's important, to not come from a place of superiority and knowing everything and trying to *disseminate that information on to students, which is how I think insti-tutions are set up at the moment.*

Victoria: *Absolutely, and I think I have said this to you, Alexis, that I need you as much as you need me. I'm the facilitator of your group, but I'm also, I feel, like I need to be in the group as much as anyone else.*

I think that can happen in psychotherapy institutes, a hierarchy of who's the expert. And actually, I'm not the expert in any of this, but what I am willing to do is to keep having the dialogue. And you asked a bit before about the intersectional lens, the reason intersectionality has become important is because it's about lived experience. It's about that multiple complexity of lived experience. And I think for me, when I'm talking about difference, I feel safer.

Alexis: *You feel safer having those difficult conversations about what people aren't necessarily always comfortable talking about. You didn't say this, but it is different from a lot of the institutions out there. Hence, why people are being recommended if they're starting difficult conver-sations, if they're asking difficult questions. You've talked about being radically open, having radically open dialogue. And I just want to kind of pick your brains about what that is, and how we, even if you're not studying psychotherapy, or you're not a therapist, how can we have more radically open conversations?*

Victoria: *So the idea, in a way, sounds so simple, doesn't it? And it's, of course, not. Hart talks about radical openness and non-defended dialogue, as he was challenging the idea of cultural competency. And he was say-ing, how on earth do we use an academic term 'culturally competent' in relating to the other, who is going to be different.*

He said there's something about us being curious about our differ-ences, taking away defensive responses, to be curious and interested. There will be times where, well of course, in this dynamic with you now, because I'm White, systemically I've been afforded more privilege and more power. And so, in being open and owning and undefended, we can then have dialogue, that can enable us to connect, yeah.

Alexis: *Yeah, that really resonates with me. Actually. I'm having a discus-sion at the moment in a group setting, and it's about race. There was an email that came in and somebody had a Black partner, and they wanted to know what steps have been taken in order for the space to be welcoming. I found the response to be a little bit defensive in terms of people of, there's this separateness. I think that people are really keen to distance themselves, especially White people, distance themselves from supremacy, from White supremacy and racism and talk about how virtuous they are, how kind they are, and how good they are, and not own the racism, that I think we all inherently have to own, being born in this society, it is the air that we breathe. And so, I'm really struggling at the moment with having that conversation* from a place of lack of ownership. I'm not really sure where to go to it. And I also own my Whiteness, I'm mixed, and whether I was mixed or not, there is still a part of me that will be perpetuating the White ideology and the systems that uphold the society, and it's just if we can start from that point, then we can start kind of uncovering and digging and dismantling things. But there's not really anywhere to go when people are really adamant about distancing themselves from being called racist.

Victoria: I am thinking about mutual consent, and that's one of the aspects of TA, where both people have got to be willing to have the dialogue, you are saying people are distancing themselves. My dilemma is when people come into psychotherapy training, there's all differences, there's a responsibility to be willing to do the work, owning their racism. It's a process, we can't make anybody else do the work or feel anything, but there's something about intention and willingness and, and White people educating themselves that racism is in this country, as you say, it is in the air that we breathe.

It's with us every day, every person is part of the system of racism and whether we are the colonisers or the colonised, we're also both. So it's like, people get very defensive and say things like, I'm not racist, which is a racist statement in itself, discounting racism. We can start from the place of yes, I am racist, I am White. I'm saying this about myself. I don't know what it's like to be Black or to be Brown or to be dual heritage. I don't know what it is like to experience racism, I haven't got to be defensive, that is the truth.

I hold power because I'm White. I also know I need to be more careful around power because I'm White. I also risk even causing harm in my presence. We can start from the place that all of us have been constructed within systemic racism, whether it's offering racism or receiving it, we can start to have the conversation.

Alexis: Yeah, conversation, and that, to me, is radically open dialogue, that, to me, is really coming from a place of ownership and acknowledgement. That there is potential harm that can be done, and that's really uncomfortable for someone, somebody to sit with that, who is adamant that they are a good person, because it's kind of like having to admit that unconsciously, you might be causing some hurt and pain to others. How does somebody sit with that? I can understand why people would like to distance themselves from it.

The above excerpt aims to give insight into radically open and non-defended dialogue and demonstrates our journeying of owning race difference and power differentials and our mutual willingness to be open, referring to Hart's ideas on 'a receptivity to that which is unexpected in relation to oneself and in relation to the other' (Hart, 2017, p. 2).

Dialoguing with radical openness and non-defence – An act of love?

bell hooks (1999) has spoken and written extensively about the act of love. As I write this chapter, I feel emotional. I feel grief, grief for all of us, what we have lost. It takes love to reach out to those who have harmed us; it takes love to have dialogue with our oppressor; it takes love to give up to and surrender to I the oppressor.

This was modelled in a dialogue between Justin Baldoni (he/him) and Alok Vaid-Menon (they/them), on podcast *Man Enough* in an episode titled 'Alok: The urgent need for compassion' (Vaid-Menon, 2022).

Justin began by asking Trans-femme non-binary Alok about the last time they 'didn't feel enough'.

Alok replied saying they had a daily relationship with a sense of inadequacy, they talked of their experience as a non-binary person in the USA and experience of imposter syndrome for being alive as people think they should not exist.

Justin replied, stating that he was feeling nervous about mis-pronouning Alok – nervous that he may say 'he' instead of 'they' – which he had done earlier and then corrected.

Justin said that he understood gender pronouns but found himself mis-pronouning and that he did not want to hurt Alok, or say the wrong thing, and did not want to take away from Alok's identity by referring to them as 'he'.

Justin, visibly anxious and emotional, was mortified to have mis-pronouned earlier.

Alok replied – acknowledging the awkward choreography of being a human – saying that humans are always going to mess up in a world that teaches us ideology not compassion for one another.

They said to Justin, you will mess up because you are alive and being alive is about messing up – say sorry and it won't happen again, say I am learning; and when it happens again, say I am sorry and then try harder. Alok stated this is what love is – trying harder for each other. Justin visibly relaxed, he had messed up and he will get better.

In bell hooks' writing on openness and love, she states: 'Commitment to truth telling lays the ground work for the openness and honesty that is the heartbeat of love' (hooks 1999, p. 53).

Alok and Justin's conversation emanates love, demonstrating radical openness and non-defence, bringing hope for all configurations of being human, along with permission to mess up. This resonates with Hart's ideas around making mistakes and bringing bias into consciousness: 'You might wind up, along the way, saying something that's not the "right" thing to say, something that may even offend. But if you approach the dialogue with a willingness to consider things that are out of your awareness (unconscious, unformulated), things that have not occurred to you before, then maybe the other can tell you about their problems with what you are asking and how you are asking it… how you got things wrong, how you failed to understand, and how you were experienced as presuming rather than listening with an open mind' (Hart, 2017, p. 3).

Another illustration of this was when I, within an education setting, acting out of awareness, was challenged to open my mind and heart. I began by spontaneously offering an intersection of my lived experience, to teach and bring alive Kliman's social matrix (2008), a visual tool for mapping privilege and marginalisation. The matrix provides a unique map for each person, offering a visual representation of degrees of privilege and marginalisation in self and in our parents. I was focusing on the intersect of 'education' named on the social matrix.

Victoria: *My maternal grandfather, left school at 10 to take care of his siblings and later worked down the mines, never having learnt to read. Both my parents left school at 15, within the social construct of working class, 'do not get above your station'. They wanted me to have a different experience and I went to art college from 16–18 years. In my family there was no expectation of a university education. When I was 18, a letter arrived offering a degree course. I went for an interview and I started a degree, quickly feeling out of my depth.*

I was called to meet with the academic adviser, I had not written an essay before, I was struggling. He instructed me to write a daily journal, slowly and painstakingly I learnt how to write in a formal way. Each week he would correct the grammar in the journal. I felt shame, and yet strived for better the following week. Eventually I learnt to write 'good enough' essays. Yet, when I came to write my final year dissertation I was told by a middle class lecturer it would be too difficult for me, and that I would get on in life working without a degree, I was deeply shamed.

From a place of determination, my working class fight, I submitted my dissertation and years later I completed my psychotherapy CTA dissertation. I deferred my first submission.

In telling of my story to the group, I cited on the matrix my education privilege, having achieved a first degree, then later my CTA and MSc in psychotherapy. I located my parents' and grandparents' education experience towards marginalisation, along with my 'learning to write academically' towards marginalised education experience – sitting between privilege and oppressed – accounting for relative privilege (Minikin, 2021).

A radically open and non-defended dialogue, in the education setting ensued:

Amara: *I just have to stop you there, I have to cut in. I have to stop you there.*
Victoria: [I was quite taken aback. I was in my archaic experience, stirred by telling my story, sharing my vulnerability, modelling intersectional nuances in self experience.]

Amara:	*You being helped, that was privilege. You were helped because you were White. I didn't have that.*
Victoria:	[I felt defensive, I wanted to explain, I felt unheard, 'Didn't she hear my struggle?' I felt my discomfort. In this moment I was not in touch with ideas of relative privilege, in relation to the other.]
Amara:	*I deferred my CTA twice, nobody helped me, I am Black, no one helped me. You got help because you were White. Black people do not get help. You did, that is privilege.*
Victoria:	[I sat in my defence, I was talking of my working class experience and my educational experience. I felt exposed. I knew it was important to hear Amara. She was telling me about her experience of racism. I paused, took a moment and reflected on my intersection of class, yet I was also protected by my Whiteness, I had been here before. I considered A's intersectional identities of Black, woman and immigrant – a very different lived reality to mine. I took a breath. I had to own my part in the system of Whiteness and racism – I had to stay open.]
Victoria:	*I hear you Amara. I hear you were not given help and support, no one reached out to you, as they did me. There was no one there for you. And I was offered help as a White person. I understand my being helped was privilege.*
	[I subsequently remembered being supported by those in power when I deferred my CTA seen as caught between an institutional split between relational and classical TA, with a subtext, it wasn't my fault – I was given the benefit of the doubt.]
Amara:	*Yes, you have privilege. Getting help is privilege. Being believed in is privilege.*
Victoria:	*Yes it is, and you had a very different experience, you experienced racism, you were not believed in. I am sorry.*
Amara:	[nodded, acknowledged.]

Across the room, another student colleague Emiliano came in, getting in touch with his anger, his rage, sharing his experience of racism in a psychotherapy institute.

Emiliano:	*You talk about deferring your CTA written exam Victoria, you deferred yours once, I deferred mine three times! I know it was racism, three times I deferred mine. No one helped me.*
Victoria:	[I sat with Emiliano's intersections of Brown identity, an immigrant and English not his first language. Both Amara and Emiliano were telling me the onslaught of racism, intersected with other oppressions. I had to accept that my experience was different. I had to give up my defence. I was getting in touch with something out of my awareness, something that had not occurred to me, in the moment that I shared my experience.]

Victoria: I am sorry Emiliano that you experienced racism. I hear your anger and your pain. I know my experience was different to yours, I deeply accept that I experienced privilege alongside the oppression I felt in my working class identity.

Insightful dialogue is a process of letting in, a giving up – authentic growth and heartbreak in many ways are essential in examining unconscious bias and prejudice.

The action of radically open and non-defended dialogue is to raise consciousness, to awaken, to account for the differences between us, in a way that we haven't been able to before. An intimacy is required with the potential of evoking anger and shame, which can result in retreat, serving to keep the cycle going.

Ultimately we keep doing the intersectional work, engaging, getting better at owning our bias. Radically open and non-defended dialogue is a journey, a journeying, it is not a one-off event, both are changed by each encounter and encountering.

Conclusion

Radically open and non-defended dialogue is not immune to risk, yet there is greater risk in hanging onto pre-knowing, where the status quo remains fixed and systemic enactment ensues. The action of radically open and non-defended dialogue serves to expand perspective: not assuming understanding, challenging perception and difference, and the illusion of sameness; staying interested in the other – giving up what doesn't fit through enquiry, curiosity, and empathy; and acknowledging that we all function in systems, hierarchical systems which sets individuals and groups against each other.

Ending here, with beautiful, heartfelt, and deeply moving excerpts from letters between psychoanalysts, Karim Dajani and Eyal Rozmarin, a Palestinian man and an Israeli man, titled 'Crossing divides' (Dajani and Rozmarin, 2024).

Both with psychoanalyst sensibility, wanting against all the odds to hear each other, and to forge connection and respect allegiances.

Karim writes:

Dear Eyal,

Thank you for your courage to engage with me. I say this knowing full well that the risks to me for speaking about Palestine are far greater than they are to you.
Nevertheless, I am grateful.
The first thing I want to say is that your approach makes sense to me. It is similar to mine. You are trying to be brutally honest while maintaining your allegiances, or while speaking from personal and collective dispositions. For me, psychoanalysis

is about truth, and a real psychoanalyst is one who refuses to lie, refuses to flinch away from painful realities.

Karim speaks of courage, risk, and gratitude, acknowledging both their positions of allegiance. He talks of truth and realness and pain.

He states:

Much has been written about 'the conflict'. None of it has reduced it or made it less malignant. To think that you and I, two individuals, can move the needle towards recognition and cooperation is… necessary despite the impossibility.

I am interested in taking the issue up analytically. The typical ways have failed. We need something new. I feel some glimmer of hope here, as I think our nascent conversation will help me learn more about psychoanalysis, cooperation, and liberation.

Eyal replies, connecting with and deeply hearing Karim:

We, you and I, are lucky. We live behind, not under the killer jets and the guns. We live from one earthquake to the next, in never-ending aftershocks of hate and violence. And yet there is so much life and beauty there as well, and this, too, animates us. We are doomed but also fortunate to belong together in Israel-Palestine.

As the psychoanalysts that we are, I believe it is our task to revive our original ambition, to strive, from our angle, to understand the human condition, which also means human society … . it is in the infinite instant between love and hate that we need to find each other.

This is the reality of radical openness and non-defended dialogue, it is not about bringing the other to the other side, it is the action of listening and the profound ability to hear 'the others' experience. It is a profound acknowledgement of who you and I are in the world, the systems we reside in and how the intersections between us intersect. It is the 'we' listening to the 'I' and the 'I'. It is the profound acceptance of where we sit in systems. It is the profound acceptance that you and I, I and you, are human. 'The heart of justice is truth telling, seeing ourselves and the world the way it is rather than the way we want it to be' (hooks, 1999, p. 33).

References

Andrews, K. (2024). *The psychosis of whiteness: Surviving the insanity of a racist world.* London: Penguin Random House.

Baskerville, V. (2022). A transcultural and intersectional ego state model of the self: The influence of transcultural and intersectional identity on self and other. *Transactional Analysis Journal, 52*(32), 1–16. http://doi.org/10.1080/03621537.2022.2076398

Dajani, K., & Rozmarin, E. (2024). 'Crossing divides'. *Room: A sketchbook for analytic action* 2.24. https://analytic-room.com/speakingofhome/

Diangelo, R. (2018). *White fragility: Why it's so hard for white people to talk about racism.* London: Penguin Random House.

Eddo-Lodge, R. (2017). *Why I'm no longer talking to white people about race.* London: Bloomsbury.

Ellis, E. (2021). *The race conversation.* London: Confer.

Hart, A. (2017). From multicultural competence to radical openness: A psychoanalytic engagement of otherness. *The American Psychoanalyst, 51*(1), 12–13, 26–27. https://apsa.org/wp-content/uploads/apsaa-publications/vol51no1-TOC/html/vol51no1_09.xhtml

Hooks, B. (1999). *All about love: New visions.* New York: William Morrow & Company.

Kliman, J. (2008). 'Intersections of privilege and marginalization: A visual teaching tool'. *AFTA.* Winter, 2010. 39–48.

Lorde, A. (1984). *Sister outsider.* UK: Penguin Random House.

Minikin, K. (2021). Relative privilege and the seduction of normativity. *Transactional Analysis Journal, 51*(1), 35–48. https://doi.org/10.1080/03621537.2020.1853349

Mullan, J. (2023). *Decolonizing therapy.* New York: W.W. Norton & Co.

Totten, T., & Neely, N. (2021). Season 4 - Between us: A psychotherapy podcast: Episode 40: Radical openness: D/@betweenusapsychotherapypod6335

Turner, D. (2021). *Intersections of privilege and otherness in counselling and psychotherapy.* London: Routledge.

Turner, D. (2023). *The psychology of supremacy: Imperium.* London: Routledge.

Vaid-Menon, A. (2020). *Beyond the gender binary.* New York: Penguin Workshop.

Vaid-Menon, A. (2022). 'Alok: The urgent need for compassion'. *Man Enough.* https://youtu.be/Tq3C9R8HNUQ

Chapter 9

The role and influence of activists

In this chapter I draw on activism and the work of activists to develop, challenge, and further the theory and practice of contemporary transactional analysis through an intersectional lens. What is clear, reflecting and reading about civil rights activists, is that each person is in some unique way fighting for their own existence within a power system, be it race rights, sexuality rights, gender rights, disability rights, and so on. Many are fighting for multiple rights – illustrated by Lorde, who states there 'is no such thing as a single issue struggle, as we do not live single issue lives' (Lorde, 1982); echoed in Chin's (2014) ideas that 'all oppression is connected'; and highlighted in Turner's (2023) themes of conscious and unconscious supremacy and the idea that patriarchal supremacy does not serve any communities.

Arguably, many activists are born into multiple marginalisation through systemic oppression, both from what they endure in the present and what they hold in their bodies historically and ancestrally (Klosin et al., 2017). Others may be awakened by witnessing the plight of others, or align with particular struggles and social movements that speak to their values and stories. Intersectionality (Crenshaw, 1989) is demonstrated in the explicit and implicit writing and activism of Lorde, hooks, Chin, Baldwin, Turner, Ellis, Rich, Vaid-Menon, and Hart, and, in its very being, accounts for privileged and oppressed experiences of the self. Using activism to frame an intersectional lens in transactional analysis takes us outside normative structures, inviting in all intersectional voices and in so doing deconstructs and decolonises normative theory, process, and practice.

Those who sit comfortably in normative structures are often unable to see the harm caused to marginalised others through power dynamics and therefore do not understand or indeed judge the drive for activism. Just as the privileged are like fish that are unaware they are in water, racism, transphobia, homophobia, sexism, classism, and so on are in the air that we breathe. It cannot be denied, and yet many want to deny its existence, which serves to keep this status quo. Transactional analysis, while a social psychiatry, has not been immune to this denial, which has served to keep social and political awareness and attention to systemic power outside of our theories and practice.

DOI: 10.4324/9781003509424-9

Often, we hear the 'personal is political', originating in the second wave of feminism in the 1960s, connecting experiences of women as rooted in gender equality. Indeed, all personal experiences can be located within systemic oppression: be it privileged – holding power, or oppressed – not afforded power. I have considered reversing this statement to the 'political is personal', demonstrating the profound influence of political ideology on the development of the personal self.

The political is personal, becoming an activist

I am an activist. I sometimes wonder how I got here. On that account, I will begin by telling some of my personal story of being born into the political, and living consciously and unconsciously into activism, with the aim of illustrating motivation for activism through social and political lived experience and the place of activism for individual and collective change.

My grandfathers on both paternal and maternal sides of my family were coal miners, as were their fathers and their grandfathers. My maternal great grandparents were immigrants from Ireland during the potato famine, when the working class had little access to other food – that being a luxury only afforded to the wealthy. As massive quantities of food were being exported to Britain, many people were evicted from their homes illegally and violently. My maternal Irish great grandparents came to Stoke-on-Trent, England, to work in the coal mines. Consequently, they changed (killed off) their Irish names to English ones, and gave up their Catholicism to become Methodists (Baskerville, 2022; Turner, 2021).

I remember conversations between my parents about real conditions down the pit. 'Coal mines were dangerous for all workers. Collapsing mines, suffocation, gas poisoning, explosions, and heavy machinery accidents were daily dangers. Before electricity, men often worked standing in water, swinging their sharp pickaxes and shovelling coal in the flickering light of their gas headlamps' (PBS, 2012).

In 1942, when my grandfathers were miners in the area, 57 men and boys died in the Sneyd Pit disaster in Burslem in Stoke-on-Trent (BBC, 2009).

Early memories of my maternal grandfather are seeing him in his back brace, following years of being bent over in the pit, he also suffered poor lung health. A grandfather who never had the privilege to learn to read after taking care of his siblings following the death of his mother when he was ten years old. Yet every evening he sat 'reading' the newspaper and one day confided to my older sister that he couldn't actually read.

During the Second World War my maternal grandmother drove a milk float and was indeed the matriarch of the family. My earliest memories of Stoke-on-Trent were smoking chimneys – the legacy of the industrial revolution – leading to nights managing acute bronchitis. This led my parents to make the brave decision to move to Blackpool, a predominately White working class seaside town in Northern England, which was at the peak of its era. In this they challenged the working class message of 'know your place' or 'do not get above your station' (Baskerville, 2022).

However, growing up in the north in the '70s and '80s, meant teatime conversations were filled with stories of strikes and picket lines. My Dad's dilemma of being on strike and having a family to provide for; my sister, four years older than me, supporting the miners and taking food bundles to picket lines. I was young, and in many ways blissfully ignorant, but somehow found my way to activism. I can recall the palpable complexity of feelings: fear, anger, rage, hopelessness, and the desire to fight. Growing up at this time, described by Morgan (2017), as the dark ages was 'Britain's gloomiest period since the Second World War .... set between Harold Wilson's "swinging '60s" and Margaret Thatcher's divisive '80s' (p. 1). Blackouts and three-day weeks for workers followed the miners' strikes, industrial conflict ensued and there was economic decline. Alongside this there were many conversations about 'the troubles' in Ireland, and IRA bombings were a palpable fear growing up, with little understanding of Britain's escalation of the conflict.

In the '80s from aged 11, I had many jobs and at 14 worked in the men's department for the large department store Lewis's. One afternoon, like every other, killing time and fantasising that one day I may purchase a Jaeger jumper I came across a shoebox amongst the neatly folded jumpers. Moments later I was taking it upstairs to lost property as instructed by my supervisor.

After three lots of escalators and a steep staircase I arrived, task done. The next part of the story becomes a blur and to this day one of disbelief and dissociation. Standing at the lost property desk I witnessed the opening of the box lid, a clock face, and wires – a ticking bomb. My next recollection is running alongside others down the escalators and out onto the Blackpool promenade waiting for bomb disposal to arrive. Thereafter I recall many experiences of bomb scares with very little understanding of the social and political context.

Both my sister and I found our way to college/polytechnic by accident rather than design, both 'knowing our place', and at the same time fighting for something different. Not surprisingly, we both went for degrees with a social and political edge: my sister took politics, while I went for community studies with community arts.

Feeling homesick it wasn't long before I was taken in by the Christian Union, an unfortunate intervention which resulted in persecution of my emerging lesbian identity. Weekly I was taken to the back of the Pentecostal church where White elderly men laid hands on me to exorcise the devil. I knew this was wrong, yet I internalised the oppression until years later when I reached safety. By now, Thatcher's Britain was taking hold and the gap between right and left-wing politics escalated and set the ball rolling to where we find ourselves today.

Placed in East London for community arts work experience, I witnessed the beginning of the gentrification of the East End. In short, the 'yuppies' (young upwardly mobile people) arrived, and working class communities were pushed out, including creatives and community artists who housed themselves in warehouses along the Thames. It wasn't long before I was marching through the streets of Tower Hamlets chanting 'Save the docklands!'.

Living and working in Mile End and Whitechapel, while still a student, came another awakening – the Bengali community. This community was the most discriminated group of the time, largely residing in high-rise blocks, experiencing poverty and many forms of alienation, particularly Bengali women and their children. Community projects involved bringing Bengali and White East London communities together.

By 1988, aged 21, I had to let go of my desire to work in community arts, Thatcher had killed it, and I became a teacher in the multi-diverse, multiply deprived London borough of Newham, planning only to stay for a few years before returning north. At this time, I was allowing myself to begin to accept my lesbian identity. Coming out was a challenge at the time of the AIDS epidemic where homophobia was on the rise, and many of our community were dying (SFGMC, 2022).

Furthermore, I was working under 'section 28', or Clause 28[a] – a legislative designation for a series of laws across Britain that prohibited the 'promotion of homosexuality' by local authorities. Introduced by Margaret Thatcher's Conservative government, it was in effect from 1988 to 2000 in Scotland, and from 1988 to 2003 in England and Wales. It caused many organisations such as lesbian, gay, bisexual and transgender student support groups to close, limit their activities or self-censor (gov.uk 1988).

Working in schools at this time was reminiscent of the laws in Florida today, banning the word Gay and banning books which dare suggest ideas outside the normative. Newham local authority was on the one hand a progressive borough, outwardly recruiting and welcoming minorities and people like me – young, progressive forward-thinking teachers – and on the other, schools had to adhere to section 28.

Working on the refugee and asylum seekers support team, I was soon placed in a Catholic primary school. Showing up in my 20s and looking 'like a lesbian', with a number one haircut, piercings, and biker's jacket, I began to feel my difference. In one sense feeling deeply welcomed while also feeling the limits of my existence. All was 'OK' if I adhered to the law. The head teacher, called me in to a senior leadership meeting. A child in my class had taken a book home from the classroom library about 'two mums'. The Catholic mother had complained to the school that this was inappropriate reading in primary school.

As I write I find myself anxiously rubbing my lips with my fist clenched: I am taken back to the room, sitting at a round table, where a decision was made in my presence to search all rooms for books of 'this nature' and to lock them in the cupboards with sex abuse books. I was stunned and perhaps more stunned by the lack of awareness of my colleagues.

Lesbians due to the beliefs of Queen Victoria, that we couldn't possibly exist, meant that we were excluded from laws, the age of consent and the gross indecency law; however, we were still deeply affected by the fate of our brothers in our community and indeed the way we were implicated as lesbians. Teaching in the '90s brought many challenges. Thatcher's Britain resulted in an upsurge of strike action, and I became a union rep partaking in strike action and organising unofficial strikes. There was much to fight for in the '80s and '90s, as every other decade I suppose, however back then there was an appetite and a freedom in the right to protest which is now being shockingly eroded. There were the wonderfully expressive early Pride marches, and the anti-racist rallies and the fight for the release of Nelson Mandela from racial imprisonment for 27 years – with the joyful celebration of Mandela's release in Trafalgar Square on February 11, 1990.

There was the shocking presence of the National Front, venomously racist and homophobic. Stickers flooded the underground, with razor blades under them in case someone dared peel them off. Looking like a lesbian in the '80s and '90s was about belonging, about resisting, and was also terrifying at times.

I found myself fleeing another bomb in Tottenham Court Road one night. I was sitting in the safety of a Queer bar one moment, then running with hundreds of others to jump on open buses to take us to safety. There are many personal stories of being Queer in the '80s and '90s: bricks smashing through windows when gathering with friends, having my car battered by a gang of police, and being driven off the road. The difficulty being that we looked Queer – and all the laws told us we were not welcome and were a danger to the wider community.

Working as an asylum seeker and refugee support teacher in Newham schools profoundly changed me. Children, largely Somalian, traumatised by war-torn countries, arrived and were placed in White working class deprived areas of the borough. It was almost like, those that didn't matter were placed together, racism and poverty interwoven. As a team, we were placed in twos in a large primary school, we were ill equipped, naïve, steeped in privilege, with little understanding of the trauma and violent racist enactment that ensued.

I witnessed children in playgrounds enacting war scenes: the lining up of their peers and then pretending to shoot them. We had refugee children attending school in babygrows, with bottles of breast milk for their lunch. At the same time active racists telling us and them to leave.

Parents evening became a terrifying event, and the walk from school to my car became one that I feared every afternoon. My feelings are still palpable as I write.

During this time, I began a relationship with my long-term partner a Catholic cis woman, brought up on Irish rebel songs and a grandfather who was in the IRA, branded by the British as a terrorist group. Her earliest memories were of coming to England, aged five, searching for a home while seeing signs: 'No Irish, no dogs, no Blacks'.

The following years brought many experiences of marginalisation and activism. Marginalisation in not being able to marry my partner, marginalisation in having to fight to have her at the birth of our children, marginalisation in having painkillers held back post c-section due to homophobia, marginalisation in not being able to have her name on our children's birth certificate; marginalisation every day through microaggressions, is she your mother?, is she your sister?, when did your husband leave you? Marginalisation as a Queer family, our story excluded from sex education, our children's family not represented in school curriculums, our children pretending we are heteronormative.

The absence of the political in the personal gained momentum in my journey as a transactional analyst – I often attempted to keep the political outside the door of my consulting room. This required splitting off parts of myself to continue to keep the 'White construct' or indeed colonisation of psychotherapy holding court. In 2018, I made the bold decision to hold the political as central to TA and psychotherapy training.

Years later, years of activism and the fight goes on… the political is personal. And my activism has been standing by and fighting with all discriminated against. My experience of othering and being witness to others being othered has fed my conviction that 'all oppression is connected' and that true liberation, will only come when all people are free.

The influence of activists informing contemporary transactional analysis theory, training and practice with an intersectional lens

'An activist is someone who is active in campaigning for change, normally on political or social issues' (COE, 2024). Indeed, activism can be aligned with the act of offering transactional analysis, or psychotherapy – journeying with another or others, to change and further self or systems – which ultimately contributes to social and political change. In fact, some would describe transactional analysis as an act of social justice, congruent with Berne's social psychiatry vision and philosophy that 'All people are OK', 'Everyone has the capacity to think' and 'All people can change'. An existential desire, somewhat radical and yet arguably a hope and perhaps naïve vision, discounting the onslaught of systemic oppression.

Many, in fact the global majority, have not been afforded the right of 'being OK' for many generations through colonisation, slavery, White and patriarchal supremacy. Indeed, many marginalised groups have not been afforded the capacity to think for themselves or indeed the right to change, illustrated through decades and centuries of legislation against those deemed to be different. The political has largely been omitted from the theory and practice of transactional analysis, perhaps overshadowed by Berne's experience of having to kill off that part of himself. (See Chapter 6.)

Contemporary authors have served to address this, yet there is still a long way to go in shifting the normative construct of transactional analysis. Activists through time have brought about political and social change and have largely served to amplify the voice of those who are marginalised. Indeed, the task of radical relational transactional analysis aims to bring about fundamental change from alienation to reclamation (Minikin, 2023).

Many activists come from a place of having experienced multiple marginalisation and have indeed struggled in their lifetime to be heard and understood. Many have drawn on their lived experience and oppression to fuel their fire, passion, and drive for change. Some have felt that activism has not been a choice but a response to what their own lives, and the generations before, have handed them.

Some have been writers, some poets, some have taken up political positions, others are known for their challenge to systems and law. And indeed, at times rule breaking to forge change. Some have spent time in prison due to their activism, others have suffered hunger strikes, isolation and even death in their plight to be heard and forge change.

Forging change requires thinking outside the box, it involves taking risks and usually requires breaking rules and challenging systems. Thus, activists are the trailblazers, the visionaries, and the change makers. I deeply honour the journeying of these activists, the bravery and the courage, the toil and the cost, the known activists and the unknown. The women who were not named. The Black suffragettes, the women and Black scientists, the gender fluid people, the indigenous communities, the native people, the Queer voices.

Taking 'the road less travelled' requires stepping out of the academic and normative realm. Activists have informed and framed my development of theories and practice: these include the historical work of Lorde, hooks, Baldwin, and Rich, as well as contemporary thinkers Chin, Vaid-Menon, Ellis, Hart, and Turner, along with local activists and spoken word poets. What they all have in common is a profound understanding of multiple selves and the interconnected systems we all reside in.

These activist voices have brought a breadth of intersectional identities through lived experience to the framing of theory, highlighting the need for representation and amplification of marginalised voices – 'I can see myself, I am heard' – as well as informing the deconstruction and reconstruction of transactional analysis original theory.

They have woken us up, they have challenged, rattled and invited discomfort, they have also been ignored, ostracised and killed off in their different communities. And they have inspired hope and the drive to keep fighting – something not often talked about in the realm of transactional analysis. Hidden underneath the 'I'm OK, you're OK' lies the fighting, the power struggles, the multi-privileged saying 'what's the problem here?', the multi-marginalised being injured over and over again. Activists fight, fight for themselves, fight for each other, for the collective, for the planet, they expose their most vulnerable selves, they express their anger, their despair, and ultimately their love and hope, in the very nature of their being. This is 'I'm OK, you're OK'. I can exist and you can exist. I will fight for you, and you will fight for me. I bow to the divine in you and you bow to the divine in me (Baskerville, 2022). Fighting isn't often acknowledged, and the risk is enactment and harm but also that of transformation, reminding me of Hargaden and Sills (2010) projective and transformative domains of transference.

Here, I look in more detail at the work of just nine activists chosen for their courage, creativity, and most importantly their profound understanding of the interconnectedness of oppressions.

Audre Lorde *(she/her)*

I begin with Lorde whose activism and writing have energetically challenged and framed the development of ideas in offering an intersectional lens to transactional analysis theory.

Lorde through poetry and writing brings a profound understanding of the complexity of the transcultural and intersectional self (Baskerville, 2022), describing her lived experience as many selfhoods, her concert of voices. Audre Lorde self-described as 'Black, lesbian, mother, warrior, poet', devoted her life to addressing injustices of racism, sexism, classism, and homophobia. Lorde was born in New York City to West Indian immigrant parents and began writing poetry aged 13 as a way of making sense of her lived experience.

Lorde made significant contributions to Critical Race studies, feminist theory, and Queer theory and was a strong voice advocating the intersections of race, class, and gender in the lens of difference. In particular, in her essay 'The Master's tools will not dismantle the Master's house' (2018), she locates patriarchy as central to all discrimination and challenges White feminists to include all women – women who are Black and poor – ultimately looking at their part in upholding the system. In many ways reminiscent of today's White cis gender-critical feminists' exclusion of Trans women and gender-fluid people.

Lorde shows vulnerability in her writing exposing the catastrophic onslaught of multiple oppression, stating: 'I have a duty to speak the truth as I see it and to share not just my triumphs, not just the things that felt good, but the pain, the intense, often unmitigating pain' (1997, 2017; Poetry Foundation, 2024).

In her essay 'There is no hierarchy of oppression' (1983), Lorde called for us to fight 'all' oppressions. Thus, highlighting the idea that there is 'no single issue'; that all oppression is born from the same hierarchical systems, that no one is immune from being destroyed by these systems, and true liberation is born from challenging all interlinked oppressions. Those who are multiply privileged, who do indeed 'benefit' from these systems, also, arguably, live with the shadow of oppression and ultimately the loss of self in the disconnection from spirituality, community and the planet. Reading Lorde's essay 'There is no hierarchy of oppression', I invite an undefended listening, a laying down of arms, a willingness to hear the privileged and oppressed parts of self and their intertwined stories.

> I was born Black, and a woman. I am trying to become the strongest person I can become to live the life I have been given and to help effect change toward a liveable future for this earth and for my children. As a Black, lesbian, feminist, socialist, poet, mother of two including one boy and a member of an interracial couple, I usually find myself part of some group in which the majority defines me as deviant, difficult, inferior or just plain 'wrong'.
>
> From my membership in all of these groups I have learned that oppression and the intolerance of difference come in all shapes and sexes and colors and sexualities; and that among those of us who share the goals of liberation and a workable future for our children, there can be no hierarchies of oppression. I have learned that sexism and heterosexism both arise from the same source as racism.
>
> Within the lesbian community I am Black, and within the Black community I am a lesbian. Any attack against Black people is a lesbian and gay issue, because

I and thousands of other Black women are part of the lesbian community. Any attack against lesbians and gays is a Black issue, because thousands of lesbians and gay men are Black. There is no hierarchy of oppression.

Lorde's essay and along with her poetry takes us to another realm, to the unspoken, it is a passionate plea to be heard, a powerful medium of change. A way of telling the stories of lived experience within systemic racism and oppression, the palpable struggle, the pain, and journeying for a different experience.

Lorde's writing is both inspiring and challenging. Inviting us to look at all aspects of our identity and identities, supporting the call for an intersectional lens across all theory and process. Lorde's activism in her writing and poetry has been integral to my reframing of transactional analysis theory, process, and practice.

bell hooks *(she/her)*

Another profoundly influential activist is bell hooks, born Gloria Jean Watkins, who adopted her great grandmother's name as her pen name, she was an African American author, educator, intersectional feminist, and social activist and focused her writing on the interconnectivity and intersections of race, class, and gender and their ability to produce and perpetuate systems of oppression and domination. Her first major work, *Ain't I a Woman?* (hooks, 1981), possibly her most read work, was followed by more than thirty publications.

Like Lorde, hooks is 'most well known for her feminist theory that recognises that social classifications (e.g., race, gender, sexual identity, class, etc.) are interconnected, and that ignoring their intersection creates oppression towards women and changes the experience of living as a woman in society' (Flores, 2016). In particular, the convergence of sexism and racism experienced by Black women. Thus, bell hooks challenged the social construct of feminism, moving away from the White construct of feminism. She was one of the first intersectional feminists, along with Lorde, bringing marginalised identities into feminism.

These ideas challenge the normative and monocultural lens in many of our TA theories. The realisation that no one benefits from systems of oppression: including cis men in patriarchy who have become alienated from the feminine, cis heterosexual women who are socially constructed to live within patriarchy, Black cis heterosexual women, who suffer racism and sexism and patriarchal power, Black Queer women turned away from both the Black community and the Queer White community, or Trans women who are ostracised by the gender critical feminists.

hooks spoke of love in her political writings, she dared to imagine the possibility of another world through love and transformation. She taught us how to dialogue, in her many interviews she taught us the power of love. And indeed, reminded me of the revolutionary act of love in TA and psychotherapy as an act of social justice, loving those who deem themselves unlovable. A tribute to hooks following her death in 2021 speaks to the essence of what she gave us. 'We have lost another whose life, whose intimate politics of transformative love has taught us how to believe that there is the possibility of another world: a world beyond this patriarchal gaze, this subconscious niggle, this anomaly of nature... I remember marvelling at how love was at the centre of her revolution, how she let the flame of desire, and the embers of loss give light to her politics' (Poetly, 2021).

In describing bell hooks, John A. Powell in an interview (Powell, 2015) says, 'there is no box that can hold her'. He stated that her work had been for the people and that she believed belonging came through connection. She wanted ordinary people to benefit from her work and her institute, a place where people could be as they are, unload burdens and find home. She wanted to include everyone. hooks wanted to understand love and self in all its complexity through community.

hooks described being called to activism, saying that her pastor asked 'is your heart ready to handle the weight of your calling?', and she asked, 'what am I called to do here?'.

bell hooks is remembered as teaching us that 'the oppression of one is the oppression of all. And that love dismantles systems of oppression'. She stated: 'The moment we choose love, we begin to move toward freedom, to act in ways that liberate ourselves and others' (hooks, 1994, p. 5).

James Baldwin *(he/him)*

James Baldwin, the grandson of a person who was enslaved, the eldest of nine was born in 1924 in Harlem, New York, grew up in poverty and developed a difficult relationship with his religious stepfather. Baldwin spending much of his childhood in libraries, briefly became a pastor and later joined the railroad, before finding his way to Greenwich as a writer.

Baldwin became a novelist, and playwright whose eloquence and passion about race in America made him one of the most important voices of the 20th century (Ostberg, 2024). Baldwin addressed race relations with complexity and passionate anger. He was also one of the first Black writers to include Queer themes in fiction.

James Baldwin had his own personal struggles as a Queer Black man living in a time of overt racism, where homosexuality was criminalised and pathologised. What strikes me about Baldwin is his profound courage to speak out about racism and homophobia. As shown in his semi autobiographical novel, *Go Tell It On The Mountain* (1953), and Raoul Peck's documentary following his death based on Baldwin's uncompleted work, *I Am Not Your Negro* (1979; 2017), he didn't shy away from speaking truth and challenging White and heterosexual supremacy and individuals in the system. His radical book, *Giovanni's Room* (1956), regarded as deviant and rejected by many publishers because of its explicit homosexual content, illustrates Baldwin's conviction that the sexual question and the racial question have always been entwined. Again, strengthening the argument for an intersectional lens in understanding self in the system (Armengol, 2012).

Baldwin's writing profoundly and powerfully advocates for working on self and giving the responsibility back to the oppressor, strongly inviting self reflection on conscious and unconscious racism and bias, both explicitly and implicitly. He states

'I am not a negro I am a man' – it is up to the oppressor to work out why they need to project racist constructs onto a Black person. His quote, 'Not everything that is faced can be changed, but nothing can be changed until it is faced' (Baldwin, 1962) speaks to his courage in his fight and his right to belong. It is a quote I have used repeatedly in inviting dialogue around difference and who holds power in the room.

Dwight Turner (2023), writes about Baldwin's experience of homophobia within his close circle of friends and human rights activists, illustrating oppressions as born from the same interconnected system (2023): 'Martin Luther King, whilst considered to this day a major advocate for human rights, was a part of a group who were uncomfortable with the sexuality of their contemporary James Baldwin whose intersectional identities as a Black gay man did not align with King's religious perspective on sexuality identity (Campbell, 2021). So that whereas in the early stages of their work together, Baldwin felt included in the dialogues around race and difference, by the end of King's life, pre his assassination, Baldwin had been very much side-lined from the fight for racial justice in America. This example here actually shows in King's case, that whilst he was undoubtedly a great man, and whilst he did undoubtedly fight against White supremacy, he too had taken up a position of patriarchal and also religious superiority over another vocal activist and man of colour, purely because of his sexuality. That we all, as activists, no matter what our position, need to work through these intersectional mazes' (p. 123).

This furthers my conviction of the importance of working intersectionally, thus challenging and rewriting the system through deconstruction and reconstruction of theory, process, and practice PBS (2006).

Adrienne Rich (she/her)

Adrienne Rich, a White cis woman, known as a poet of ideas, essayist and activist was born in 1929 in Baltimore. She began writing poetry from a young age and published numerous poetry and nonfiction collections (1995, Rich and Gilbert, 2019); her lifetime work explored themes around the Vietnam war, identity, sexuality, patriarchy, and revolutionary ideas about radical feminism, which she preferred to cite as women's liberation. Adrienne Rich won the National Book Award in 1974 for *Diving into the Wreck* (1973). She refused to accept the award individually, instead sharing it with fellow nominees Audre Lorde and Alice Walker. They accepted it on behalf of all women everywhere who are silenced by a patriarchal society (Napikoski, 2019).

Adrienne Rich (1980) popularised the phrase 'compulsory heterosexuality' in her essay 'Compulsory heterosexuality and lesbian existence'. She argued from a lesbian feminist point of view that heterosexuality is not innate in human beings. 'Nor is it the only normal sexuality', she said. She further asserted that 'women can benefit more from relationships with other women than from relationships with men'.

On feminism, or indeed lesbian feminism she wrote: 'Much male fear of feminism is the fear that, in becoming whole human beings, women will cease to mother men, to provide the breast, the lullaby, the continuous attention associated by the infant with the mother. Much male fear of feminism is infantilism – the longing to remain the mother's son, to possess a woman who exists purely for him' (Rich, 1979, p. 123). Furthermore, on challenging patriarchy and cis male supremacy, Rich, in her commencement address at Smith College stated: 'No woman is really an insider in the institutions fathered by masculine consciousness. When we allow ourselves to believe we are, we lose touch with parts of ourselves defined as unacceptable by that consciousness; with the vital toughness and visionary strength of the angry grandmothers, the shamanesses, the fierce marketwomen of the Ibo's Women's War, the marriage-resisting women silkworkers of pre-Revolutionary China, the millions of widows, midwives, and the women healers tortured and burned as witches for three centuries in Europe' (Rich, 1979). Here Rich challenges the patriarchal colonisation of women, all that has been 'done to' women through the decades and centuries. She draws on the strength of ancestors, the native and indigenous women that have come before us, that sit across race, sexuality, and nations. The murdered women, named as witches, killed for their autonomy.

Rich also challenged the cost of individualistic culture, capitalist supremacy. In her poem collection *Dark Fields of the Republic* (Rich, 1995), she highlighted the nature of individual happiness set against community need. I witnessed this, illustrated beautifully, in Will Tuckett's 'Then or now', blending Black classical ballet, music, and the poetry of Adrienne Rich to ask the question: 'In times like these, where do we each belong?' (Ballet Black, 2023). This poem, set with music and ballet, had a profound impact on my understanding of the loss of the 'we' for the 'I'. The catastrophic loss of community, the loneliness and isolation, the idea that individual need is greater than community need. The risk of the 'I' in psychotherapy and the loss of the 'we' in individualistic culture (poetryfoundation, 2024).

Staceyann Chin *(she/her)*

Staceyann Chin was born in 1972 in Jamaica, and now lives in New York. She is of Chinese Jamaican descent. She is a spoken word poet, performer, and political activist known worldwide. She has shared her struggles growing up as a gay person in Jamaica. Chin's first full-length poetry collection *Crossfire: A Litany for Survival,* was published in 2019 (Chin, 2019). Through impassioned spoken word poetry, she brings into sharp focus the profound reality that 'all oppression is connected', and that we cannot profess to make a stand against racism and not stand up for the Trans community. We cannot profess to be anti-oppressive and not understand the plight of the Palestinian people, alongside standing up with those of Jewish descent. Watching Chin perform her poem *All Oppression is Connected* is a rude awakening of the hard truth, not wrapped up, painful, messy, rageful, urgent, aggressive, violent, heart rending. Her poem speaks loudly of the harrowing onslaught of all oppressions presently and historically, the complexity of intersectionality, the interconnected nature of all oppressions.

Staceyann Chin's poem, *All Oppression Is Connected* impels action: acting now while we still can before it is too late and, as Chin warns, 'they come for you'.

The poem (Chin, 2014), which I urge people to read, speaks the unspeakable, yet the truth, the painful catastrophic truth. The truth that usually resides on the edge and is not welcomed to the centre. She dares to use slurs and words not usually spoken, some reclaimed, many want to keep them in the past and want to disown them as being part of their ancestral story. Some words have been reclaimed, Queer for example, and yet it depends on who reclaims them and how they are used as to whether they sit easy with the recipient.

Chin's spoken word poetry takes us to discomfort, yet when I listened to her in the safety of my home, I did not feel discomfort, I felt seen, I felt safe, I felt passionate, and riled up to keep taking the journey. Yet when I shared it with a group, I felt exposed, disturbed, and my internal shame kicked in, shame around daring to expose my anger, my grief, and my despair.

The political is personal, this is the work as transactional analysts, taking the action, taking up our therapeutic swords and taking the splinter out, thus furthering our radical roots, the deep learning, the willingness to account for all voices, all in the training room, in our consulting rooms, in our communities, in our world.

Indeed, the process of deconstruction and reconstruction of our theories and practice is stirring, disturbing, serving to derail the normative, hence an awakening, and the profound awareness that many of these stories have been kept out of White individualistic institutions, through White privilege, White bias, Whitewashing, White reframing, and all that colonisation brings.

Alok Vaid-Menon (they/them)

Alok Vaid-Menon, born in Texas, US, 1991, a Yale scholar, is a renowned gender nonconforming and Trans feminine author, activist, poet, and comedian, who eloquently fights for the Trans and non-gender-conforming community, stating that Trans people are free and modelling true autonomy. Alok comes from a place of love, and challenges those who discriminate others as enacting their internalised oppression. They invite creative expression and imagination and see the gender critical feminists and all who are transphobic as fearing their own freedom.

Alok tours worldwide bringing their lived experience, modelling free expression. Their books serve to educate and to challenge the construct of gender. Alok has authored *Beyond the Gender Binary* (2020), *Your Wound, My Garden* (2021), and *Femme in Public* (2021).

In the podcast, 'Man Enough' (2022), 'The urgent need for compassion', Alok is interviewed and engages in an important dialogue around use of pronouns, the interviewer is concerned about miss-pronouning. Alok says: 'You will miss-pronoun, you will mess up, but keep learning and trying harder'. A human yet potent response – get better. He writes avidly on Instagram challenging the social construct of sex and gender and links the sex binary with racism, he states: 'The sex binary (the idea that there are only two distinct opposite sexes) is a 19th century colonised intervention'. Alok's activism challenges the social construct of gender through their way of being in the world, through fashion, through comedy, interview, poetry, podcast, and authoring short digital books.

The Trans movement aligned with Queer theory challenges the binary in all social and political constructs and opens capacity for true autonomy and inclusion. The ultimate aim of transactional analysis is autonomy inviting awareness, spontaneity, and intimacy. Yet the focus on the normative, has missed the social, cultural, political, and historical contexts and has not considered who is afforded/ allowed autonomy. Black people have not been afforded autonomy, Trans people have not been afforded autonomy, Women have not been afforded autonomy, and so on. All are caught up with the binary, be it Black and White, cis and Trans, cis women and cis men. Our original theories set in the context of their time, bring a White, binarygendered and heterosexual lens. The Trans movement challenges these social constructs, inviting movement between binaries, ideas of non-gender-conforming – arguably bringing a freedom beyond the vision and dreams of Lorde, Baldwin, and Rich.

Anton Hart

Anton Hart, a Black American psychoanalyst, teacher, supervisor, writer, and associate co-producer for the film, *Black Psychoanalysts Speak*, presents and consults nationally and internationally on issues of diversity and is interested in issues of otherness, race, racism and racial trauma. He describes his intersectional identity as: 'I am multiracial with a Black father whose ancestors were African American, Native American and Western European, and a White, Jewish mother whose ancestors were from Russia and Poland. I consider myself to be both Black and White, and, also, not simply either'.

Hart (2017) states: '"Multicultural competence" – I wish that term would be banished from this earth. Competence? We're going to be competent in relating to the other?' (p. 1). Further arguing that 'Multicultural competency training promotes a defended, prepared manner of addressing differences... and is a lost opportunity for personal reflections and deeper engagement'. Hence, he coined the idea of radical openness and non-defended dialogue, inviting curiosity and enquiry, stating: 'The heart of the matter is learning how to become increasingly undefended around matters of diversity and otherness such that you can be open: open to the other person who will be, in some significant ways, most certainly different from you. A psychoanalytic sensibility suggests to us that genuine openness can only emerge in the context of an unscripted dialogue, one that involves making contact with and participating in an exchange that will, necessarily, threaten the dialogic participants' understandings, identities and perceptions' (p. 1).

Hart's ideas around radical openness and non-defended dialogue invite an open and honest curiosity around 'the difference between us', rather than 'others are different', which can result in othering. This invites an honesty and an openness, a permission to tell our stories, to know and share our transcultural narrative, our transgenerational stories and to be interested in the stories of others. Moreover, moving away from the preconception and projection of monoculture, it invites curiosity and empathy and a non-threatening interest in intersectional identity in ourselves and in the other. Being interested in the intersects that connect us, the ones that cause tension between us, the ruse, the killing of each other, the shucking and the jiving (Turner, 2021). Hart's ideas bring to light themes around disclosure, the place of transference and countertransference, the real relationship and the relational field of both the client and therapist, educator and student, facilitator and organisation.

Eugene Ellis *(he/him)*

Eugene Ellis, pioneer, founder and director of The Black, African and Asian Therapy Network (BAATN), created a safe space and community in the UK over two decades ago for people of Black, African, Asian and Caribbean heritage and other people of colour affected by oppression due to the colour of their skin and global White power. Ellis responded to the need for racially marginalised therapists to come together as a community, to address the race inequalities in the psychotherapy profession.

Today, as a not-for-profit social enterprise, BAATN aims to address the inequalities of access to appropriate psychological services for these communities by providing events, training and partnerships with therapy organisations that recognise the impact of racism. Thus, providing a home and solidarity in 'striving to integrate a Black empathic approach into mainstream psychotherapy and advocate for its inclusion in training and practice', thus 'working towards mental health equity'. https://www.baatn.org.uk

This is a vision shared by TA East, striving to attend to systemic racism within TA East and the transactional analysis and wider psychotherapy community. Actively inviting dialogue around race and difference across races in training and consulting rooms. Raising awareness across the race divide, attending to the race construct as described by Ellis, the construct of Black and the construct of White and the polarised binary, constructed decades and centuries ago, through colonisation and White supremacy.

The work is learning to have the dialogue and to keep doing the work on ourselves, however the time is now, reminding me of Martin Luther King's quote, as well as the shift in urgency following the murder of George Floyd, Ellis (2021) stated 'talking about race had always been hard work, but, after George Floyd's killing, it had somehow become hard work, not to' (p. 4).

Ellis (2021), in his book *Race Conversation: An Essential Guide to Creating Lifechanging Dialogue,* explores the intersection of race and trauma and the non-verbal communication of race and how to navigate oppressive patterns. Ellis shares some of his own journey, in being called to have conversations about race and his own ancestral story and transgenerational trauma, experienced in his body.

Moreover, Ellis's chapter in Ababio and Littlewood, eds. (2019) *Intercultural Therapy: Challenges, Insights and Developments* entitled 'Finding our voice across the Black/White divide: Race issues in therapy', reflects on the therapists' process when issues of race become foreground for the therapist, the client, or the trainee therapist and what processes encourage and maintain the ability to stay with race dialogue.

Ellis (2021) models ways of having the race conversation and my hope would be that future courses include facilitated intersectional dialogues around the binaries of race and oppression challenging systemic enactment. However, tutors, students, transactional analysts, educators, and psychotherapists need to take the journey, White and people of colour, working through their transgenerational trauma to come to a place to dialogue, to own the part they play, to be open and non-defended, to walk the unknown territory, and to forge a different path.

Dwight Turner *(he/him)*

Dwight Turner is a course leader on a Humanistic Counselling and Psychotherapy degree course, a PhD supervisor, and a psychotherapist and supervisor in private practice. His publications include *The Psychology of Supremacy: Imperium* (2023) and *Intersections of Privilege and Otherness in Counselling and Psychotherapy* (2021).

Turner is a current activist and has been, in my view, instrumental in reshaping and shaking up the counselling and psychotherapy profession. His presence on Twitter/x and Instagram is generously spirited inviting solidarity and collective activism for all oppressions. Turner uses social media as a platform and writes avidly about themes of othering, race, difference, and intersectionality. He eloquently translates his academic skill into a form of palpable activism. His books and blogs are vehicles for change and speak to counsellors and psychotherapists, inviting greater self-reflection around intersectionality, otherness, and supremacies.

Crenshaw stated, 'intersectionality was always a lived reality before it became a term' (Crenshaw, Washington Post, 2015). I think Turner has brought intersectionality alive in a new way, citing privilege as having its part in constructing otherness. At the beginning of Turner's (2021) *Intersections of Privilege and Otherness in Counselling and Psychotherapy* his relational and open style sets the scene by naming his intersectional identity and sharing his experience of otherness. This in itself is stirring and moving, thus inviting practitioners to consider their own intersectional identity consciously and unconsciously and their place within systemic oppression.

Turner's writing on the mini deaths experienced by minoritised cultures on a daily basis and the killing off the other to comply with White supremacy and normative culture is particularly powerful. Indeed, these ideas informed the Transcultural and Intersectional Ego State Model (Baskerville, 2022), where A_1 intuits and code switches safe and unsafe spaces; and, moreover, bringing depth to the dialogue, for example asking: what did I kill off in this unique encounter?; which supremacy played out in this relationship?

Turner's second book, *Psychology of Supremacy: Imperium* (2023), explores delicately and powerfully the intersections of the triumvirate of supremacies: capitalism, White supremacy, and patriarchy. His ideas are groundbreaking for the counselling and psychotherapy profession, taking us to a new level in addressing and deepening understanding around themes of power enacted in the consulting room and wider world. He attends to the multi-complexity of multiple levels of systemic oppression, structures and systems and their histories and places them within the context of supremacy.

Turner has profoundly opened up a dialogue around the influence of supremacy on self-identity and the idea that these are socially constructed through the intersects of supremacy, developing ideas around internalised unconscious supremacy and how this manifests in relational dynamics. His ultimate call is for us to really evaluate ourselves internally (Baskerville & Kannathasan, 2023; Baskerville, 2023).

Calling for collective action and change in our profession, Turner asks us to keep questioning: where is the patriarchy in this?; where is the capitalism in this?; where is the White supremacy in this?

Conclusion

I have drawn on activism and the work of activists to develop, frame, further, and challenge the theory and practice of transactional analysis and psychotherapy through an intersectional lens. Activism challenges social and political constructs and activists have used their marginalisation and privilege to tell their stories and fight for themselves and others. Fighting isn't usually seen as an act of transactional analysis, yet we do fight for our clients, our organisations, and our educational institutes with love, passion, anger, and conviction. It is not found behind the paywall of academia, activism finds us, reaches into us, through the mediums of social media, blogs, protest, art, dialogue, podcast, youtube, poetry, spoken word, music, rap, street art, and so on. It has served to inform the development of contemporary theory, offering a challenge to, and critique of, normative structures within systemic oppression.

References

Ababio, B., & Littlewood, R. (2019). *Intercultural therapy: Challenges, insights and developments*. Hove, East Sussex: Routledge.

Armengol, J. M. (2012). In the dark room: Homosexuality and/as blackness in James Baldwin's Giovanni's Room. *Signs, 37*(3), 671–693. http://doi.org/10.1086/662699

Baldwin, J. (1953/2001 edition). *Go tell it on the mountain*. London: Penguin Random House.

Baldwin, J. (1956). *Giovanni's room*. New York: Dial Press; London: Penguin Classics (2007).

Baldwin, J. (1962). Quote from *New York Times,* January 14, 1962.

Baldwin, J., & Peck, R. (1979; 2017) *I am not your negro*. London: Penguin Random House.

Ballet Black. (2023). https://balletblack.co.uk/events/barbican-2023-ballet-blackpioneers/

Baskerville, V. (2022). A transcultural and intersectional ego state model of the self: The influence of transcultural and intersectional identity on self and other. *Transactional Analysis Journal, 52*(32), 1–16. http://doi.org/10.1080/03621537.2022.2076398

Baskerville, V. (2023) Book review: Intersections of privilege and otherness in counselling and psychotherapy. *New Psychotherapist,* Summer 2023.

Baskerville, V., & Kannathasan, N. (2023). Book review: The psychology of supremacy: Imperium by Dwight Turner. *The Transactional Analyst, 13*(4).

BBC. (2009). https://www.bbc.co.uk/stoke/content/articles/2009/02/14/history_mining_staffordshire_feature.shtml

Campbell, J. (2021). *Talking at the gates, a life of James Baldwin.* Edinburgh: Polygon

Chin, S. (2014). 'All oppression is connected' [Video]. https://www.pbslearningmedia.org/resource/fp17.lgbtq.oppression/all-oppression-is-connected/

Chin, S. (2014). http://whyaminotsurprised.blogspot.com/2014/07/staceyann-chin-all-oppression-is.html

Chin, S. (2019). Crossfire: A litany for survival. Chicago: Haymarket Books.

COE. (2024). https://www.coe.int/en/web/compass/hre-and-activism

Crenshaw, K. (1989). 'Demarginalizing the intersection of race and sex: A black feminist critique of antidiscrimination doctrine, feminist theory and antiracist politics'. University of Chicago Legal Forum, Issue 1, Article 8. https://chicagounbound.uchicago.edu/cgi/viewcontent.cgi?ar-ticle=1052&context=uclf

Crenshaw, K. (2015). 'Why intersectionality can't wait', September 24, 2015, *The Washington Post.* https://www.washingtonpost.com/news/in-theory/wp/2015/09/24/why-intersectionality-cant-wait/

Ellis, E. (2021). *The race conversation.* London: Confer.

Flores, M. (2016). 'bell hooks – intersectional feminist' https://info.umkc.edu/womenc/2016/01/04/bell-hooks-intersectional-feminist/

gov.uk (1988). https://www.legislation.gov.uk/ukpga/1988/9/section/28

Hargaden, H., & Sills, C. (2010). *Transactional analysis: A relational perspective.* Hove, East Sussex: Routledge.

Hart, A. (2017). From multicultural competence to radical openness: A psychoanalytic engagement of otherness. *The American Psychoanalyst, 51*(1), 12–13, 26–27. https://apsa.org/wp-content/uploads/apsaa-publications/vol51no1-TOC/html/vol51no1_09.xhtml

hooks, B. (1981). *Ain't I a woman?: Black women and feminism.* London: Pluto Press.

hooks, B. (1994). Love as the practice of freedom (chapter 20). In *Outlaw culture: Resisting representations.* New York & East Sussex: Routledge; e-book 2015. https://doi.org/10.4324/9780203822883

Klosin, A., Casas, E., Hidalgo-Carcedo, C., Vavouri, T., & Lehner, B. (2017). 'Transgenerational transmission of environmental information in *C. elegans. Science*, 356(6335), 320–323. https://pubmed.ncbi.nlm.nih.gov/28428426

Lorde, A. (1982). Learning from the '60s, Malcolm X Weekend, Harvard University. https://www.blackpast.org/african-american-history/1982-audre-lorde-learning-60s/

Lorde, A. (1983). There is no hierarchy of oppressions. *Homophobia and education.* Bulletin. New York: Council on Interracial Books for Children. Retrieved on December 29, 2021, from http://www.pages.drexel.edu/~jc3962/COR/Hierarchy.pdf; https://theanarchistlibrary.org/library/audre-lorde-there-is-no-hierarchy-of-oppressions; https://sites.williams.edu/engl113-f18/marr/there-is-no-hierarchy-of-oppression/

Lorde, A. (1997). *The cancer journals.* San Francisco: Aunt Lute Books.

Lorde, A. (2017). *Your silence will not protect you.* San Jose: Silver Press.

Lorde, A. (2018). *The master's tools will not dismantle the master's house.* London: Penguin Random House.

Minikin, K. (2023). *Radical-relational perspectives in transactional analysis psychotherapy: Oppression, alienation, reclamation.* London: Routledge.

Morgan, K. (2017). 'Britain in the Seventies – Our unfinest hour?', Revue Française de Civilisation Britannique [Online], XXII- Hors série | 2017, Online since December 30, 2017, connection on February 16, 2023. http://journals.openedition.org/rfcb/1662;

Napikoski, L. (2019). 'Biography of Adrienne Rich, feminist and political poet'. August 4, 2019. https://www.thoughtco.com/adrienne-rich-biography-3528945

Ostberg, R. (2024, June 13). 'James Baldwin'. *Encyclopedia Britannica*. https://www.britannica.com/biography/James-Baldwin

PBS. (2006). https://www.pbs.org/wnet/americanmasters/james-baldwin-about-the-author/59/

PBS. (2012). 'Slavery by another name'. https://www.pbs.org/tpt/slavery-by-another-name/themes/life-coal-mine/

Poetly. (2021). Obituary tribute to bell hooks https://poetly.substack.com/p/poems-frombell-hooks-when-angels

Poetryfoundation. (2024). https://www.poetryfoundation.org/poets/audre-lorde (accessed August 2024).

Poetryfoundation. (2024). https://www.poetryfoundation.org/poets/adrienne-rich

Powell, J. (2015). John A. Powell & Bell Hooks: Dialogue at the Othering & Belonging Conference, 'Belonging Through Connection, Connecting Through Love: Oneself, the Other, and the Earth'. https://youtu.be/0sX7fqIU4gQ?si=LLd-73TyCX8_6l7i

Rich, A. (1973; 1994). *Diving into the Wreck, reissue: Poems 1971-1972*. New York: W.W. Norton.

Rich, A. (1979). *What does a woman need to know?*. Speech Smith College. https://www.coursehero.com/file/66234961/Adrienne-Rich-What-Does-a-WomanNeed-to-Know-TPO-4-71-76pdf/

Rich, A. (1980). Compulsory heterosexuality and lesbian existence. *Signs: Journal of Women in Culture and Society* (University of Chicago Press Journals), 5(4), 631660. http://doi.org/10.1086/493756.

Rich, A. (1995). *Dark fields of the republic*. New York: W.W. Norton & Co.

Rich, A. (1995). *On lies, secrets, and silence: Selected prose 1966-1978*. New York: W.W. Norton & Co.

Rich, A., & Gilbert, S. M. (2019). *Culture, politics, and the art of poetry: Essential essays*. New York: W.W. Norton.

SFGMC. (2022). https://www.sfgmc.org/blog/aids-crisis-1980s

Turner, D. (2021). *Intersections of privilege and otherness in counselling and psychotherapy*. East Sussex: Routledge.

Turner, D. (2023). *The psychology of supremacy: Imperium*. East Sussex: Routledge.

Vaid-Menon, A. (2020). *Beyond the gender binary*. London: Pocket Change Collective Series, Penguin Random House.

Vaid-Menon, A. (2021). *Your wound, my garden*. Audible Studios (2023).

Vaid-Menon, A. (2021) *Femme in public*. https://www.alokvmenon.com/writing

Vaid-Menon, A. (2022). 'Alok: The urgent need for compassion'. *Man Enough*. https://youtu.be/Tq3C9R8HNUQ

Chapter 10

The evidence, 10,000 cuts

Research on inclusivity and exclusivity in counselling and psychotherapy training and the experience of trainees, in particular with regard to difference

Victoria Baskerville, Nilufar Ahmed, Vikki Nelson, and Gillian Neish

In a final summary report, this chapter offers the findings of a two-year UKCP research project into inclusivity and exclusivity in counselling and psychotherapy training. The report was published in the UK's *The Transactional Analyst* magazine (Winter 22/23, 13:1), the UKCP's *New Psychotherapist* publication (2023), and presented at the UKCP conference (2022).

The evidence of exclusion was painful yet familiar, accounting for the human cost of oppression and marginalisation. The experiences of inclusion were moving and optimistic, accounting for good practice and calling for practitioners to do the work on themselves and take decisive action around themes of difference, inclusion, and exclusion.

FINAL UKCP RESEARCH PROJECT REPORT

Inclusivity and exclusivity in counselling and psychotherapy training and the experience of trainees, in particular with regard to difference.

Background

In September 2020, following a Twitter discussion in response to the Black Lives Matter protests, an intersectional diverse group of counselling and psychotherapy colleagues who had never met in person got together to apply to the UKCP research bursary to research inclusivity and exclusivity in training. The group was successful and the iterative, creative, research took off. Almost as soon as the funding was confirmed, the group number shrank as people weighed up their commitments, and what was a group of nine quickly became five and then finally a core of four cis women representing a broad cross section of diverse cultural and social intersectional identities.

The group met monthly to explore and process our intersectional identities in relation to training experiences and to pave the way for research tasks through dialogue and group process. The intention from the start was to model inclusivity in our

DOI: 10.4324/9781003509424-10

research process by drawing on creative and non-traditional forms of data collection. At times the meetings were raw and emotional as we shared our stories and vulnerabilities around multiple levels of exclusion in the therapeutic field with each other.

A common experience among us, and one we were familiar with through our networks, was the gulf of inequalities which permeates psychotherapy and counselling, and most central to that was the way in which training perpetuated and intensified social inequalities and injustice. There was a need to critically interrogate how White privilege, unconscious bias, and institutionalised oppression operates within our curriculums, to explore what changes can be made to both widen the representation of diversity amongst trainees entering and succeeding in their training.

While there is limited research in this area, there is anecdotal evidence that indicates training spaces are experienced as unsafe and exclusionary by marginalised groups (Powell et al., 2015). This was the focus of our work: to explore experiences of current trainees and the ways in which the curriculum impacted their sense of inclusion and exclusion in the process. The findings can inform ways to update and develop the delivery of training to be less exclusive and oppressive, both in terms of content and process (Arnold, 2022/23).

This report summarises our work and the multiple interactions and outputs we have had over a two-year period.

Research questions

We began the process by sharing our own personal experiences of inclusion and exclusion in therapy and counselling training. We asked ourselves three key questions at the outset of the research in November 2021:

1 What brought you to this research group?
2 How have you experienced yourself in the research group?
3 What outcomes are you hoping for from the research?

From these discussions, the importance of our intersectional identities and their interplay with power and privilege in creating spaces of inclusivity and exclusivity became a salient theme that we kept returning to – each time uncovering new links; and the ways in which parts of our identities had to be silenced in different spaces including our therapeutic training and journeys. Thus, we decided intersectional identities should be the focus of our research – to create a space where people could explore and share their intersectionality.

Following this, the research group released a 40-minute film, which is BSL signed, naming our unique intersectional identities and exploring these questions as our first piece of research (Research Team Interviews, 2021).

Methodology

We used critical participatory action research, as the methodological framework for our work. It has been described as 'research in collaboration with communities, groups, and individuals living at the margins, that is those with relatively little sociopolitical power' (Fine et al., 2021, p. 345). It recognises the different positions people hold and the ways in which identities intersect with power in the research process. Within this framework we all brought our different identities, strengths, and knowledge. A mix of practitioners, trainers, and academics, we offered unique perspectives and skills to the research process.

Central to our ethos has been to ensure that not only is our research accessible to all, but that we promote a wider discussion within our profession on issues of inclusivity. In keeping with our overarching aim of increasing inclusivity, we embraced methodological pluralism, and used a range of qualitative research methods available to us. Thus, we chose to facilitate workshops, to amplify the voices of those who have been silenced, and to offer support to allies who wish to understand lived experiences of exclusion, as well as documenting examples of good practice that we have fed back to the wider therapeutic community. This method allowed us to ensure we created safe spaces, that participants were able to connect with us, rather than sending out questionnaires and surveys which felt distant to the relational journey that we, as researchers, had gained so much from. This creative methodology foregrounds narratives, stories, intersectional maps, videos, and blogs to document lived experiences and the change we want to see.

We have shared our outputs throughout the two-year process (see Table 10.1).

Participant recruitment

We had planned to recruit participants from a broad range of counselling and psychotherapy institutes across the UK through direct appeal to the courses, and also via social media and snowballing techniques. Due to an unexpected delay (see below '*A note on Ethical Review*') we rethought our approach and focused on finding participants through conferences to maximise recruitment. This was an iterative process, and drawing on the success of the first workshop at the UKATA conference (2022), the team decided to hold its own conference to explore these themes in more detail. The participants included a range of trainees and graduates from a number of modalities and institutions with normative and marginalised identities. In total 65 people participated in this study, representing 12 institutes, and we collected 65 intersectional maps.

In the spirit of participatory research, as well as recruiting participants to the study, the research team members were active participants in this project, asking ourselves the same questions we wished to explore with trainees and practitioners.

Data collection

Data was collected at the UKATA conference, April 2022, and the Research Conference held at TA East, July 2022, through experiential workshops. We presented our study aims and invited participants to share their intersectional identities and their experiences of inclusion and exclusion. We chose to ask broad questions to allow participants to bring whatever was salient for them in that time and space.

Table 10.1 Research timeline

Time period	Activity
Sept–Dec 2020	Forming research group.
Jan 2021–	Formalised research strategy and design.
Apr 2021	Prepared participant information sheets and consent forms.
May 2021	Research documents ready for submission to ethics.
Nov 2021	**Published Research Project Report 1, in *The Transactional Analyst* magazine**
	• Interviews recorded with the team.
	• Victoria Baskerville becomes guest editor for *The Transactional Analyst* magazine themed issue 'social justice' and interviews marginalised voices and develops an amplified voices column; Victoria Baskerville writes an article on 'Evolving an inclusive training'.
Dec 2021	**Researchers' interviews filmed and released for public access.**
	• The interviews were shared in Dropbox for students, practitioners and trainers to see this raw unedited data, we shared our experiences with the viewer who may find in our words echoes of their own experiences. This process was important for us to embody the research questions, to allow ourselves to be vulnerable and honest. https://www.dropbox.com/s/dkh23gzj6dbawld/Introducing%20Research%20Project.mp4?dl=0
Feb 2022	**Published Research Project Report 2, in *The Transactional Analyst* magazine**
April 2022	**UKATA conference**
April 2022	
	• Facilitated research workshop at UKATA conference with 20 participants, representing 6 Institutes collecting data and presented themes for inclusive practice.
	• Themes from these fed into the data collection process to define and refine the emergent ideas.
	Published Research Project Report 3, in *The Transactional Analyst* magazine
	• Victoria Baskerville reports on the UKATA research workshop and some emerging outcomes, held at the UKATA conference in April, focused on inclusivity and exclusivity in counselling and psychotherapy training.
	• Workshop participants co-wrote the article, bringing their voices and experience.
June 2022	**Presented Research project at UKCP Annual Research Conference**
July 2022	**Published article and developed new theory in *Transactional Analysis Journal***
	• Baskerville, V. (2022). 'A Transcultural and Intersectional Ego State Model of the Self: The Influence of Transcultural and Intersectional Identity on Self and Other'. Transactional Analysis Journal, 52:3, 228243, DOI: 10.1080/03621537.2022.2076398

(Continued)

Table 10.1 (Continued)

Time period	Activity
	Hosted Research Conference at TA East London Institute
	• Facilitated focus groups, collected data, and presented workshops on themes of inclusive practice.
	• 65 participants, representing 12 multi-modality institutes.
October 2022	**Research cited in the *New Psychotherapist* magazine**
November 2022	**Research Project Report 4, in *The Transactional Analyst* magazine**
	• Report on TA East Research Conference
	Amplified Voices article
	• Interviewed trainee/practitioner on his experience of the conference and inclusivity and exclusivity in training.
December 2022	**Final analysis carried out after data collection ended**
	• Identifying themes and theories of inclusivity in psychotherapy training.
January 2023	**Writing up and dissemination of themes of research**
	• Disseminating findings to counselling and psychotherapy training establishments through Dropbox platform, articles, films, powerpoints, and social media platforms.
	• Report aims to inform training addressing inclusivity within psychotherapy and counselling training institutes.

We shared information sheets detailing our study, and workshop attendees were provided with a consent form to sign for anonymised contributions to be shared in research outputs. For those who did not consent to their contributions being used, we ensured that we did not record their experiences.

Interviews with the research team

In order to fully immerse ourselves into the research and hold the position of the participant, we spent time exploring our intersectional identities, and conducted videoed interviews (BSL signed) with each other, asking each other the same questions on our own experiences of inclusion and exclusion in therapy training. We all took it in turns to be the interviewer and the interviewee. This shift in power and position allowed us to occupy different spaces as both the observed and the observer. As we were all based in different parts of the country, online interviews were the most appropriate.

Data analysis

There is no scope in this study to undertake a rigorous data analysis process. We present a summary of findings below.

Findings

All participants recognised the western bias in training and expressed frustration at the lack of change on this front. Regardless of modality, participants all spoke about the lack of space to explore intersectional identities. It remained the case that training courses tended to approach diversity and inclusion as '*an "add on" or "tick box", rather than an integral, holistic part of the training*' (workshop participant).

Everyone was in agreement that it needed to be '*woven into the curriculum: not a one-off weekend!*' (workshop participant), and wanted '*action and not lip service on oppression and racism*' (workshop participant). Many recognised the intrinsic unquestioned inclusion and exclusion that arose from the intersection of gender, race, and class in counselling: '*(I am) included by being White and a woman*' (workshop participant); and '*(I am) seen as a leader being a White, well spoken male*' (workshop participant).

The impact of factors such as financial barriers to training was raised. While some organisations offered bursaries and support, others did not, and this directly impacted who was included and where. The importance of intersectionality in inclusion was summarised by this participant sharing they felt excluded, '*when I feel I'm not able to be vulnerable as a White person to explore my full intersectional identity*' (workshop participant).

Inclusivity

Representation

Representation in the teaching staff helped foster a sense of inclusion, one participant said they felt included through seeing their sexual identity represented and '*feeling mirrored by gay tutors and supervisors in my sexuality*' (workshop participant); while another felt recognised and included when '*working with a South Asian tutor mirrored me and my "OKness"*' (workshop participant).

Representation was not only about similarity, but about a shared sense of difference, '*my peer group are all visible outsiders in a way*' (workshop participant), from difference came a sense of solidarity and belonging. Equally importantly was acceptance, even when in the minority '*feeling accepted as "the only one"*' (workshop participant), highlighting the difference between being a minority on a training course and being 'minoritised' by a training course.

Accepted for whole self

There was a sense of relief that came with being able to bring all parts of oneself to the process, '*I feel included because I can bring my life experience, which is valid and valued in this space. I feel I belong and am accepted for who I am*' (workshop participant); '*(my) age and life experience is valid and valued*' (workshop participant); '*(my) religious beliefs are included*' (workshop participant); '*I feel heard, an appropriate designated space is assigned to openly explore intersectionality*' (workshop participant); '*being invited to contribute, especially if in a group where I'm a minority*' (workshop participant); '*positive modelling and definition of self by staff members, eg. if we listen and understand one another in the group's lived experience, we in turn can feel included*' (workshop participant). Thus experiencing '*acceptance of intersectionality*' and '*feeling I'm OK, you're OK*' (workshop participant), and bringing '*lived experience, living anti-racism and anti-oppression*' (workshop participant) – all contributed to an acceptance of whole self.

Feelings of safety

Participants wanted to have '*psychological safety to access and express feelings*' (workshop participant); to feel safe enough to express the '*courage to ask for what you need*' (workshop participant). They felt safe when they did not need to ask for '*permission to talk about diversity*' (workshop participant). The lack of safety on training courses came up repeatedly in the discussions. Having strong tutors who could '*hold the process*' (workshop participant), was recognised as critical for inclusion, many shared experiences of tutors unable to hold the space around difference and the jeopardy that put the group in, creating unsafe spaces. This highlights the need for staff to 'do the work' particularly around social, cultural, race, and political awareness. Otherwise, there is '*little discussions on difference*', resulting in '*issues of difference being ignored*' and the loss of safety through '*discounting the oppression in ourselves and others*' (workshop participant).

Participants talked about the importance of being heard as integral to feeling included and safe. TA East was named and singled out for its approach from the start, one participant felt it from their '*first day at TA East discussing and placing our cultural selves / identities*' (workshop participant); another described it as a place where '*diversity is embraced and encouraged*' (workshop participant).

Another stating '*TA East is seeking out people who would not normally be there*' (workshop participant), and '*culturally aware and open-minded tutors challenge and confront oppression*' (workshop participant). Similarly, finding organisations that were supportive was identified as important, one participant said '*joining BAATN felt like a homecoming*' (workshop participant). When diversity goes unexplored feelings of '*experiencing the sense of being not safe with the White women in my training group*' (workshop participant) can exacerbate a sense of exclusion. The lack of safety led to '*Black people repressing experiences in groups in training – didn't feel safe, maybe denied. Shamed and blamed*' (workshop participant). As well as a lack of exploration of diversity of trainees, it was noted there was '*no discussion about practicing with Black/Brown community*' (workshop participant).

Space for discussion

All attendees wanted to have space to explore intersectional identities and have discussions, to ask '*open questions around our differences*' (workshop participant); and work towards '*understanding other people's narrative through dialogue*' (workshop participant); and '*understanding other people's narratives and cultural context*' (workshop participant).

Exclusivity

As would be expected, many of the issues around exclusion were the opposite of the processes that created feelings of inclusion, for example: '*no representation: all White tutors*' (workshop participant); and financial access, '*I couldn't join the last year of training due to financial restrictions and I was told that if I left, I might not have had a space in the following years*' (workshop participant). There was a loneliness that came with being excluded: '*never having a lunch buddy in my majority White class*' (workshop participant); or being '*the only gay*' (workshop participant); or feeling '*misunderstood – a lack of attunement*' (workshop participant). Theory and curriculum were experienced as excluding: '*script matrix drawn heteronormative*' (workshop participant); '*over emphasis on dual parent, nuclear family*' (workshop participant); and '*intersectionality not in core curriculum, race, class, neurodiversity, sexuality, disability, culture etc*' (workshop participant).

Not enough

Participants spoke about not belonging to any space, and therefore excluded from all, '*being constantly "not enough" to belong to any group, for example, female, LGBTQ+ – the essence of "you" is missed*' (workshop participant). Frustrations and sense of exclusion arose from the silos of modalities, the '*levels of TA pyramid scheme – am I TSTA, PTSTA, CTA?, who supervises me – snobbery and not feeling wanted or good enough*' (workshop participant); and '*finding psychoanalytic training organisations hierarchical and heteronormative*' (workshop participant). The feeling of not being enough was also extended through questions about the right to be on the training course: '*I didn't have a degree prior to training and I was questioned as to how I got onto the training without one*' (workshop participant); the sense of '*not feeling "academic" enough*' (workshop participant), was a common experience of exclusion.

Assumptions and unconscious bias

Participants spoke about exclusions that arose '*when people assume things about you*' (workshop participant), these included simplistic ideas, for example, '*"you're privileged" being thrown at you – in some ways perhaps yes (and a person can own that themselves), but in some ways, perhaps not'* (workshop participant). Or being told *'I don't think of you as gay'* (workshop participant); and finding people *'making assumptions about my class / culture / religion'* (workshop participant); and *'treated as the exotic representation of a culture/ethnicity'* (workshop participant), *'reinforced by assumed cultural norms'* (workshop participant); and *'lack of acknowledgement of history of minorities'* (workshop participant).

Positioned as an outsider

Minoritised students spoke about *'feeling like issues of diversity and difference were "my issue" not a group opportunity to share and learn'* (workshop participant). These were seen as missed opportunities for training resulting in a *'fear of taking off masks'* (workshop participant) in the learning space for fear of rejection and exclusion. One participant spoke about having to have *'Brown bits split off'* (workshop participant) in order to survive training. It was also suggested that the *'dominance of women in training can minimise male experience'* in training (workshop participant).

Institutional exclusions

Participants discussed *'cultural blindness'* (workshop participant) on their courses which left them feeling excluded, and voiced frustration at lack of diversity in teaching materials, *'reading lists: no authors of colour!'* (workshop participant). Trainers present felt ill-equipped to know how to embed inclusion in their work and training. Their lack of confidence was picked up by trainees, who recognised the resistance but felt the work needed doing, *'tutors need to model doing the work and taking risks of getting it wrong'* (workshop participant). Participants also spoke about a lack of awareness around difference: *'lack of respect when sharing experiences of placement clients'* (workshop participant), which sent out conflicting messages about ethics and confidentiality; and made them feel excluded for wanting more respect for clients.

Course delivery was also recognised as being geared towards a normative or 'ideal' student with comments around fixed library opening times not being accessible for working students, or *'assessments always to be written assignments, which are more challenging for anyone neurodiverse or if English isn't their first language'* (workshop participant), and *'training is excluding for dyslexics'* (workshop participant). One participant shared: *'as someone who experiences overstimulation of senses, even venues in terms of building / structure / environment are not accessible'.* Reinforced by: *'I sometimes experienced heightened sense, open echoey spaces can be too noisy during group activities which can make it difficult for me to focus'* (workshop participant); they felt there was no inclusivity or accommodation for individual difference. Another participant felt judged for *'having to work fulltime to fund training and then being questioned why I wasn't building up clinical hours quicker'* (workshop participant).

There were also practical factors that communicated messages of exclusion such as a lack of lifts or lack of subtitles on recorded lectures which reinforced messages of ideal students with no disabilities or health and inclusion needs.

Intersectionality

The importance of holding space and awareness of the complexities of intersectional identity was expressed in this quote: '*I felt excluded when I saw support groups for minoritised groups, even though I'm seen as in the majority, I don't feel part of the majority*' (workshop participant). An intersectional lens allows conflicts to present and be explored safely, one participant simply listed '*Blackness: Pride. Shame*' (workshop participant). It also helps uncover the nuances of experience, as with one participant who talked about their experience of access to the profession and exclusion through the intersectionality of class and health: '*working class and work part time as a result of disability (social model) claiming benefits and PIP. No financial support for course fees*' (workshop participant); another stated, '*broad labelling excludes nuances and true intersectionality*' (workshop participant). Participants were asked to map their intersectional identities. They went beyond broad categories of race, gender, sexuality, class, disability, language, ancestry, to include relationships, hobbies, politics, health, employment, hopes, experiences, worldviews, and offered a window into aspects of self that emerged when there was safety and permission to be present. They show the breadth and depth of identities that form our profession.

Discussion

This study has offered an insight into contemporary training and the experiences of inclusion and exclusion. In summary, factors contributing to inclusion were: representation; feelings of safety; acceptance of lived experience and being seen and heard for full intersectional selves; and having tutors and institutions that were able to recognise, hold space for, invite in, dialogue, and fully embrace and account for diversity. Factors that contributed to exclusion were: a lack of representation; being made to feel 'not enough' because of difference; financial barriers; assumptions around different cultural contexts; being made to feel like an outsider; having to split off parts of self; and a host of institutional factors around lack of representation and diversity in teaching materials, theories and the expectation of normative trainees.

Repeatedly, participants spoke about feeling '*excluded by double standards*' (workshop participant), a direct opposition to what was being taught in training (inclusion, acceptance, curiosity), and what was being modelled in training (exclusion, rejection, no space for discussion). It is notable that many of the exclusions experienced in training are the same issues clients present with – not being heard, made to feel not good enough, experiencing discrimination, having to silence parts of intersectional self.

If training courses cannot make space for dialogue around race and difference, it raises the uncomfortable question of how we can expect trainees to be competent in challenging oppression and discrimination in the therapeutic dyad, inviting clients to feel heard in all their identities? When those delivering training were repeatedly unskilled around themes of difference, trainees were left feeling unheard, unsafe, and in some cases harmed. Many participants spoke of being made to feel 'not enough' because of their race, ethnicity, sexuality, financial position, health needs, etc. Again, it is common for clients to present with such feelings, and the lack of resolution or perpetuation of this feeling for marginalised students risks losing vital trainees, and also not giving trainees a valuable experiential learning experience of processing complex feelings and their intersection with institutions.

It is crucial that courses find time to hold spaces for dialogue and exploration of diversity, difference, intersectional identities, and power dynamics. If this does not happen on training courses, trainees enter into the profession lacking cultural competence and risk alienating clients by seeking to have their clients educate them on cultural context, or indeed leave parts of themselves outside the therapeutic relationship. It was noted that as a profession we ask our trainees and clients to sit with discomfort, yet many trainers exhibited a lack of awareness and skill to do so when it came to race and other themes of difference.

Training institutions that fail to offer inclusion are at risk of exacerbating negative feelings of trainees, potentially having marginalised students drop out, and perpetuating the structural racism and supremacy that persists in the profession. Everyone loses in this scenario: trainees who drop out, lose out on their hopes, vision and dreams; trainees who stay lose out on the value of shared cultural and social diversity and the benefits that it would bring to their client work; the profession loses out on therapists who can incorporate different world views into existing modalities to improve them and make them more relevant for the society we live in; and, most importantly, our clients who seek therapy lose out by having therapists who lack the skills and competence to work with a diverse experience of clients.

Ultimately the experiences shared by participants who were in current, or had recently completed, training mirrored those of practitioners who had trained decades ago. There continued to be exclusions and discrimination. This raises critical questions for therapy and therapy training regardless of modality. Questions about who holds power, who delivers training, and the auditing of the quality of training and teaching materials become pertinent, when asked to list exclusions the names of professional bodies kept coming up, indicating a lack of trust in the actions of professional bodies to address issues of exclusion. It raises questions about measures such as SCOPEd that seek to assign value to therapists based on education – if the education is impaired, how can the therapist be deemed skilled to deliver?

However, there were wonderful examples of inclusion experienced at the research workshops, that can be integrated into training, one being creating space for cultural dialogue, as named by a research workshop participant: '*I thought it was just incredible, from a starting point to hear about cultural context and the intersectional experiences of yourselves and others running the conference was a massive change, in terms of just setting the scene with it within our experience. And starting with that, the dialogue around difference was just there. With your [trainers'] experiences, it felt like a massive change and felt more intimate, I think. And as a consequence of that, giving everybody license and the opportunity to do the same. So really, I think for me, it opened up further desire to be more open about my background and what I am feeling – as a super power rather than something I have to hide'.*

Another example was the importance of '*an intersectional lens applied throughout models, not just a one-day workshop – difference and identity, power, privilege, unconscious bias, social political contexts – as part of our everyday. An inclusion of all difference, for me reduced my feelings of otherness*' (workshop participant); alongside, '*training which has a non-pathological approach to difference has helped me to feel that all parts of myself are accepted in the room*' (workshop participant).

Recommendations

Recommendations came directly from our participants.

- **To be heard, seen and understood:** '*An appropriate designated space is assigned to openly explore intersectionality*' (workshop participant). '*For there to be a designated staff member on the training, who a student can speak with if they are feeling excluded in any way on the course, in a training supervision group, or for support if experiencing whilst on placement*' (workshop participant).
- **For trainers to be aware of different lived experiences and to be able to hold intersectional space and dialogue:** '*Trainers take time to explain to all students at the start that cultural identity and intersectionality is part of being a human being, so for any "group process" it may feel inequitable and difficult to explore, but it is essential*' (workshop participant). Change is always difficult and adapting training is not easy, this is a process, it is a journey of personal development and social and political awareness, however, there are multiple resources and trainers equipped with knowledge and skills that can support institutions and individuals on their journey.
- **For courses to reflect inclusive therapeutic aims:** '*Positive modelling and definition of self by staff members, for example, if we listen and understand another in the group's lived experience, we in turn can feel included*' (workshop participant).
- **To offer a curriculum representative of intersectional identities and power dynamics, to encourage development of theory:** It is crucial that curriculums reflect our diverse communities: '*Having diversity woven into the curriculum, not a one-off weekend*' (workshop participant); awareness of '*holding dual roles, oppressed and oppressor' (workshop participant);* and '*the collective versus individuality*' (workshop participant). '*Open questions around our differences*'

(workshop participant); *'encouragement to write about personal experiences and theory'* (workshop participant) – all leading to a diversified and decolonised curriculum.

- **Diversify styles of teaching and learning:** Attention to learning styles and neurodiversity is essential in offering inclusion, described as: *'An acceptance of individuals' different realities'* (workshop participant); and an integration of *'different learning styles are considered'* (workshop participant).
- **To consider how we invite those marginalised into training – representation matters:** For example, *'seeking people who may not normally be there'*, thus *'being acknowledging and welcoming'* (workshop participant); positively seeking and inviting difference, *'people who reflect parts of my identity'* (workshop participant)*; 'being invited to contribute, especially in a group where I'm in a minority, it feels like the person inviting me in is genuinely interested'* (workshop participant).
- **For tutors to 'take the journey in knowing, owning and modelling dialogue around their own lived experience of privilege and oppression, accounting for the power dynamic in the therapeutic dyad and training context:** Thus *'action not lip service on oppression and racism'* (workshop participant); *'owning and sharing vulnerability about difference'* (workshop participant), where *'the tutors need to model doing the work and taking risks in getting it wrong'* (workshop participant).

Additionally, there is a need for greater action by institutions to take responsibility for cultural competence training of staff and a re-evaluation of how the curriculum and teaching are delivered through an anti-racist and anti-oppressive lens, to ensure greater inclusivity for marginalised students. It is recommended that there be more stringent auditing of requirements and accountability for inclusion and diversity by professional and awarding bodies. As well as a more active focus on funding, bursaries, and creative assessment processes.

Further questions

This study sought to ask the question to see where current training stood. As a team we were not surprised, yet still overwhelmed by the experiences of exclusion that define training experience. We propose ongoing and further questions for exploration which have arisen from this work:

- How do normative/marginal trainees experience counselling and psychotherapy training?
- What would inclusive training look like?
- How can an intersectional lens be utilised to examine who we invite into training and how?
- How is the curriculum constructed in terms of privilege and unconscious bias?
- How can we deconstruct bias and privilege in training?

- What are experienced as the hierarchical structures, power structures, and institutionalised oppression in training? How can these be addressed?
- What are the alternatives for exclusivity in counselling and psychotherapy?

Outputs

To date we have published four research articles in *The Transactional Analyst* (Ahmed, 2021/22; Baskerville, 2021, 2022a, 2022b, 2022/23); been cited in and interviewed by the editor of the *New Psychotherapist* (2023), and published our final findings in an article in the *New Psychotherapist* (2023). We have presented at the UKCP research conference, presented a workshop at the national UKATA conference and hosted a day research conference at TA East London Institute. Alongside these we have released films on dialoguing and interviews around our own experience of inclusion and exclusion, published articles on inclusivity, interviewed those who are marginalised in *The Transactional Analyst*, begun an Amplified Voices column for each issue, reviewed books, and interviewed authors inviting marginalised stories and developed new theory.

Research group

Nilufar Ahmed (she/her) or Nilu (pronounced nee-loo): I'm a Muslim, female, Asian, academic, heterosexual. These are the top layer identities, under that there are national identities – I identify as European, Welsh, British, Bangladeshi. My parents are immigrants from Bangladesh and they are both buried in Wales. I was born here, but the colour of my skin means for large swathes of the population I will always only be a Brown outsider. A Chartered Psychologist, Senior Lecturer in Social Sciences at Bristol University and BACP registered intersectional psychotherapist, and a diversity and inclusion trainer.

Vikki Nelson (she/her): I'm a White woman, middle aged, heterosexual, deaf from birth. My heritage is a mix of Irish and North east working class, although brought up middle class. A UKCP registered psychotherapist and founder of Deaf4Deaf counselling and psychotherapy services.

Gillian Neish (she/her): I'm a Black woman, old, heterosexual and non-disabled. I was brought up by White carers via a private fostering arrangement. My background is working class, but I now have the means to live a middle class lifestyle. Diploma in transactional analysis counselling and a trainer focusing on anti-racism and antidiscrimination.

Victoria Baskerville (she/her): I'm a British, White, Northern cis woman. I was born in the Midlands, grew up in the north and have lived in East London for 30 years. I have Irish heritage and working class roots and values, and a middle class lifestyle now. I am neurotypical and identify as lesbian and Queer, though I was brought up heterosexual. UKCP registered relational intersectional transactional analyst psychotherapist, educator, supervisor, and founder of TA East London Institute.

A note on ethical review

We recognised the limited reach of academic publishing with research often hidden behind paywalls, thus we decided we wanted to do something different, that was more inclusive, but also could be situated within traditional models of knowledge production. To that end, we intended to publish in magazines and share videos. Ethical approval would have positioned our study differently in terms of outputs, however, the work we were undertaking remained the same and valid in its own right. The stories and experiences we collected would not have been any different had we had ethical approval or not. One of our team is an experienced academic with over 20 years of experience leading research projects. This gave us confidence in the methodological rigour of our work, plus we worked within the UKCP research ethics guidelines and the BACP ethical framework for research.

References

Ahmed, N. (2021/22). 'Research project 2'. *The Transactional Analyst 12*(1): Winter.

Arnold, C. (2022/23). 'What's the point of research?'. *New Psychotherapist*. Issue 82: Winter.

Baskerville, V. (2021). 'Research project [1]'. *The Transactional Analyst, 11*(4): Autumn.

Baskerville, V. (2022a). 'Research project 3'. *The Transactional Analyst, 12*(2): Spring.

Baskerville, V. (2022b). 'Research project 4'. *The Transactional Analyst, 12*(4): Autumn.

Baskerville, V. (2022/23). 'UKCP research project final report'. *The Transactional Analyst, 13*(1): Winter.

Baskerville, V. (2023). 'The unseen, how many trainees are feeling left out?' *New Psychotherapist*. Issue 83: Summer.

Fine, M., Torre, M. E., Oswald, A. G., & Avory, S. (2021). Critical participatory action research: Methods and praxis for intersectional knowledge production. *Journal of Counselling Psychology*, *68*(3), 344.

Powell, D., Dada, M., & Yaprak, R., (2015). 'Black and minority ethnic (BME) trainee counsellors reflections on their training and implications for practice', Lewisham Counselling & Training Associates.

Research Team Interviews (2021). https://www.dropbox.com/s/dkh23gzj6dbawld/Introducing%20Research%20Project.mp4?dl=0

Chapter 11

Amplifying voices

A collection of dialogues

Since 2022, I have had the privilege of interviewing and dialoguing with 'voices' within the UK's TA and psychotherapy community. These have been published in themed issues of UKATA's quarterly magazine, *The Transactional Analyst*. The aim has been to invite an intersection of voices and stories. The regular column is titled 'Amplified Voices', defined as 'increasing the sound', and aims to honour all voices, the difference between us, and the breadth of our cultural and social narrative individually and collectively.

In this chapter, I offer short excerpts from a selection of interviewees, bringing themes of race, gender, class, heritage, religion, spirituality, neurodiversity, dis/ability, and sexuality through lived experience.

My hope is that we will see ourselves and the other in these stories – aiming to inspire continued intersectional curiosity through the nuances of cultural narrative, inviting in all voices, through the intersections of privilege and oppression – striving for deeper empathy and meaningful connection.

Being Trans... identity and transphobia

Blythe Hunt (they/them/theirs)

> [My intersectional identity is]: White/Queer/Trans/posh/neurodivergent/non-disabled/thin/privately educated/t4t
>
> I'm neurodivergent, I was diagnosed as dyspraxic when I was nine, and now dyslexia and ADHD is the full gamut. I'm Queer. I'm a non-binary lesbian, that is how I describe myself now. I love being Trans, is the really important thing to say; obviously it is an oppressed identity – non-binary isn't even a legal category in the UK. So, you know, if I was to get married, which I want to do, I wouldn't be able to get married as the actual gender category that I identify as. I would need to be married as a woman or a man. One of the two.
>
> Being Trans is a massive source of joy in my life. It's one of the most important things, being Queer and Trans, both politically and personally, the personal is political, I really believe that.

DOI: 10.4324/9781003509424-11

When people talk about the Trans experience, I think I always have a little bit of, am I Trans enough? That's the first thing that comes up for me when people talk about how difficult it is to be Trans at the moment. I think, because of my class privilege and the fact that I'm completely cis passing, people don't really look at me and feel confused about my gender identity, even though they should be.

I know that transphobia is a huge part of the culture war and has been for a while. I had the unfortunate experience of thinking that someone was my friend, and they turned out to be enormously transphobic and that came out of nowhere. That was a few years ago. But it's starting to be just evident in the environment constantly.

It's something like 0.5% of the British population are Trans, but maybe 95% of the people that I know, are Trans. I would have loved to have trained with a whole cohort of Trans people, that would have been unbelievable.

(Baskerville & Hunt, 2023)

Unconscious bias and racism – Black in a White space

Ngozi Cadmus (she/her)

[I am a] Black woman of faith, CEO and founder of Frontline Therapist, social worker, psychotherapist and pursuing a doctorate.

I began the journey of evolving Frontline as I wanted to provide something culturally sensitive. I wanted to say, you have power and choice, you know, where a Black person can ask for a Black person, there's still limitation, as we can't always be that specific and say a Black woman from Nigeria. But the ability to say I would like to be with a Black woman or I would like to be with an Asian person.

As a woman of colour, you have little option to say, 'what is going on here?'. It is unconscious bias. So, my experience being both painful but also empowering – I've learned a lot about myself. I've also become unashamed, because I can't change who I am. I can't change how I present myself. I can't apologise for the sound of my voice. I can't apologise for just how I am. So that's kind of my experiences. I've been reflecting on one of the microaggressions experienced in supervision in TA and I remember being told in my training that my voice is quite harsh, "soften your voice".

So … I reclaimed my voice – being proud of how I speak and how I sound because that's just how I am you know, I can't change my tempo.

Yes, it's hard to put it in words, and I think it's because of the subtle terms, a lot of the things are not obvious, they're not blatant. They're not you know, in your face, it's the questioning after a conversation, it's the feeling of being undermined.

It's not always about saying a person's racist, it's about saying there are things that happen consciously and unconsciously that can cause harm and when there are no spaces to help hold that, it just continues.

(Baskerville, Nelson & Ngozi, 2022)

Islamic faith, identity, and relational psychotherapy

Nada Khader (she/her)

I hear the word 'intersectionality' being used more frequently. It's a theoretical concept, but I think of it in terms of lived experience – it's an expression of our reality. I am a therapist; a Muslim; and a Palestinian; I am a mother; a woman; an immigrant; heterosexual; middle class; educated. Taken as a whole, these facets, and many more as well, make me a unique person – no facet stands by itself, in fact each facet impacts on every other and makes each a unique expression of my reality. I grew up in the Middle East and North Africa – my family were Palestinian Muslim refugees.

Faith, religion and spirituality are all a part of who I am and what I offer as a therapist. For me, religion and psychotherapy overlap. Both are about the human search for truth and meaning: Who am I? What do I want? What is my purpose? What is the meaning of life? For me, religion and spirituality are about seeking truth. My faith inspires me to learn about myself, and who I am in the world. And the more I've progressed with my psychotherapy training, the more I see this overlap with therapy: the two fit together.

When I was younger my culture taught me that the British passport was a great privilege, and I believed that. As I have grown, the passport has changed from a symbol of privilege to a symbol of the cost and oppression of my Palestinian heritage. Despite all this, Britain has still been my home for my entire adult life and has changed much about my life and beliefs.

The more I am freed from barriers, the better I am able to relate to others, the more I am able to be in the moment and relate to their pain and suffering as equals, rather than seeing cultural differences.

Once Islam is separated from culture, politics and various types of oppression, it can be seen as a code of ethics that encourages love, compassion, empathy, equality, forgiveness and social justice.

"I'm OK, you're OK" speaks to the reciprocity of being. There is an Arabic phrase " انت وانا سواسيه " that literally means "You and I are equal". But it means so much more than that, it too speaks to the reciprocity of experience and being. Something that I was trying to hint at throughout the interview is that for me, Islam really is a religion for social justice.

There is a section of the Koran called *Surat An-Nisa*, literally the 'Passage of the Women'. I would like to leave with a quote that speaks to the heart of Islam for me from this passage: 'O you who believe, stand firm for justice even against your own selves' - *Surat An-Nisa* 4:135.

(Baskerville & Khader, 2022)

Intersectionality and reflections on inclusivity and exclusivity in training

Luq Adejumo (he/him)

I describe myself as bicultural. I grew up in Lagos, Nigeria, until I was seven.

From a race perspective, I grew up in a country, in the city, where pretty much everyone was the same, to being in the UK in a school, where we were the first Black kids of my kind and quite different economically, because we were kind of a relatively well-to-do Black family.

I come from a polygamous family. Something I wasn't aware of until five years ago, when my mother let me know. So, this is a key facet in terms of my experience, given that up until that point I had a sense of my family being a monogamous family unit, and actually now it makes more sense of an understanding of how we all fit together and some of the challenges within the family as a consequence of that.

So, there was lots of difference there in terms of experience, as well as my parents coming from two different tribes... I've straddled lots of different groups and tribes and religions throughout my life. So, defining where I sit with that has been an important part of my journey.

When I was training, I worked at LGBTQ+ charities, there was a real mixture in terms of diversity of clients there and trying to make sense of the modality that I was in and what I was being taught. And then how that related to my client base was really challenging because there were lots of different things that were going on that didn't sit within the traditional model that I was being taught.

The power dynamics, for example, the challenges with clients deciding they didn't want to continue. And the charity that I was working with at one point said, well maybe race is part of the equation, but then also that having to sit with me and thinking this is an unsaid in the room, but also needing to have a dialogue.

Thankfully in supervision, I could explore what that meant for me, and then how my insecurity affected my acumen as a therapist.

And having to manage expectations of what Blackness is, what Brownness is. It isn't one homogenous whole, and trying to relate to a client's individual experience. I think these intersectional conversations are not within teaching institutions.

(Baskerville & Adejumo, 2022)

Trauma and old and new racism

Karen Minikin (she/her)

[I am] a dual heritage, heterosexual, cis woman.

I sense I have been an undercover agent. I have at times stood up and shouted and railed against the system. But I've also tried to keep people engaged. So, the psychotherapy training, especially the relational influence, has been very much about building bridges – as I have tried to build bridges into different worlds. And I am an embodiment of different worlds, with my heritage and my experience also of living in Africa. Sometimes I've tried to maintain those bridges while also challenging people and that's not always an easy thing to do. And I say undercover agent, because I've always tried to have one eye on keeping the other engaged, while also confronting minds or processes that I've experienced as oppressive.

And, I also want to acknowledge that in some ways, my quest to keep the other engaged has potentially a defensive quality. I don't like falling out with folks. I want to have a poke, but I also don't want to lose people.

One of the people I draw on is Valerie Batts, as a figure who's written and spoken very powerfully about racial trauma in our world. Valerie Batts writes about old racism and modern racism. In many respects, as a woman of my age, I've experienced both of those versions. The old racism being the entitlement to call names, physical violence, violence against homes, all of these things that have happened in the communities when I was much younger and that I witnessed and experienced. To the way perhaps, in our more middle class profession, I experience attacks which are much more subtle than that, and consist more of an undermining of authority, which isn't necessarily traumatic in that it doesn't threaten life. However, it can evoke the memories from the old racism, which are life threatening. So, there are times when in my countertransference, when at the receiving end of a more subtle attack such as an undermining of my authority, or a demand for me to prove myself, justify myself, those sorts of things, I get that old, very primitive process, aroused in me, that feeling that I'm about to die. Which, over the years of course, thankfully, I'm much better at holding and being with and so the freezing, that comes with the trauma process, is less gripping. I can have it without being had by it.

That dilemma ... I need to survive around here, so I will keep my mouth shut and belong... but actually, I need to hold my integrity, so I need to speak out. So, the constant moving between the desire to belong and the desire to speak our truth, whatever that is.

(Baskerville & Minikin, 2023)

Student voices: Reflections on essay writing – Academia, cultural contexts, neurodiversity, intersectionality, and the unseen

Lauryn McKinson-English (she/her)

I am Black, British, Afro/Caribbean young woman. Born in the UK but identify as of Caribbean heritage.

I think it's very layered. In society there's unconscious stereotypes that as an individual of ethnic background I'm not as educated as my White passing counterparts. Then there's also a cultural pressure to achieve well as a means of making my family's sacrifices worthwhile, whilst not requiring 'too much' help – there's a real clash.

One limitation is that people of different backgrounds have to code switch continuously in order to succeed in a professional or academic capacity.

Accessibility is a main thing for me especially in terms of funding, and providing opportunities to under-represented members of society. Having the option to explore these spaces which have been gate-kept for so long, are in fact places they'd thrive.

I would like to highlight the value in being tutored and experiencing theory written by individuals who acknowledge and share your lived experience.

Crena Watson (she/her)

I am a White cis gendered female. I have dyslexia and ADHD.

I have had no formal education. I was born in 1957, I was illegitimate, and my mother was an orphan who was brought up in Dr Barnardo's children's home. We were on our own in the world, we were poor. I now live a privileged life.

I have come to enjoy writing essays. In the beginning it was traumatic as I had never written anything in my life, I am unable to spell. I have embraced technology that helps with spelling, and I've spent many hours learning to write. It was an enormous challenge.

I may not have been able to do the essays if I didn't have extra time in my life to achieve this. I felt at times I was not going to be able to achieve this requirement, I felt full of shame.

In my experience, academics do not make the best psychotherapists. They sometimes lack emotional intelligence. Uneducated people for instance who have been let down by society can make good therapists, in my experience they are often far wiser than formally educated people.

Julia Pool (she/her)

I am of mixed-heritage (British/Maltese with Syrian, Armenian and Iraqi heritage), bisexual, cis female, middle class.

It's been a very rocky process for me. Having been to a socially and economically challenged inner-city, large comprehensive school in London and coming from a complex and chaotic family dynamic with significant transgenerational trauma – my education has been chequered with large gaps in learning. I did pretty badly at all levels of education. I returned as a mature student to study education and teaching, and later psychotherapy, doing well in these areas, but my low confidence around my intellectual ability can still haunt me.

I think people can feel isolated and excluded from academic language and a potentially brilliant therapist can get missed in training if they can't put down what is needed in written assignments and exams within the tight constraints of a marking criteria. I have met some really good, naturally gifted trainee therapists who have not gone on to do their CTAs. Many of them were multiply marginalised and are exactly what the field needs so that the mystifying and deceptive dynamics of systemic oppression can be sensitively worked through in safe enough spaces. I think the training and assessment process can appear opaque, exclusive and it is very expensive. This is such a shame, and it does feel like something needs to change in how people are assessed.

I think that our ability to really sit with another's pain and trauma, to have a keen ear for the pernicious effects of systemic oppression on our clients, cannot be mirrored or done justice by the written exam/assessment process as it stands, and a lot of great therapists will get lost along the way as a result.

Caroline Matthews (she/her)

I am of Black African origin. I was born and brought up in Africa and migrated to the UK as a grown up. I am married with two children and been a stay-at-home mum for a while to take care for our young family.

Because English is not my first language, I struggle sometimes to interpret what exactly is being asked. Also, when it comes to responding whilst I may know exactly what I want to say, I really struggle with how to say it. I find that there is an element of interpretation happening internally when I speak as well as when I am writing.

I find that my counterparts who were born in the UK (hence English is their first language) are very good at saying what they need to say, in a concise manner.

It may be worthwhile to explore how assessment can be achieved through oral presentation or learning portfolios. General writing and essay writing skills and support should also be part and parcel of training.

Most African cultures are very hot on respect for others especially those in authority, not challenging or questioning authorities in one's life is a value we are taught very early in life. I reckon that this impacts on how we may be open to offering our opinions especially where they differ from others. We are open or not open to debating and this could also be misconstrued as lack of confidence.

Jubriel Hanid (he/him)

I would call myself a degree-educated, neurodiverse, heterosexual, Black, male introvert.

Essays for me are a bit of a mind-dump. I tend to formulate them in my head, so that the first draft is pretty much the finished article. I struggle to edit and rewrite my essays, as I find it uncomfortable seeing myself reflected back at me. I tend to avoid looking in mirrors unless necessary, so this may have a common root. I also struggle with producing bibliographies. I experience them as an interruption to my thought process. I don't like interruptions.

Although marking is supposed to be standardised, markers will always come with their own ideas of what is right, or wrong, good, or bad. The dominant culture will set the rules. It reminds me of the racist 'English Canon' in literature; veer from the mould at your peril.

When compared with the 'norm', the stress and anxiety that goes into producing an academic piece, may be totally out of proportion to the reward. Sometimes this is experienced, and sometimes this is avoided by producing poor, or no work. This aspect is missed, or put down to lack of effort, when not everyone has to dig so deep.

This work is important for the sole reason that the people who are disengaging with the process are the people with the potential to change the system.

Rosa Trout (she/her)

I am of East and West European heritage, first generation British born, Christian, heterosexual married (second time) working woman, student and mother.

I am the first member of my family to have a degree, which I achieved in my 40s. My parents (both economic migrants) were not academic and had a very naive view that school was the place to be taught, so we (siblings) were not really encouraged to go onto college etc. We were taught by my parents to be "in work" and to ensure it was done well!

My cohort are mature students, working in paid jobs alongside study and some with families. The requirements for therapy, supervision and to be in placement has a huge impact on home life and the time available for study.

Mayuri Patel (she/her)

I am an Indian woman. I was born in East Africa and moved to the UK aged 10 years. I am 49 years old. I am a mother. I work in the NHS as a primary care pharmacist. I identify as heterosexual. I am educated to Masters level.

On some level, I can see that it is sensible to have high standards, to give the public assurance that their therapist has a high level of education, is knowledgeable, but on the other, it precludes many who may not have had opportunities to become educated to such levels. Is it right that we exclude people who may make wonderful therapists because of their humanity and rich lived experience?

English may not be a trainee's main language, so it may be challenging translating complex thoughts and process from your own language to English.

Our lived experiences may be missed if training is seen simply through the academic lens.

I have lived in the UK for many years and consider it my home, so I have absorbed the wider culture, but the training is from a western perspective, and there is little room for diversity of thought, around cultures, race, religions and values.

I like the concept of BAATN and BACP mentoring schemes for those from marginalised groups. However, my training at TA East weaves an awareness of difference and culture into every aspect of learning as much as possible, so I feel seen for who I am and that my experience matters.

Clodagh McCahill (she/her)

[I am] White British/Irish/Scottish; middle class; neurodivergent.

The thought of writing [essays] causes me anxiety, I have learnt to deal with this and now try to just write a good enough essay.

My neurodivergence has meant that I associate essay writing with school, which was often problematic for me. There is a lot in my cultural script around survival, which means that my 'be perfect' and 'try hard' drivers really come into play when I write essays. I don't feel either met or missed, I see essay writing as essential to my training, but I do think there could be scope for other forms of assessment.

I don't view the academic aspect of training to be of primary importance and see the relationships that we have with our clients and supervisors to be paramount, with the theoretical knowledge underpinning this. Focusing overly on the academic aspect of training can mean that people from marginalised groups are not coming into psychotherapy training.

In my view psychotherapy can either perpetuate privilege and the status quo or challenge it. To me it should be challenging it and to do this more people from marginalised groups need to be joining.

Shabazz Nelson (he/him)

I am an able bodied, English-speaking Black male from a working class background who grew up in London. I am married with two children, I have a Caribbean background, I coach and am a Taoist.

I feel met by an institution with a shared interest in my story and perspective, whose staff have considered what it means and how I am impacted by learning to navigate the world of TA from a diverse learning position. There is also room for and consideration of the learning potential and self-realisation of the world as seen through a cultural lens, and how that initially appears and subsequently changes as knowledge is applied through experience and sensitive teaching.

The range of the question may not allow for deeper analysis; the question may not account for the specific lived experience of the writer; the marker may miss the person answering the question; the writer may misunderstand the question.

I think this is speaking about the application of criteria to all people on the assumption that all people have access to the same starting point economically, socially and culturally. I think there are cultural and social benefits for marginalised people to qualify, yet there are economic restraints that may hinder those from a poorer or financially restricted start point, from having the same access to the opportunities that could benefit them.

(Baskerville et al., 2022)

Queer voices on the UKCP's decision to leave the Memorandum of Understanding on banning conversion therapy

In April 2024, the United Kingdom Council for Psychotherapy (UKCP) made the decision to leave the Memorandum of Understanding (MOU, 2017, 2022) on banning conversion therapy. 'The Memorandum of Understanding (MOU) is a joint document signed by over 25 health, counselling and psychotherapy organisations which aims to end the practice of conversion therapy in the UK. Conversion therapy is the term for therapy that assumes certain sexual orientations or gender identities are inferior to others, and seeks to change or suppress them on that basis' (MOU, 2017, 2022).

Consequently, many Queer practitioners, including those who have personally been witness to conversion felt vulnerable and angry. This is expressed in the following excerpts (Baskerville, 2024), which are in response to the first two of the following questions asked: *What is your lived experience of being Queer? What was your response when receiving the email that the UKCP had decided to withdraw from the MoU? How do you make sense of the action socially and politically? How has leaving the MoU and the subsequent notices from the UKCP and UKATA impacted you? What do you think needs to happen now?* (For full answers to all the questions, see Baskerville, 2024.)

Blythe Hunt (they/them/theirs)
White, Queer, Trans, posh, neurodivergent, non-disabled, thin, privately educated, t4t

What is your lived experience of being Queer?

Being Queer and Trans is the best thing in my life. The Queer and Trans community is where I feel the most alive and the most myself.

What was your response when receiving the email that the UKCP had decided to withdraw from the MoU?

It is bitterly disappointing to understand that a culture war is being fought over your right to exist and that that war is being fought not only in the news, in parliament, schools (where I worked before becoming a counsellor), and the feminist movement but also in your place of work. It is an alienating, infuriating experience.

Chris Colcomb (he/him)
White, gay male, Queer, cis gendered, middle class.

What is your lived experience of being Queer?

I knew I was gay around the age of 12 or 13 but didn't really come out until my early 20s as a result of feeling oppressed by Clause 28 and the HIV/AIDS crisis. I was a scared gay teenager. I have spent the last 20 years of my life bringing LGBTQ+ communities together through owning bars and nightclubs across the country. I have recently retrained as a psychotherapist, and I am Level 7 UKCP registered and practicing just outside Hull. The feeling of alienation as a teenager and beyond has been ever present for me, and bringing people together has been my way of helping others out of their own alienation narratives.

What was your response when receiving the email that the UKCP had decided to withdraw from the MoU?

I was utterly horrified. This happened following some earlier UKCP pronouncements on gender ideology which felt alienating to the Trans community. As they withdrew from the MoU, I felt directly alienated by the organisation who I had just accredited with. I felt the script backlash into teenage injunctions of don't be you, don't belong, don't exist. Their use of the term exploratory therapy appears, on the face of it, to be OK. However, it hides something that appears more sinister. What do we therapists do with clients? We affirm. We do not try to dissuade our clients from being anything. Whether that is a career choice, a relationship choice, a sexuality, or how to identify their gender. We also ALWAYS explore alongside the client, we never dissuade as to 'convert' someone into a choice that is not congruent for them.

Fi Firman (she/her)
White, cis woman, lesbian, daughter, partner, Northern Irish.

What is your lived experience of being Queer?

I grew up in Northern Ireland at the height of the troubles and was raised within the Evangelical church. Any sense of difference was not tolerated, and I learnt from an early age that being gay was not OK. It was regarded as sinful, an abomination, and evil. I knew from a young age that I was gay, and I grew up feeling so confused, so not OK, and with a deep sense that there was something inherently wrong with me, simply for being me. I couldn't talk to anyone about how I felt, because it wasn't safe to, and so I internalised all my self-loathing and sense of not being OK in the world, and over the years it manifested in eating disorders, self-harm, and suicide attempts. I left Northern Ireland 22 years ago, and I know now that if I hadn't left when I did, I would have taken my own life. Today, I am out and proud, however I still live with the trauma and impact of having grown up in such a toxic culture, where my very existence was denied.

What was your response when receiving the email that the UKCP had decided to withdraw from the MoU?

I felt absolute despair, dissociated, and it opened up a lot of early trauma. Having grown up completely isolated as a child, with no safe adult to confide in about my sexuality, I was not safeguarded. I did not choose to be gay. It is who I am. Similarly, I did not choose to have hazel green eyes. They are a part of me. I am deeply concerned by UKCP's decision, for what if parental choice and rights are not in the best interests of their child? It certainly was not in my best interests.

Denise Fowler (she/her)
White, British, working-class, heterosexual, married, 52-year-old cis woman

What is your lived experience of being an ally?

I have no lived experience of being Queer, I have worked alongside people with lived experience, and I am here to speak up and support in any way I can.

What was your response when receiving the email that the UKCP had decided to withdraw from the MoU?

I did not fully understand what was happening and wanted answers, I feel heartbroken to think I am a member of an organisation that would demonstrate this behaviour.

Chris Rolls (he/him)
White, British, Queer, neurotypical, lower middle class, graduate educated, able bodied

What is your lived experience of being Queer?

As a person (and a psychotherapist) I have always experienced intersectional complexity. On the one hand, I have a lot of privilege and unconscious bias in my backpack (White, British, neurotypical, etc.), and as a gay/Queer man who grew up in the '80s and '90s with the AIDS crisis and Section 28, I experienced external and internalised homophobia. We still live with the Queer phobias of patriarchy and capitalism. I have swung between the need for self-protection (through closeting) and activism (visibility and fighting back).

What was your response when receiving the email that the UKCP had decided to withdraw from the MoU?

Disappointment and (out)rage. The move seemed crass, clumsy, and transphobic. It struck me as, once again, a group of normative experts speaking on behalf of Trans people. The Trans communities don't need speaking on behalf of. They demand inclusion and representation in all decision making. There was a way for UKCP to work towards its concerns about treatment for Trans minors without withdrawing from the MoU and taking into consideration the wider impacts of this move.

Carole Shadbolt (she/her)
White, working class originally, older woman, cis gender, LGBT.

What is your lived experience of being Queer?

To give a feel of what it's like to live in a so called minority, here are some questions that I and others might have been asked about their sexuality or gender. Asked in circumstances of inequality, and power dynamics. The questions reversed become preposterous, ludicrous non-questions. It's fun to learn like this, except there are real people and real lives whose mental health and freedoms are at stake, and a sinister shadow falls and a dystopian landscape of inequality, and discrimination and judgement borne out of insouciance can be felt: 'Why do you think you are heterosexual or cis gendered? Have you ever been disciplined or sacked because of your heterosexuality? Have you ever considered suicide because you are cis or heterosexual? How did you explain to your family that you and your opposite gender partner share the same bed? What is the psychotherapy treatment plan for clients tormented by their heterosexuality and cis gender? Have you ever been physically attacked when being openly heterosexual or cis?'

What was your response when receiving the email that the UKCP had decided to withdraw from the MoU?

The process of homophobia and transphobia – the familiar embodied radar 'smell' and taste of discrimination and systemic power comes first. Like a physical blow. Followed by something of a disbelief… then a realisation, a recognition of the presence of prejudice, and a patronising manipulation and misuse of power, amounts to a being 'done-to'. It's like grief. It's like feeling left out of something you don't want to be part of in the first place. It's a feeling of betrayal, loneliness. A confirmation of a not belonging. If these hatreds are internalised as many are, self loathing takes root, and an internalised homophobia and transphobia grows.

Mark Widdowson (he/him)
July 1973–August 2024
I am a Northern working class gay man with multiple disabilities. Being Gay and being working class form the core of my identity. As for the disabilities, I have had epilepsy since I was a kid, I'm a long-term survivor of HIV, and I also have ADHD.

What is your lived experience of being Queer?

I'm certain I was born Queer. I always knew I was different and can't ever recall a time I didn't feel my difference. The moment of realisation came when I was about five and watching the film *Spartacus*. There was a scene in the Roman baths and there was a conversation on screen between a group of semi naked men which was ulterior sexual, but even though I didn't understand the question, I understood that I'd just seen something that I knew related to me. I came out on my 16th birthday and went to a gay pub that night and have been unashamedly in your face gay ever since. That was during the AIDS crisis when people were dropping dead left, right, and centre. My very first counselling client back in 1994 was a gay man in his 50s who had never told anyone before that he was gay. Shortly after that, I got a part time job as a gay and bisexual men's health worker to supplement my counselling work. I've worked with hundreds of people from the LGBTQ+ community over the years, including more than one person who was previously subjected to conversion therapy. I am also a psychosexual therapist and have done some work in a gender clinic many years ago.

What was your response when receiving the email that the UKCP had decided to withdraw from the MoU?

My response to the UKCP's decision to withdraw from the MoU was initially one of disbelief and shock which rapidly turned to rage. Although I am still angry, I am more sad now and disappointed. I feel utterly betrayed by them, and I have lost faith in the integrity of the people in charge of the organisation. I have never felt like that towards the UKCP in all the time I have been registered with them, and I am really upset that they have taken this action.

Geoff Hopping (he/him)
Queer, gay, raised working class, family affected by war and poverty, White, parent, grandparent.

What is your lived experience of being Queer?

My experience has been the lived experience of marginalisation, fear, and shame. Homosexuality was an imprisonable offence until I was 16. Homophobia was rampant in every social situation. When I came out in my late 20s, I immediately faced the AIDS crisis where there was a double oppression – I remember being physically threatened by residents of the local council estate when we were planning to open the London Lighthouse. I worked with dozens of people impacted by HIV/AIDS. It was harrowing and yet strangely enlivening being on the front line. Then my therapy training was completely heteronormative and middle class and I spent most of it feeling angry but believing it was my personal pathology. There was also the tremendous joy of being part of what was the then 'scene' and yes, I loved the ghetto!! It was the only place I felt I could breathe and be myself.

What was your response when receiving the email that the UKCP had decided to withdraw from the MoU?

On first reading the decision to withdraw from the MoU I felt that this was a retrograde step and was reminded that freedoms and rights can easily be removed in an essentially undemocratic society that has moved to the right.

Karen Minikin (she/her)
Cis, heterosexual, dual heritage woman, LGBTQ+ ally

What is your lived experience of being an ally?

Oppression conscious and unconscious hurts everyone. People want, need, and deserve to belong to society, communities, and groups safely, without having to carry the shame and blame that gets discharged onto folks who are seeking to be themselves, to love and to live. I am an ally politically and spiritually to groups who are discriminated against.

What was your response when receiving the email that the UKCP had decided to withdraw from the MoU?

I was horrified when UKCP withdrew from the MoU… I thought it a big error and a fear response. The clause about children is uninformed.

Victoria Baskerville (she, her)
Brought up heterosexual, Queer, lesbian, cis woman, White, Northern British, lives in East London, working class DNA, Irish heritage, Mother, Activist.

What is your lived experience of being Queer?

Growing up there was an absence of a positive lesbian mirror. I got caught up in a religious cult in my late teens/early twenties resulting in exorcism of my lesbian identity, a violent form of conversion therapy. I came out in the late '80s during the height of the AIDS epidemic. I was a teacher working under Section 28 – a law banning the discussion of sexuality in schools. I have lived with my gay brothers, through many laws criminalising homosexuality. I was chased off the road by police simply for looking like a lesbian. I was not allowed to marry my partner; she was not allowed to be on the birth certificate of our children. We as a family experience homophobia everyday.

What was your response when receiving the email that the UKCP had decided to withdraw from the MoU?

Initially, I could not make sense of it and at the same time I felt like I had been physically punched, winded. The next day I found myself dissociating and retraumatised, experiencing flashbacks. The ban on conversion therapy had protected me, protected us, the Queer community for many years. I was in shock to the core.

(Baskerville et al., 2024)

Endnotes

I have offered these excerpts with the intention of hearing, experiencing, and being witness to the breadth of intersectional voices in our UK TA and psychotherapy community. With the hope to invite dialogue across our world community, accounting for intersectional differences, power dynamics, and commitment to amplifying all voices.

References

Baskerville, V. (2024). 'Amplified voices: Queer community and allies'. *The Transactional Analyst, 14*(2), Spring/Summer.

Baskerville, V., & Adejumo, L. (2022). 'Amplified voices: Luq adejumo'. *The Transactional Analyst, 12*(4), Autumn.

Baskerville, V., & Hunt, B. (2023). 'Amplified voices: Blythe hunt'. *The Transactional Analyst, 13*(3), Summer.

Baskerville, V., & Khader, N. (2022). 'Amplified voices: Nada khader'. *The Transactional Analyst, 12*(2), Spring.

Baskerville, V., & Minikin, K. (2023). 'Amplified voices: Karen minikin'. *The Transactional Analyst, 13*(1), Winter.

Baskerville, V., Nelson, S., & Ngozi, E. (2022). 'On the frontline, in conversation with esther Ngozi'. *The Transactional Analyst, 12*(1), Winter.

Baskerville, V. et al. (2022). 'Amplified voices: Students and essay writing – Lauryn McKinson-English, crena watson, julia Pool, caroline matthews, jubriel hanid, rosa trout, Mayuri patel, clodagh McCahill, shabazz Nelson'. *The Transactional Analyst, 12*(3), Summer.

MoU (2017, 2022) https://www.bpc.org.uk/professionals/registrants https://www.bpc.org.uk/professionals/registrants-hub/guidance/memorandum-of-understanding-on-conversion-therapy-in-the-uk/hub/guidance/memorandum-of-understanding-on-conversion-therapy-in-the-uk/

Chapter 12

No time

'Our house is on fire', climate change and colonisation

'Our house is on fire' says Greta Thunberg. This chapter will explore all the supremacies that influence the onslaught of climate change including White supremacy, capitalist supremacy, and patriarchal supremacy. Ecological transactional analysis will be considered through oppression and privilege, inviting in intersectional voices and calling for collective action.

We are climate change

We cannot save the planet without uplifting the voices of its people – especially those most often unheard.

(Thomas, 2022, p. 3)

'Our house is on fire', said Greta Thunberg at the World Economic Forum in Switzerland in 2019. Her words were a call to action urging world leaders to take immediate and drastic measures to reduce greenhouse gas emissions and prevent catastrophic climate change. It seemed like the world was listening to the voice of a 'White' 16-year-old Autistic young woman, who was indeed centred, as well as marginalised, as being of no threat to the patriarchal and capitalist structures.

Critics have argued that Thunberg's Whiteness, privilege, and 'western' heritage enabled the amplifying of her voice across mainstream media and audiences. And consequently, Thunberg's rise to prominence overshadowed existing activism and contributions of indigenous and minoritised communities, who have been advocating for climate justice for decades.

Thunberg's voice has been important and has been centred through privilege, yet with further social, cultural, and political insight she has been protesting against the plight of the Palestinian people and intersecting climate justice with racial justice. This has resulted in her falling from her idealised positioning, where mainstream media has turned on her – her authentic intersectional voice is not welcome.

Intersectional voices are paramount in standing up for climate justice. Climate change disproportionately affects indigenous and minoritised communities, and climate activism must centre these voices in being part of the change and the decision-making processes.

DOI: 10.4324/9781003509424-12

This chapter aims to consider the intersections of climate change and supremacies, and the White construct of psychotherapy that is impacting on eco therapy, calling for, along with Marshall and Barrow (2023), deconstruction and reconstruction through an intersectional lens.

In this, it is important to account for my Whiteness and the reality that I will bring a 'White gaze', to my reflections, along with the complexity of my other privileged and marginalised identities and social and political awareness. In decentring Whiteness, and mirroring this commitment, the dialogues below – with TA East student colleagues Alexis and her partner Corynne, and with Jubriel and Dhruva – invite intersectional voices and lived experience around themes of racism, colonisation, decolonisation, spirituality, and community. The aim is to further a different path towards climate awareness and amplify the importance of the ecological and the eco-systemic (Marshall and Barrow, 2023) in transactional analysis.

Climate change and colonisation: Informing ourselves – Historical context

'Mountains hold the echoes of history. The vibrations and shock waves of the climate crisis are written in stone, absorbed over the course of geologic time dating back more than four billion years' (Goffe, 2025, Introduction, p. xix).

Goffe (2025) writes about the origin of climate change spanning billions of years, yet she argues that the climate crisis originated in the 15th century with Christopher Columbus' arrival in the Caribbean, marking the beginning of globalisation and western capitalism's exploitation of natural resources.

Goffe's work emphasises the connection between racism, colonisation, and environmental transformation. She contends that racism is fundamental to the climate crisis, as it was integral to its origins, and explores the intersection of colonisation, racism, and environmental degradation. She tells the historical story of the current climate crisis through climate exploitation: from colonial powers extracting valuable resources and destroying sacred ecologies, to the legacy of slavery, forced toil, stolen land, ravaged environments, and the displacement of indigenous communities.

She states that: 'Freedom for everyone requires a confrontation with the capitalist greed upon which western society was founded' (p.xxi), calling for a new kind of climate storytelling that no longer prioritises colonial capitalist expansion.

Yet as I write this, colonial capitalist expansion is continuing to happen in real time across the globe. On a daily basis we are witness to wars, genocide, displacement, and forced migration. Trumpism is the epitome of capitalist exploitation, destroying and seeking to erase marginalised communities – racism, misogyny, and transphobia are legitimised. There is an attempt in ethnic cleansing, forcing some groups out of the country. The threat of land grabbing and the stealing of resources all move us closer to the catastrophic destruction of the planet through deliberate greed and disregard for human and more-than-human existence.

In the UK, protestors are being imprisoned for climate action, organisations like Extinction Rebellion and Greenpeace are being silenced by the courts, seemingly an attempt to kill off humanitarian effort. Climate agreements to reduce emissions are being violated, and policy and laws seem to be on the side of the perpetrators, while activists are policed, demonised, and silenced for having the conviction and courage to stand up against climate injustice.

Social injustice and climate injustice: Informing ourselves – Social and political context

Thomas (2022), states:

> Social injustice and environmental injustice are fueled by the same flame: the undervaluing, commodification, and exploitation of all forms of life and natural resources, from the smallest blade of grass to those living in poverty and oppressed people worldwide. It's a point that many ecofeminists, environmental justice scholars and leaders, indigenous rights and land sovereignty advocates, and climate politicians have argued for decades, but it hasn't been embedded deeply enough in modern environmental education.... In the largest environmental movements in the U.S. and worldwide, issues of race have been met with hostility, downplayed, questioned, and placed on the back burner. Because environmental justice activists, who are primarily Black, Latinx, indigenous, and people of color, haven't been given the support from the global environmental community that they deserve, we are still fighting for climate justice all these years later.
>
> *The intersectional environmentalist* (p. 5)

Thomas (2022), emphasises the connection between social justice and environmentalism. It has to be said that climate change intersects with racism (Williams, 2021) along with poverty, class, women issues, and marginalised communities. As transactional analysts, who hold social justice at our core, connection to our planet and the survival of humans and the more-than-human is integral to our values, ethics, and practice – hence, an intersectional and interconnected ecological lens is paramount in addressing the climate crisis and furthering climate justice.

Climate justice and the survival of our planet

> If we can create the future we want despite the realities of not only racism, but also sexism, poverty, and other oppressive systems, imagine what all of us can do and be when those systems crumble and we are all free. As Leah [Thomas] says, the future is intersectional — just as the past and present are too.
>
> (Gloria Walton, CEO of the Solutions Project – Foreword, Thomas, 2022, p. ix)

Achieving climate justice and ensuring the survival of our planet requires a multifaceted intersectional approach that addresses the root causes of climate change by challenging climate narratives, amplifying and centring marginalised voices, addressing climate inequality, and consequently promoting sustainability by prioritising human rights and protecting all species.

Climate justice requires collective action, intersectional activism, with a 'We' focus, accounting for systemic inequalities and challenging supremacies through social, cultural, political, and historical awareness; thus accounting for the impact of patriachial, capitalist, and White structures (Turner, 2023).

Ecological transactional analysis

Hayley Marshall and Giles Barrow, both transactional analysts, co-founded the Ecological transactional analysis movement (2020, 2023).

And, for the last five years, Carol Wain (UKATA Registered Training Director) has developed the Red Kite in Liverpool into an Ecological TA training institute. She has been instrumental, alongside the leadership of Hayley Marshall, in bringing the systemic into the ecological. Marshall and Barrow's most recent writings (2023), accounts for our predominately White TA community in the UK, citing intersectional consideration as paramount.

Ecological transactional analysis (Eco-TA) is an approach in understanding human experience in connection with the natural world. It is an interconnected process of both human and more-than-human encounters within ecological contexts. As the climate crisis surges, we, as transactional analysts, are having to consider the ecological in our clinical and educational spaces.

'The ecological self', coined by Marshall and Barrow moves from the individual to a broader sense of self that incorporates the natural world, distinguishing between relational space and ecological space. Physis (Berne, 1957, 1972) – 'the drive towards wholeness and health' (Tilney, 1998, p. 98) – is seen as universally present and promotes a deeper connection with self and nature.

Marshall and Barrow (2023) reflect on the indoor and outdoor mindset systemically; the indoor mindset is described as 'human centred only' (p. 11) and seen as 'restrictive and patriarchal'. And the 'outside mindset' as an embodied experience of 'being nature' in the here and now, described as an 'encounter with the wider living world, to become awakened participants' (p. 12). They reflect on themes of intersectional difference in outdoor practice – bringing social and political awareness to their writings – asking questions about who owns the land, who has previously owned the land, and considering colonised land and the consequent impact on human relations. They also account for themes of race in the countryside, stating 'ecological practice and, in particular, outdoor work brings into sharp relief the impact and implications of issues associated with intersectional interest, perhaps more so than when working indoors' (p. 15). Barrow describes how he was impacted when working alongside a Black woman colleague in the countryside; he accounts for their difference, and his privilege as a White cis man.

Marshall and Barrow invite an opening up of the outside mindset, the emergence of the ecological self. It can be said that the ecological self is intersected with the intersectional self. And, that to connect with land – be it our ancestral or born into land – invites an unconscious emerging of what came before: the generations and ecological encounters before us (eco-lineage) and between us (eco-systemic: Marshall & Barrow, 2023). Thus accounting for our journeying across lands and landscapes, and the shaping of our identities through changing social, cultural, and political contexts – the interconnected nature of the environment and systemic oppression.

Furthering the deconstruction and reconstruction of the ecological through Eco-TA and an intersectional climate justice lens

The practice of ecological transactional analysis (embracing all four fields) is in itself a form of decolonisation – taking practice outside, connecting with land and becoming one with the more-than-human, returning to ancient land, rituals, and healings. And yet, born from a privileged profession, eco psychotherapy has largely attracted Whiteness ultimately risking becoming another form of colonised practice. Ecological psychotherapy, alongside psychotherapy *per se,* has the potential in perpetuating the White construct of psychotherapy, marginalising the cultural and spiritual practices of indigenous and non-western communities.

Some of the criticisms of ecological psychotherapy for example, have included the risk of cultural appropriation – not honouring indigenous cultures; or cultural homogenisation – focusing on similarities and risking the killing off of differences; and the underrepresentation of diverse communities and limited accessibility.

Certainly, within Eco-TA the latter two have been addressed by Marshall and Barrow (2023) by considering racial difference, disability, and accessibility, I am interested in further exploring these ideas and to consider what action can be taken to invite in more difference, and how we can adjust our normative frame of reference to widen access?

Having said this, over the last few years I have experienced an impasse, in some ways an impotence, as to whether as a White founder of an intersectional training institute – similarly to Barrow and Marshall – Whiteness can invite in difference? (see Chapter 2).

And, while I do not have the embodied experience of working in an outside mindset in the way Marshall and Barrow have, I am open and curious – taking permission to work out and ask, along with Barrow, Marshall, and Wain, what ecological transactional analysis may look like with an intersectional lens?

What does, for example, Eco-TA look like in the urban in the 21st century, across multi-diverse intersectional communities?

What does it mean to invite a person with a history of colonisation, partition, war, and/or displacement, to connect with an outside mindset? How may we consider transgenerational trauma when 'being with land and nature' that does not feel like homeland?

How may we reflect on Eco-TA and psychotherapy and the intersection of race and gender? How may we account for racism and other forms of marginalisation in the countryside? And indeed everywhere? Are the racially marginalised and other marginalised identities safe enough in the countryside, or even in city parks? How do we consider the intersect of access and ableism, women and Queer safety in the countryside and parks? Indeed, those with Trans identities are currently targets of attack and many spaces can be unsafe. Does this mean the outside mindset, for those who are marginalised, has to take place inside the consulting room, as explored by Marshall and Barrow (2023). And, is this potentially a reinforcement of systemic oppression?

To reflect further on these themes, I have engaged in three dialogues aiming to centre indigenous and marginalised voices and to gain insight into the complexity of bringing an intersectional lens to ecological transactional analysis.

Dialogues, and further intersectional reflection on the eco-systemic

First, I engaged in conversation with TA East student Alexis Lee (she/her) and her partner rapper artist Corynne (she/her) talking about a predominately Black fishing community they have evolved on the south coast of England: 'We are Black Fish'.

Second, I offer a conversation with TA East advanced student Jubriel Hanid (he/him) on his experience of racism in the countryside, and what this may mean for the ecological transactional analysis 'outside mindset' with an intersectional lens.

And finally, I talk to TA East student and Hare Krishna priest Dhruva Maharaj Das about the interconnection of land, spirituality, healing, and psychotherapy within Krishna Consciousness, demonstrating 'being nature'.

I found the dialogues emotional and stirring and I offer my reflections on how they may inform the development of the ecological intersectional self.

'We are Black Fish' – Human conversation, connection, land, nature, sea, community, and being

Corynne: *I identify as a Queer Black woman from the UK. My heritage is Jamaican. My ancestry is supposedly West Africa, but I feel very aligned to Malawi.*

Victoria: *Can you tell me about your connection to Malawi?*

Corynne: *It's a feeling of being, going to a place, and feeling home. In Malawi, I can walk out of the airport and just walk left or walk right. There isn't a sense of, I need to carve something out here, those things don't come to my mind. It's home.*

I don't have that in Jamaica; in Malawi I don't need to build up the imagination. It just lands.

Victoria: *No preconception or planning, a being, a knowing.*

Corynne: *That's because I'm leaving that behind. I think that's what makes it home.*

Alexis: I think it's interesting to talk about how you are in that country.

Corynne: I have something called Paresthesia, which is experienced as tin-
             gling sensation in my face and cheeks, nerves. And in Malawi, that
             was completely gone. It didn't happen. I get quite over stimulated,
             as someone probably on the spectrum, I have ADHD, but perhaps
             AUD-ADHD. A lot of sounds make me jump, in Malawi I was calm
             as a cucumber. As soon as we got back on the plane, it started to
             kick in.

Victoria: I can relate to you, returning to the north, to the coast, my body knows
             I am home, an ease. My ancestral home was Ireland. I only discovered
             this more recently. I've always had a yearning and connection with
             Celtic heritage across the sea.

Alexis: So you're both speaking to the body experiences and remembering be-
             fore you even have any cognitive awareness where home is. You feel it
             in your body.

Victoria: What about you Alexis?

Alexis: I am 44, British, London-born, a mother. I identify as Queer and neu-
             rodiverse. I have Irish and Caribbean heritage. I have a very strong
             affinity to the water. I have always loved water. Anytime I need heal-
             ing, my instinct is to go to the sea, a real solace for me. In my DNA. I
             also have some really irrational fears around water, that I don't have
             a memory of, definitely felt in my body. One of them is big chains and
             anchors. My body reacts, and I don't know where that's come from,
             it's like you're on a boat and you see the anchor, I see it going down. I
             have a real fear.

Victoria: I am thinking of all the ancestors we hold in our bodies.

Alexis: There's something about the vastness, the unknownness of the sea that,
             that is scary and attractive.

Victoria: I am thinking about 'We are Black Fish', about its emerging.

Corynne: It was an idea I had from the documentary Blackfish, about the killer
             whale in 'Sea World' captivity. Seeing the connections and the similari-
             ties between how this beautiful creature was captured, enslaved, and
             then the response to its enslavement, and how, how much that reminded
             me of the African slave trade. I developed a love of fishing. When Alexis
             and I met, it came up in conversation early, I just didn't think I would
             find another woman of colour going fishing. I've never seen that. It
             was a wild connection. We started fishing regularly and 'We are Black
             Fish', grew quickly, when the universe moves everything out of the way
             for you.

Victoria: Finding yourselves, your place, your peoples, creating communities
             that we need to be in.

Alexis: Exactly. I think things are borne out of necessity. What we need in our-
             selves, what we need to create, and hopefully it resonates with other
             people.

Corynne: *In terms of Black Fish, we knew we wanted community. And the documentary Blackfish, there was something about being displaced, being taken out of your environment, and not really knowing how to connect and belong and thrive, essentially in a new environment, that has always been your home. We've been told it's your home, but yet, where is your home?*

Alexis: *There's no other home to go back to, if we go back to our ancestral homes, it's still not necessarily home, because you're still an outsider or a tourist and you're seen differently. So where do I belong? And trying to find a connection with the land helps that process. And that's what fishing gives me. It gives me the skill of fishing and survival, and the healing of being by the water, and the community that I so desperately need.*

Victoria: *You were talking in the beginning, about carving out something that can become home and your experience of Malawi. We are Black Fish, feels somewhere in between, because it doesn't feel like there was a toiling in carving out.*

Corynne: *It's like it's the two things being true at the same time, captured land that we're experiencing. There's a scene, in one of my favourite Black British films from the '80s, it's about a crew that sets up a sound system and they're practicing. And there's a White English lady that bangs on the door telling them, shut up. And the guy comes out because she says, go back to your own country. And so, the young Black guy, who's equally as cockney as Jamaican, because he's born in England, right? And he comes out and he says, 'This is my f... g country, and it's never been lovely', and that has always stood out to me.*

I love it because it so captures the nuance of, this is my country, and it's never been lovely. With Black Fish, we're out fishing, and there's this boat. This boat could have brought us over here. So how can we now say that we can't stand here and fish.

Alexis: *It's quite a dichotomy, really, isn't it?*

Corynne: *I think being Black or Brown British specifically, the dichotomy of this place kind of hates me and also this is my home. Even with fishing, what fish we're supposed to eat and how we're supposed to eat it. What is acceptable and who makes the rules and how we are supposed to follow them. So, there's size limits on fish. Even if you're outside talking to someone about sea bass, they want to tell you about it. English, they're very authoritarian. I'm imparting these rules on you without you asking me, it has to be 42 centimetres, right? But the thing is, if you're only going to eat the filet of the fish, then it would make sense to have a big fish. If you're going to eat the whole fish, which would be the most sustainable way to eat it, it doesn't have to be that big. These rules are made, away from what is indigenous.*

Communities across the world have never had an issue with the size of fish. The West, has a way of thinking that has pushed against indigenous practices. I only want to eat the fish that has no bones. I only want the white flesh, which, is in itself interesting. What are you actually saying? People won't eat brown crab meat. I only eat the white part of the meat. You know, there's different levels to this, it's a psychology. The rules, going against indigenous practice, and it's not a way that we're going to save the planet. And you're not getting the health benefits. Science has proven, indigenous people have known for centuries, that fish head is brain food.

Victoria: *I am thinking about constructed truths, the 'truth' through Whiteness, only the white meat. I'm wondering whether you can say a little bit about the people that come to you. What does it look like on the Folkestone beach?*

Alexis: *We attract people who are like us, Queer, mostly women and people who identify as women, mostly Black and Brown. We have White people too, who feel very at home and welcomed.*

Corynne: *People who come feel grateful, we're passing on our passion for community and fishing, to anyone who's interested. There's certain fish that fishermen don't like catching, and they're in abundance. They're sustainable. So, we're supporting the eco-system. There's people that come because we're a group of Black women, there's people that I can see myself in, which is particularly important in areas where there's a very low percentage of Black people.*

Victoria: *From your experience, what do you about think about the realm of psychotherapy and connecting with the land, sea, and nature.*

Alexis: *It's odd to have therapy sitting in a small room with two chairs facing each other. It's never felt natural, most of the time it feels awkward. In psychotherapy there's an over emphasis on theories pathologising human behaviour, and there's a lack of connection with the environment and being out in it. I know that you're hot on how systems affect the individual. I think all of that is really important in terms of where I see psychotherapy going. I don't separate psychotherapy in terms of being with people, talking, embodying community. As well as joy we also end up having some deep conversations on the beach, talking about divorce, talking about sexual abuse and trauma. These are conversations I want to be having, they feel natural, it just happens. It's the sharing.*

Corynne: *It's making me think it's not top to bottom.*

In this interview/dialogue I was of course impacted by Corynne's and Alexis's experiences 'of home', felt and held in their bodies, somatic responses, both experiencing disturbance in being born in Britain and 'not being quite welcome'. I was struck by Corynne's having to keep carving out home in order to belong, something I have not had to encounter/navigate as a person who is White.

And I was moved by the deep soothing Corynne experienced in Malawi, when she was able 'to just land'– a profound sense of being home.

I was witness to the palpable racism experienced by Corynne and Alexis, and the idea that one of the Folkestone boats 'could have brought them both to the shores of Britain'. And Corynne's experience of patriarchy and capitalist structures, informing how to fish, and what to eat. And the powerful analogy of white meat being more significant, and brown meat discarded, and the killing off of indigenous lived experience. Along with Alexis's powerful dreams of chains and anchors, conveying palpable fear, maybe transgenerational wounding, along with a deep connection to the water. And yet inspired by their *physis*, in creating Black Fish – bringing together a Black inclusive community, on Folkestone beach, to share in the indigenous experience of 'being' with land, sea, and each other, enabling intimate and connecting moments.

And, at the same time, attending to the flattening of power, while being held by the interconnectedness of the ecological landscape; giving insight into the possibility for 'outside mind' within the intersectional-ecological. In Alexis' voice, moving away from the restrictions of the indoors (indoor mindset) and not separating psychotherapy from being with people, community, and the natural environment. Ultimately connecting with sea and land and 'people like us' – finding home.

Intersection of racism and autism in the countryside – Implications for ecological transactional analysis/psychotherapy

Jubriel: *I am a second-generation immigrant from Africa. My father was Nigerian. My mother is Congolese and Greek Cypriot. I grew up in Kingston upon Thames, which is a White, middle class suburb of London. I went to grammar school. My dad was a doctor, pretty much middle class, university degree. I am diagnosed autistic, I was undiagnosed for my whole life, heterosexual, cis, married, two children to a White English woman who was born in Zambia.*

I live in a semi-rural area. If you go out of our front door, you're in a suburb. It's a conservative affluent area. If you go out the back door, there are woods and fields.

They have livestock in there, sometimes sheep or cows.

I grew up in Kingston, so there's Richmond Park. So it's not like I was born in inner city London. There's no reason why I shouldn't feel perfectly comfortable in rural settings.

I should be, but I'm not OK.

I'm always very conscious being out on walks, I feel a lot better when I've got the dogs with me. I'm always worried about meeting people, there's an intersect there, social anxiety and knowing what to say, or whether you should say anything, or should you say hello or not. I wonder about being a Black man. This is just one Black man, what are their first thoughts when they see me? I don't look in the mirror much. If I did, I will realise that I am totally unthreatening. I imagine my glasses and my eyes and my friendly face, but I'm always looking very serious when I'm walking around the countryside. My cousin visited with her three sons. And they're 22, 18, and 14 and quite tall. I was very conscious walking around with them, when we took the dogs out, Black men in a group, unheard of around here, that's virtually a gang.

Victoria: *I imagine a White man going out with his three nephews would be described as going out with his family? And what you say is 'that's virtually a gang'. We know that racism exists. How are you perceived by the White other? How are they seeing you, you said that if you looked in the mirror, you'd see a man with a friendly face and glasses. And what do you think the White other sees?*

Jubriel: *I feel like they will see some sort of threat. They see difference in a negative way, the stereotypes, the characteristics that they would have seen on the news or in dramas. The unconscious bias. The thing about crossing the road – are they just crossing the road because I'm walking towards them, or were they just planning to cross the road? Or would they have crossed the road if anyone's approaching, I don't know.*

I can't even know if it's a threat, when you're perceived as different, threat or not, do I feel threatened, or is it backlash?

I definitely feel vulnerable, because I might get a look, or I might be ignored. Those are really hurtful. It doesn't even have to be a physical thing.

You're sort of shunned, or you feel stunned, and I think this might be the intersect again, I've got autism, I need to follow rules for a start, like greeting people. I can't pass someone when there's only two of us and not say hello or smile, just find it really difficult to do so.

Victoria: *Not being seen, or 'being seen' as a threat. In a look, or the way you're passed, is it a microaggression, racism? It's hurtful and you feel vulnerable as soon as you step outside your front door, in a semi-rural area, you somehow feel unprotected.*

Jubriel: *And the dogs are my protection, and, and I suppose it's the same with my wife, I just feel validated somehow in both situations, either walking a dog or with a White person.*

I've got a reason to be there.

Victoria: *I think it's really sad. It's sad because the land was there before any one of us were there. It doesn't belong to anybody, but it is, that's how we've all been socialised.*

Jubriel: *But it was one of those things, with the eco stuff, it's very much the same.*

Victoria: *The land before us, a land you were born into. And yet you're not feeling safe in walking in your own land. And you have your heritage land and your ancestral land. And these lands have all always been here, and in this time now you feel vulnerable walking out.*

Let's talk about what you just said about eco psychotherapy.

Jubriel: *I suppose it's a group within a group. The Eco people, Greenpeace, the activists, the White people, the White environment again. Coming from the countryside, from the rural. For whatever reason they didn't need to embrace diversity, they focused on the trees, on nature. That's my impression of eco, and I can't see a great shift in Eco-TA/psychotherapy.*

Victoria: *I'm really struck by what you've said, I know it, I feel it in my body. It is the place of Whiteness. I think you are talking about the absence of the systemic lens. We are formed by the generations before us, we have been shaped by our journeying across lands and continents. Jubriel, what would you do, to decolonise, to deconstruct, if we were to centre indigenous people and people of colour, what would it look like?*

Jubriel: *I'm feeling emotional now, I can't help thinking about back home in Africa. I mean Lagos is overbuilt, a mega city, but you don't have to go far out of Lagos to find people living on the land, most of Africa is like that. And on the allotment here, it's another space where I think I just have to be really on my best behaviour. I just have to be as middle class as possible. I feel I have to be, I can't be myself.*

Victoria: *I see your emotion, returning to Lagos and walking out of the city of Lagos, and feeling a connection to the land. And you can't imagine that here in Britain, because of Whiteness.*

Jubriel: *I have claimed, at least the metre around me. I can take myself out into nature, a lot better than I could before, the anxiety is not as bad. I would love to get to the point where I can go anywhere, to the colonial mansions that you find dotted around the countryside, built on slavery, cordoned off after common law.*

Victoria: *I hear you, you've been in a process and in many ways you're saying I am going out into this space. You don't feel comfortable. You feel vulnerable. You can protect yourself enough. I wonder if the opening up of ecological TA/psychotherapy is being able to talk about the experience of the outside mind, to be able to have these radically open and non-defended dialogues around colonial land, the legacy of slavery, the impact of White supremacy in creating racism, the stereotyping of Blackness. What is the work together? What do I need to own? How can we work this out? All marginalisation, Black, Queer, women, disabled? There's a long way to go processing the out there, the outside mindset, finding a way to be nature.*

In dialoging and hearing Jubriel I was impacted by his experience of living in the countryside as a Black, autistic, cis man; his social anxiety and experience of racism. I was struck by Jubriel's vulnerability, having to act in a certain way to feel and be safe enough to step out of his home, protected by his White wife or his dogs, and code switching by heightening his middle class voice at the allotment.

I was struck by the impact of the colonial mansions, built on slavery potentially provoking transgenerational trauma. I realised that, while I can feel stirred by the class system and the heterosexism in these spaces, I am protected in my Whiteness and I do not experience the somatic annihilation caused by racism. 'I can' call the countryside my home, even though I feel uncomfortable in my difference, yet Jubriel has described claiming a metre around him, similarly to Corynne, in the previous dialogue, who has had to carve out home.

Jubriel's experience was in stark contrast to his deep connection to Lagos and his ancestral lineage, home. In contrast, I have the privilege of being seen as being home in my Whiteness. I was born here 'and' I am welcome, and in my Whiteness my ancestral lineage is not questioned in the way a Black person's is.

Jubriel certainly experiences eco psychotherapy/TA as a White construct and not a context he can belong in. In this, we have a long way to go in furthering an intersectional lens. Certainly, moving from the 'indoor mindset', which can be described as a colonised construct, to the 'outdoor mindset' which we could describe as a freeing up, a decolonising, is going to take time in addressing themes of privilege and oppression.

The work is in continuing the dialogue, inviting in all voices, and having the difficult conversations around the outside mindset, owning privilege and marginalisation, and the part we each play in the systemic. Thus accounting for the intersectional self within the ecological self.

Mother earth, sacred cows, temple, spirituality, healing, psychotherapy, and Krishna Consciousness interconnected with the human and more-than-human

The TA East community had the privilege of being invited to the Bhakitvedante Manor. The Manor is a Hare Krishna spiritual sanctuary spread over 78 acres of land, with gardens, an organic farm, a protected herd of cows, a temple, a monastery, and a community interconnecting humans, the more-than-human, and collective spiritual consciousness.

I have spent time being with Brahmin Hindu priest Dhruva Maharaj Das (he/him) on many occasions. He describes himself as British, an East Londoner and having Indian ethnicity and heritage. While sitting in a garden surrounded by community, we dialogued about the intersection of land, spirituality, healing, and ecological psychotherapy, within Krishna Consciousness.

Victoria: *Dhruva can you can you tell me about the Hare Krishna movement.*
Dhruva: *The Hare Krishna movement is 'Krishna Consciousness' which has its roots in the ancient teachings of the* Vedas, *which are historical philosophical treatises dating back to over 5,000 years. The movement was brought to the western world in 1965 by His Divine Grace Bhaktivedanta Swami Prabhupad.*

Victoria: Dhruva, being here at the Manor can you explain what you mean by Krishna Consciousness? And what this means for you?

Dhruva: Krishna Consciousness, emphasises humility, tolerance, and service to others, focusing on the spirit soul (Atma) and its eternal nature, as described in the Bhagavad Gita (sacred teachings).

Victoria: Can you say more about Atma, and the focus on the spiritual soul rather than the body? I know you have challenged me before, focusing on body, my White body, your Brown body.

Dhruva: The body is a cage and the spirit soul is the bird. For me the spiritual world is a place free from anxiety and suffering, compared to the material world's constant pressure and focus on ego.

Victoria: Yes my focus on the systemic, rather than what Marshall and Barrow talk about as the eco systemic. We are here at the Manor, can you explain to me how Atma and community interconnects with the ecological, with the land.

Dhruva: The Manor is a place where people from diverse backgrounds, come together to worship and serve, experiencing transformation through Atma. Farming and growing vegetables is part of community life and there is deep gratitude and connection to the sacred Mother Earth. The gardens are dedicated to different spiritual directions and elements, and their healing properties.

Victoria: I can feel the sacred here, please tell me more about Mother Earth? And the cows?

Dhruva: The Hindu tradition reveres mothers, Mother Earth. We revere sacred mother cow, she provides practical and spiritual benefits, milk, plowing the land, and being a symbol of spiritual bliss.

Victoria: I can see and feel you deeply respect the healing power of Mother Earth and mother cow and the importance of interconnection with all living beings.

Dhruva: Throughout the day there are rituals feeding and worshipping the sacred cow. We make offerings to the cow at the alter, you saw this, the Ratha Prasadam. The care of the cows and the care of the community is connected, intertwined, fostering a sense of honouring, gratitude, service, respect and responsibility.

Victoria: Witnessing Ratha Prasadam, I experienced the beautiful connection and deep honouring of interconnection of all living beings as sacred. Can you say more about your experience at the Manor?

Dhruva: I grew up in an East London area, school was unsafe, I was dyslexic and I was lost. At around five years old I went to the Manor and felt in awe. I remember the large lake. When I was older, I returned seeking solace, I found confidence in myself. The Manor's peaceful and loving atmosphere helped me develop self esteem and faith. It became my true home, offering a sense of belonging and purpose.

Victoria: We have talked before about your early story, can you say something about the connection between healing and TA psychotherapy.

Dhruva: There are parallels between the principles of the Bhagavad Gita and trans-
            actional analysis, particularly in terms of ego states and self awareness.
            And the philosophy of making therapy accessible to everyone. My spiritu-
            ality, service, and TA training have complemented each other, helping me
            grow as a therapist and priest. Openness, honesty, and respect are in both.

Victoria: Dhruva, can you speak to ecological TA/psychotherapy: the role of
            the land and nature and the outdoor mindset in psychotherapy, talked
            about by Marshall and Barrow. I get the sense that Krishna Conscious-
            ness is the outside mindset, reminding me of Martin Wells' (2012, 2018)
            idea of the Adult ego self not being confined by circles, the Adult in the
            present, the spirit soul Atma interconnected and not separate from the
            cows, land, nature, and community.

Dhruva: The 'outside mindset' enhances therapy and spiritual practices, respecting
            and caring for the environment and all living beings, drawing on the prin-
            ciples of Krishna Consciousness, that all is sacred. Walking bare foot, feel-
            ing the earth and being at one with nature. Outdoor therapy includes being
            alongside those in conflict zones, finding some peace through community,
            through ritual, and the sharing of sacred food, bringing deeper awareness
            and compassion. This is about service. I am the servant of the servant.

Victoria: Is this 'being nature' called to serve all life?

Dhruva: Yes, God and creation, serving all others to make a harmonious com-
            munity. Thank you for being with me Victoria and for sharing the trans-
            formative power of love, service, and respect in creating a better world
            for us all.

Being with Dhruva in the Manor, was a deeply moving experience, I had a sense
of the inter-connected nature between self, other, the collective, the more-than-human, and the land and spirit soul Atma, the non-physical essence of being. I fleet-
ingly experienced the embodiment of the ecological self within the eco-systemic.
Moreover, I experienced a flattening of power in honoring and 'being nature' as described by Marshall and Barrow, and in stepping out of my White body, challenged
by Dhruva, into a deeper Krishna Consciousness – an interconnected experience.
I understood that the ecological self is rooted in community, the collective, and in
service to the human and more-than-human.

Moreover, I considered the need to reflect on soul and spirit, when accounting
for the ecological, and in the honouring of indigenous practices across all lived
experiences.

This is true of all communities, including indigenous White communities, long
ago, long before these communities were stripped and destroyed through invasion
and latterly individualism and capitalism. We do not often hear about indigenous
Whiteness, and the reality that Whiteness has experienced the impact of colonisation, almost turning on itself – severed from its indigenous roots and ancestry. In
particular, Whiteness intersected with women, queerness, Trans identities, disability, working class, Irish, neurodivergence, has been colonised through the systemic

powers of White, patriarchal, and religious supremacies and latterly capitalism. I would go as far as to say that these supremacies have served to 'alienate' peoples from themselves, each other and the planet, even 'deceived' those holding power, turning on its head Wycoff's (Steiner et al., 1975) formula of oppression – privilege + deception = alienation – alienation from the feminine, the divine, the collective and 'being nature'. This said, it is important to continue to own the devastating impact of multiple privilege on those multiply marginalised and the risk of what could be deemed as cultural appropriation.

Conclusion – Intersectional ecological transactional analysis

Mullan (2024) states:

> The truth is we cannot decolonize anything without getting curious and doing our part to learn about the history of the land we reside upon, the history of our original homeland (if we are settlers on the current land in which we reside on), and have a more emotional-social worldview around how these experiences affect the way we view the world today. It is my belief that we cannot dismantle, smash, decolonize anything without unlearning – without understanding our role, our kin's role, how we have been conditioned, where we continue to participate in the socialisation of others, and where our wounded parts lie.
>
> (p. 170)

Ecological transactional analysis, with an intersectional lens is a 'reconnecting' with community and land, for *all* peoples. A returning to spiritual practices, and the reclaiming of the feminine and the deep connection with nature, believing in the sacredness of land, sea, and sky. In accounting for, and honouring, these practices we must also be mindful. Whiteness still holds power and privilege and is a system that is responsible for creating racism and many other forms of marginalisation. It is important to ask, 'how may my Whiteness be perpetuating racism in this ecological space now, on this land?'.

'The systems of oppression that have led to the deaths of so many Black people were the same systems that perpetuated environmental injustice', seeing the 'need for intersectional environmentalism Thomas started a project to spark conversation and mobilise the environmental community to be anti-racist and non-complicit.' (Williams, 2021, p. 149)

Ecological TA with an intersectional lens, or intersectional ecological transactional analysis, is an approach that considers the interconnectedness of all human experience and the natural environment, accounting for the impact of, the manifestation, and the internalisation of systemic oppression. It acknowledges the complex relationship between intersectional identities and eco systems and ancestral lineage.

Not attending to these will arguably contribute to the catastrophic loss of the 'outside mind' as we hurtle towards climate disaster. We must begin with reaching out to multi-marginalised communities, centring indigenous voices, offering cultural sensitivity and humility and accounting for ancestral connection and disconnection to our land and planet for all peoples. We must see the role of activism as central to ecological practice.

The era of a single-saviour, top-down, and siloed approach to change is over. The old way of thinking about environmentalism as a single, distinct issue is long gone, because people are seeing that the solutions to our problems come from within ourselves, and from within our communities. People are empowered and coming together to create the change they want to see, the future they want that reflects their values and visions. And our intersectional lives are at the center of it.

(Gloria Walton, CEO, of the Solutions Project – Foreword,
Thomas, 2022, p. ix)

'To us the aches of our ancestors are sacred and their resting place is hallowed ground.'

Chief Seattle, Chief of Dwamish, upon surrendering his land to
Governor Isaac Stevens in 1855 (McLuhan, 1972, p. 27).

References

Berne, E. (1957). *A layman's guide to psychiatry and psychoanalysis*. New York: Simon & Schuster.

Berne, E. (1972). *What do you say after you say hello?* New York: Grove Press.

Goffe, T. L. (2025). *Dark laboratory – On Columbus, the Caribbean and the origins of the climate crisis*. London: Penguin Random House.

Marshall, H., & Barrow, G. (2020) 'Launching eco-TA – A movement of our time'. *The Transactional Analyst, 10*(2), Spring.

Marshall, H., & Barrow, G. (2023). 'Revisiting ecological transactional analysis: Emerging perspectives'. *Transactional Analysis Journal, 53*(1), 7–20. https://doi.org/10.1080/03621537.2023.2152528

McLuhan, T. C. (1971/1992). *Touch the earth: A self portrait of Indian existence*. Victoria, Canada: Promontory Press.

Mullan, J. (2024). *Decolonizing therapy: Oppression, historical trauma, and politicizing your practice*. New York: W.W. Norton & Company Ltd.

Steiner, C., Wyckoff, H., Marcus, J., Lariviere, P., Goldstine, D., & Schwebel, R.; Members of the Radical Psychiatry Center (1975). *Readings in radical psychiatry*. New York: Grove Press.

Thomas, L. (2022). *The intersectional environmentalist: How to dismantle systems of oppression to protect people+planet*. London: Souvenir Press.

Tilney, T. (1998). *Dictionary of transactional analysis*. London: Whurr Publishers.

Turner, D. (2023). *The psychology of supremacy: Imperium*. Oxon: Routledge.

Wells, M. (2012). 'From fiction to freedom: Our true nature beyond life script'. *Transactional Analysis Journal, 42*(2). https://doi.org/10.1177/036215371204200208

Wells, M. (2018). *Sitting in the stillness: Freedom from the personal story*. Hampshire, UK: Mantra Books.

Williams, J. (2021). *Climate change is racist*. London: Icon Books Ltd.

Chapter 13

Pivotal themes and concluding thoughts

This book has largely accounted for a living into 'transactional analysis through an intersectional lens' to the embodiment of 'intersectional transactional analysis' over the last seven years – since the inception of TA East London Institute.

It has been a process of progressing TA theory and practice from the ground, viewing the self within systemic oppression. These ideas have been born out of the lived experience of a breadth of intersectional voices, deconstructing, reconstructing, and evolving theory and practice that represent our diverse intersectional selves and communities.

As psychotherapists and transactional analysts, we do not separate the self of the practitioner from who we are in the world. We bring our subjective selves to our therapeutic, educational, and organisational relationships – and it is in relationship that transformation can take place. In this, the intersectional work on ourselves goes on in our everyday lives – attending to both our privileged and marginalised intersections, and how these impact each relational dynamic.

There is a sense that once we begin the journey of self awareness, in this instance intersectional awareness, it becomes an embodied experience in all aspects of life. Many have said that the political does not belong within the realm of psychotherapy or transactional analysis. However, it can also be said that not being political is a privilege – and for many of those who are not 'political', the system is likely working for them. Yet for those who are multiply marginalised there is no choice but to either stand up and say 'I matter', or stay impotent in receiving what society has handed out.

At the beginning of this book, and now at the close of it, I have stated that the political is personal and the personal is political, and, consequently, I think that the action of psychotherapy and transactional analysis is a political action. As seen in UKCP research evidence (see Chapter 10), it becomes a political act, be it unconscious, when a client/student/colleague experiences exclusion in the consulting room, in education or in our organisational settings – for example when a neurodivergent person's needs are not considered; when racial differences are not attended to; when a deaf person is excluded; or when pronouns respecting gender identities are not used. Of course, the essence of being in relationship is one of making mistakes, and the essence of psychotherapy is one of enabling not knowing and getting

DOI: 10.4324/9781003509424-13

things wrong. Yet as TA practitioners, I believe we have a responsibility to keep taking the intersectional journey.

Ultimately that journey is about evolving awareness of the transcultural self, getting to know our transgenerational stories, accounting for ancestral lineage, passed down through DNA, all informed by epigenetics and ideas of 'transgenerational memory' (Shafak, 2021), striving for individual and collective transformation, and the healing of our 'soul wounds' (Mullan, 2023).

An intersectional lens has always been about looking out, in making sense of looking in – by attending to social, cultural, political, and social contexts. For this reason, much of my learning has been in going out into the world, and experiencing a breadth of intersectional lived experience including community initiatives, arts, street art, music, spiritual practices, spoken word and poetry. And through the allies I have found on social media platforms, where there is a space for the unspeakable, for other truths and lived experiences, outside of normative systems and ideas. There has been a sense of finding and building community, where we can find solace, solidarity, and hope.

It is on these platforms that I, along with many others, have been witness to the harrowing scenes across our planet, the live streaming of catastrophic dehumanisation and killing of many minoritised peoples, all too painful to bear. And yet I have been witness to *physis* – people's innate drive to survive – to grow and to thrive. Amongst the devastating scenes, we have witnessed profound interconnection with land and peoples and collective liberation.

There has been deeper connections through the practice of radically open and non-defended dialogue and through centring of intersectional voices by way of interviewing and dialoguing with 'amplified voices'. All inspired by the work of novelist and activist James Baldwin, who brought candour, courage, and unflinching honesty to the emotional intensity of lived experience of race and sexuality.

There has been reflection on the cost of individualism – bringing to the fore Rich's (1995) ideas of the catastrophic loss of the 'We' for the 'I'. And, the most challenging realisation: the reality of our world hurtling to climate disaster and the stark reality of climate injustice intersecting with racial injustice.

In concluding, I acknowledge that this is not the end of a journey, and there are many themes to further consider that have not been fully attended to in this book. One being the transpersonal – accounting for spiritual experiences and the transcendent aspects of human experience, along with faith and the risk of prejudice when intersecting spirituality with religion.

A glaring intersectional gap for example is the education and financial, or even class, caste and race privilege required to engage in psychotherapy/transactional analysis training and in accessing practitioner services. Eric Berne's vision was to make psychotherapy, in particular, more accessible. In some ways he achieved this back in the 1950s, '60s, and '70s – bringing a palpable version of psychotherapy to the layperson. Seventy years later the world we live in has changed beyond recognition, and we have been further propelled into individualism and capitalism across both northern and southern hemispheres.

Individualism and capitalism sit at the core of psychotherapy in the UK, and sadly, across the world transactional analysis, in all its fields, is not immune to becoming an exclusive endeavour (Hart, 2017). This is, of course, fuelled by the cost of training, supervision, and, in the psychotherapy and counselling fields the important requirement for personal therapy. And, while there is a surge in group therapy being offered (in the UK) – going back to our founder's vision – it is still not enough to alter the exclusive nature and privilege needed to qualify in transactional analysis (psychotherapy, counselling, and other fields). Alongside this is the dichotomy for many, who, as a consequence of having struggled financially through their years of training, then need to charge fees which are accessible only to the few, thus keeping the profession privileged and exclusive.

And yet, behind closed doors, many practitioners and training organisations do their part in offering lower fees, offering bursaries, and some free spaces. There are also initiatives like Project TA 101 (2025) through ITAA, USATAA, Southeast Institute, IESA committee, which have widened access to TA, alongside the free Ed Fest gathering in the UK (Barrow, 2025), Cornell's project in Philadelphia on supporting mental health professionals through free programs in psychoanalysis and TA, and Jusik's (2022) projects in Guatemala, among many other offerings of psychoeducation and self help initiatives across continents.

There is also work to be done around models of *short-term* intersectional counselling and psychotherapy.

What also needs to be addressed is the 'elephant in the room' with regard to TA's unique qualification structure, from CTA to PTSTA to TSTA and SCoPEd (2025) in the UK. While there is certainly great merit in continuing to learn and accounting for experience, it has generated a hierarchical system in our communities (Minikin, 2024; Pandya, 2024), resulting in a 'Don't make it' and even 'Don't exist' in our community. TSTAs are deemed to have more experience, which may or may not be the case, and for many there is a sense of 'never being able to take their place' – or to arrive. There is also, within the three titles, stages of how long people have been qualified for, serving to keep people in their place, so ensuring the status quo.

It is challenging and painful to address these issues of power that, although incongruent with our philosophy, mirror privilege and marginalisation across societies, nations, and the world. Some would say that every community has its leaders and its followers and those in between. Yet, if we look through a lens of intersectionality, it is those with multiple privilege that sit within the positions of power. Although many generously give of their time and wisdom, it is vital that those of us holding such privilege make space for intersectional voices. In this, there is a defensiveness and to be human is to feel defence when challenged, yet Whiteness as a system needs to look at its White fragility (Diangelo, 2019), even its White psychosis (Andrews, 2024; Tudor et al., 2022).

If only we could 'depersonalise' the personal in order to understand we are all born into systems – and there is nothing we can do about that – but what we can do is acknowledge our place in it, which serves to soften defence and enter into dialogue.

Anton Hart has featured throughout this book, as has Dwight Turner, Alok Vaid-Menon, and Jennifer Mullan, all have been influential in my intersectional journeying. I have spoken of radically open and non-defended dialogue (Hart, 2017) – where there is no arrival point, no end, yet a flow between defence, uncertainty, an opening up, more defence, reflection, and curiosity aiming to account for the difference between us. Dwight Turner's (2021), important permission to all of us, to own both the colonised and coloniser in our psyches and bodies. And Alok Vaid-Menon's (2022) significant voice in challenging binaries – their message about the Trans community being deeply human, and ultimately about freedom, autonomy, and liberation for all. And, returning again to my mantra, 'that all oppression is connected', inspired by Chin and brought alive by the narratives of Lorde and hooks.

Ultimately, our task is to further reinforce the intersectional lens as pivotal in attending to systemic differences, intersecting with power differentials, towards autonomy.

This book has brought to life some of the core intersectional identities within the UK's multi-diverse context. It has shone a light on some identities and intersections more than others. I would have liked to have specifically said more on the intersection of poverty, which has multiple manifestations across the binaries of the global north and the global south, countries, and societies. Each intersection bringing a unique experience, for example: White intersected with poverty; Black intersected with poverty; disabled intersected with poverty; single parent intersected with poverty.

Often these groups are set against each other, which was prevalent during the rise of Black Lives Matter – where Whiteness, intersected with poverty, asked 'What about *my* life?' serving to discount the brutal reality of racism.

While writing I have been starkly aware of my White-British-London-Eurocentric lens, and I have wondered about colleagues in the global south. Wondering about identities and intersections, for example, that our South Asian colleagues are uniquely grappling with, be it caste intersected with gender, with religion, with sexuality, and so on (Dhananjaya, 2022). I have wondered about the application of an intersectional lens across the four fields hoping that the ideas in this book have spoken to them through deconstruction and reconstruction and viewing models within systemic oppression. I have considered neurodivergence throughout (Aldridge & Stilman, 2024; Leong & Graichen, 2024; Oates & Moores, 2024; Rupchand & Kormann, 2024) – and continue to ask who will be missed?

I've continued to wonder what else needs to be considered? I will pursue the decolonising journey, where intersectional identities are envisioned through all aspects of theory and practice, through deconstruction and reconstruction bringing cultural sensitivity and social and political awareness to theory, hypothesis, and practice. I will continue to revisit the notion at beginning of the book 'that once I have arrived, I have lost my way': as identities change, social constructs change, we grow older, and the world changes. It is paramount to consider each person's unique identity, and when we think we know, we listen again.

Reality is an ongoing construction project, and we, too, hold the tools. The only way we can create change is by recognising that we must continually exceed our own paradigms, expand our imagination of freedom. Today, I will speak from the pieces of my broken heart to show you what they are teaching me about love. I believe the movement against the gender binary is a love letter to the world, offering a more expansive definition of love. Are you ready to receive it?

(Alok Vaid-Menon (they/them), 2022)

References

Aldridge, B., & Stilman, R. (2024). Unmasking neurodiversity: Revisiting the relationship between core self and sense of self to examine common neurodivergent script decisions. *Transactional Analysis Journal*, *54*(1), 47–62. https://doi.org/10.1080/03621537.2024.2286576

Andrews, K. (2024). *The psychosis of whiteness: Surviving the insanity of a racist world.* London: Penguin Random House.

Barrow, G. (2025). Annual Ed Fest Event. https://gilesbarrow.com/docs/edfest-25.pdf

Dhananjaya, D. (2022). We are the oppressor and the oppressed: The interplay between intrapsychic, interpersonal, and societal intersectionality. *Transactional Analysis Journal*, *52*(3), 244–258. https://doi.org/10.1080/03621537.2022.2082031

Diangelo, R. (2019). *White fragility: Why it's so hard for white people to talk about racism.* London: Penguin Random House.

Hart, A. (2017). From multicultural competence to radical openness: A psychoanalytic engagement of otherness. *The American Psychoanalyst*, *51*(1), 12–13, 26–27. https://apsa.org/wp-content/uploads/apsaa-publications/vol51no1-TOC/html/vol51no1_09.xhtml

Jusik, P. (2022). Systemic oppression and cultural diversity: Putting flesh on the bones of intercultural competence. *Transactional Analysis Journal*, *52*(3), 209–227. https://doi.org/10.1080/03621537.2022.2076981

Leong, C., & Graichen, R. (2024). Decentering neuronormativity: A transactional analysis impasse theory perspective for understanding ADHD masking and authentically honoring the da Vinci archetype within. *Transactional Analysis Journal*, *54*(1), 91–106. https://doi.org/10.1080/03621537.2024.2286581

Minikin, K. (2024). Leadership, intersectionality, and feminism: Radical-relational perspectives. *Transactional Analysis Journal*, *54*(3), 203–215.

Mullan, J. (2023). *Decolonizing therapy – Oppression, historical trauma, and politicizing your practice.* New York: W.W. Norton & Co.

Oates, S., & Moores, J. (2024). What is psychological and what is neurological? A political and phenomenological exploration of neurodivergent identity and encounters with third-ness. *Transactional Analysis Journal*, *54*(1), 63–77. https://doi.org/10.1080/03621537.2023.2286575

Pandya, A. (2024). System imago: A new perspective on leadership and power. *Transactional Analysis Journal*, *54*(3), 216–230. https://doi.org/10.1080/03621537.2024.2359287

Project TA 101 (2025). ITAA, USATAA, Southeast Institute, IESA committee begun 2018. Retrieved 29/5/25 from https://itaaworld.com/about-ta/project-ta-101/

Rich, A. (1995). *Dark fields of the republic.* New York: W.W. Norton & Co.

Rupchand, F., & Kormann, S. (2024). Intersubjective discoveries on parenting autistic sons: Challenges to ableist, normative narratives of deficit. *Transactional Analysis Journal*, *54*(1), 31–46. https://doi.org/10.1080/03621537.2024.2286580

SCOPed (2025). https://www.bacp.co.uk/about-us/advancing-the-profession/scoped/

Shafak, E. (2021). *The island of missing trees*. London: Penguin Books.

Tudor, K., Green, E., & Brett, E. (2022). Critical whiteness: A transactional analysis of a systemic oppression. *Transactional Analysis Journal*, *52*(3), 193–208. https://doi.org/10.1080/03621537.2022.2076394

Turner, D. (2021). *Intersections of privilege and otherness in counselling and psychotherapy*. Abingdon, Oxon: Routledge.

Vaid-Menon, A. (2022). 'Have the courage to break your own heart': Keynote Creating Change conference: National LGBTQ Taskforce.

Appendix 1

ITAA social engagement committee

Intersectionality focus group, 2021

As part of the Social Engagement Committee of the ITAA, Samia Nelson and Victoria Baskerville co-facilitated a focus group on intersectionality in 2021. The published report in *The Script* (Baskerville & Nelson, 2021), reprinted below, reflects the need for the group and the emerging intersectional awareness of the complexity of intersectional identity and the embodiment of intersectional transactional analysis.

The intersectionality focus group report – ITAA, The Script, July 2021

The intersectionality focus group is seen as an emerging group process where members will live into an awareness of the complexity of their intersectional identity and what this means for us as transactional analysts. Twenty ITAA members met online from around the world, including India, Turkey, the USA, Iran, and the UK; within this group was a diversity of cultural identities, bringing a complexity of transcultural experience.

We began by asking what has brought you here? This set the scene for musing the unconscious. And, like many other groups of this nature, people came either because of their intersectional experience, bringing their experience of oppression, or because they held an awareness of the need of holding the political and social as central to their practice.

What was evident in a world group was whether individuals located themselves in their country of residence or their home country – home country being their place of birth, having either immigrated years ago or moved away from more recently, or indeed the place of their ancestors.

Both facilitators set the scene by introducing themselves through their cultural narrative, inviting radical openness and non-defended dialogue (Hart, 2017), inviting members' willingness to tell their cultural story and to locate both the oppressed and privileged aspects of self.

In these groups, what can emerge for those who are predominately oppressed is both a vulnerability and a sense of relief in having a space to voice their experience and struggle. Alongside this, those holding predominately privilege can go to a place of feeling 'should I be here?', 'am I an imposter?'. Which, of course, mirrors the imposter experience of minorities on a daily basis.

When considering a meta perspective on this group, it was important to acknowledge and account for the fact that the group was being facilitated in English and led by two UK facilitators, which in itself could become an oppressive dynamic. However, it was also noted that both facilitators have complex cultural narratives experiencing both the oppressor and oppressed in self.

The way we introduced ourselves led to a discussion on the palpable hierarchy within our TA organisations with particular regard to professional status. We chose to name this as potentially another oppressive structure in the group.

Intersectionality has become a popular term; however, it was evident in the shared space that we can only truly embody intersectionality, as a lived experience, as we begin to account for our part in systemic oppression and the understanding that all oppression is connected.

For the second part, we asked members to respond to two reflective questions in order to offer a collective lens and to bring alive the lived experience of intersectionality.

What brought you to the group?

'Intersectionality is a big buzzword but what does it mean for therapists and our work?'

'My curiosity about and deep regard for people's journeys and diversity of human experience.'

'My need to be mirrored, for my story to be heard and for my voice to matter.'

'My genuine belief that we can create collective wellness through learning about and embracing our differences as well as similarities.'

'Working in practice where I hold an intersectional framework in mind to uncover and support both the privilege and oppression my clients' experience, I joined the group so I could not only share my perception of the value of this way of working, but also listen and learn from others whose identity, or that of their clients, hinder or support a forward motion of change.'

'I came to the group to talk about my own culture and the challenges I had with the Islamic culture and politics. But when I heard that people talked about TA community and discriminations, I realised I had a deep feeling that I had repressed so much that I couldn't even see anymore.'

'I became curious about my own journey of remembering certain parts of my identity as a consequence of being a Brown Muslim woman and psychotherapist, not to mention an academic and an immigrant. My understanding of intersectionality is about making sense of partially overlapping and partially disjointed aspects of the self.'

'I am curious about intersectionality and maternal mental health, particularly as I work with a culturally diverse client group, but with a common thread – they are all emotionally distressed mothers.'

'I am quite interested in intersectionality as I have lived most of my life in an international environment and have experienced prejudice regarding my nationality. I am quite interested in radical psychiatry and the concept of alienation and oppression.'

'Curiosity and interest in the experiences of others and myself.'

'A desire to make training in psychological therapies more accessible and inclusive and to increase access to psychotherapy for marginalised and underprivileged individuals.'

'To finally be able to be part of a supportive group in which we can all share life experiences.'

How did you experience the group?

'I felt privileged to be invited to be part of the group and to hear people's stories.'

'I felt both excited and anxious. Will my voice matter? Will people learn anything from hearing my story? Will I be understood? Will I be able to understand and empathically challenge?'

'I love that it provided me with a safe space to talk and to learn about mine and others' experiences.'

'I found the space itself respectful and permission giving, and it was a warming experience to hear the stories of those who attended, their difference and how this impacts on them personally, the impact of their own narrative on the work they undertake, and also how the focus of difference can support a positive existential position between client-therapist.'

'I enjoy the group being global TA folk with whom I can broaden my lens and safely explore and experience the meanings, implications, and potential triggers of intersectionality.'

'I was very excited to be part of such a diverse and international group which reflects who I am.'

'I really enjoyed the diversity of people and experience in the group and the beginnings of finding an essence of intersectionality and how it impacts psychotherapy processes and is accounted for; but also, to explore my own senses of oppression, exclusion through an intersectional lens.'

'I realised I had a deep feeling of inferiority because of my nationality when I'm talking to my friends. This group was the first place I could talk about these feelings and become aware of them. I hope there'll be more of these groups to talk about what we have repressed to feel better and healed.'

'For me, entering a group with so much cultural diversity and minoritised experience felt psychologically safe. I also felt excited and inspired.'

'I found it both engaging and I learnt something about myself in the context of difference with others.'

Victoria Baskerville (she/her), TSTA(P), SEC member and focus group co-facilitator.

Samia Nelson (she/her), CTA(P) SEC focus group co-facilitator. Samia is a culturally sensitive psychotherapist based in North London. She belongs to a therapeutic learning community that holds social justice at its heart.

References

Baskerville, V., & Nelson, S. (2021). *The script*, July 2021, *51*(7), ITAA.

Hart, A. (2017). From multicultural competence to radical openness: A psychoanalytic engagement of otherness. *The American Psychoanalyst*, *51*(1), 12–13, 26–27. https://apsa.org/wp-content/uploads/apsaa-publications/vol51no1-TOC/html/vol51no1_09.xhtml

Appendix 2

The multi-complexity of difference, a conversation

An intersectional lens brings more curiosity around the multi-complexity of difference within cultural constructs and relationships (Hart, 2017). That radical openness and non-defended dialogue can facilitate making sense of and working through the complexity of difference and power differentials was illustrated by a moving exchange initiated by a student, Edward, who had been inspired by reading the dialogue with J around difference in the transcultural article (Baskerville, 2022; the dialogue with J is republished in Chapter 4). He (the student) wanted to challenge the idea of similarity by talking in a non-defended way with Ade (the tutor), both of whom shared cultural identities of being British Nigerian cis men.

Edward argued that at first sight they shared a culture, yet the dialogue profoundly challenged the construct of shared identity.

Ade was born in Nigeria and moved to the UK with his mother and siblings at the age of seven. Thus, he grew up with a Black mirror in Nigeria and did not experience racism until he arrived in the UK. His father continued to live in Nigeria and was a positive role model.

Edward was born in the UK; his father came as a student in the 1950s and took on the cloak of colonisation and embraced all things of western culture in the hope to protect against the onslaught of racism.

Both of their fathers were from the Yoruba tribe, yet the intersection of social status and family structure, and the influence of northern versus southern hemisphere culture, made them distinctly different.

Ade's father, a highly regarded public figure in Nigeria, brought him high status. Moreover, his father had a polygamous family, which meant he had another wife and older children. He lived in Nigeria and visited his family in the UK. His visits were frequent, and Ade maintained a strong connection with his Nigerian identity and collective family. He experienced racism in school and talked of being strong offering him some protection.

Edward's father faced the challenge of arriving in the UK, training to be a doctor, and finding his way through the racism and raising a family in south London, a White borough at the time. He did not experience a 'Nigerian' mirror growing up, yet he related to Ade with stories of his grandparents. Edward did not visit Nigeria until more recently, yet in his dialogue he talked about going back to Nigeria, clearly illustrating a sense of home.

This snapshot of an hour-long conversation offers a spotlight on the intricacies of difference within sameness, and the hairline between oppressed and oppressor, described by Ade as 'the complexity of intertwined intersectional cultural identities'.

References

Baskerville, V. (2022). A transcultural and intersectional ego state model of the self: The influence of transcultural and intersectional identity on self and other. *Transactional Analysis Journal*, *52*(32), 1–16. http://doi.org/10.1080/03621537.2022.2076398

Hart, A. (2017). From multicultural competence to radical openness: A psychoanalytic engagement of otherness. *The American Psychoanalyst*, *51*(1), 12–13, 26–27. https://apsa.org/wp-content/uploads/apsaa-publications/vol51no1-TOC/html/vol51no1_09.xhtml

Appendix 3

Critique and development of the Transcultural and Intersectional Ego State Model of the Self, 2022, to the 2025 updated version

It has been three years since the Transcultural and Intersectional Ego State Model of the Self (Baskerville, 2022), was first published, and I have received many personal testimonies about its impact. More recently, a student colleague wrote to me describing the model as a kaleidoscope, shifting identity depending on the view. This analogy develops my idea of the juke box (Baskerville, 2022), moving between identities and orbiting distinct aspects of self, depending on the systemic landscape (Jusik, 2022).

As stated in Chapter 4, I have always seen the model as evolving, as social constructs change and social, cultural, and political contexts shift. Through my own evolving social and political awareness and further uncovering of unconscious bias, I have updated social constructs in the original model as well as reconsidered my intersectional identity – thus proving the ever-changing nature of the transcultural and intersectional self, and staying true to my ideas around deconstruction and reconstruction of theory through an intersectional lens.

It is important to note that the original model (2022) based on the dialogue with J, served to offer a 'snapshot' of a few intersectional identities (viewed through a British context); and like Kliman (2010), I appreciate that we have a multitude – certainly many more than the original six identities.

I invite the reader to continually consider their evolving and changing lived experience informing intersectional identity and to continue to take the journey in furthering social and political awareness.

Some specific critiques of the original 2022 model

P_2 located intersectional identities (P_3, A_3, C_3)

I have reconsidered the socially constructed intersectional identities I named in the 2022 model located in P_2 – including race, class, neuro/disabled, gender, religion, and sexuality.

Originally, I offered six identities, placing neuro, as in neurodiversity and disability together. This sat uneasy with me as my social and political curiosity has evolved. Consequently, I have separated neurodiversity and disability, and

I have added ethnic identity in order to make a distinction between race and heritage.

I have updated the 2025 model to eight core identities, including: race, class, gender, religion, sexuality, neurodiversity, disability, and ethnic identity. I offer some thoughts and critique of my updates, separating neurodiversity and disability, and adding ethnic identity. The other five socially constructed identities remain the same in both the 2022 and 2025 models.

Neurodiversity and disability

Oliver and Barnes (2012, cited in Goodley et al., 2019) state: 'To contemplate disability is to scrutinise inequality. Disabled people's organisations posit a simple but powerful idea: disability is a phenomenon associated with the discrimination of people with sensory, physical, and cognitive impairments'.

In the original model I placed neurodiversity and disability together as these experiences can be understood and discriminated against similarly. In this 2025 model I separated them, as they can be viewed as distinctly different identities (Rupchand & Kormann, 2024).

And, at the same time, some readers may choose to locate their neurodiversity within disability, supported by Oates and Moores' article (2024), inviting 'readers to think with them about the politics of identity and inclusion and ask whether neurodivergence is a disability, a difference, or both' (p. 63).

Disability

Disability studies intersected with Queer theory views disability in general as a social construct, meaning that ideas about disability and who is disabled are defined by humans.

In the *Collins Dictionary and Thesaurus* (2020), disability is defined as 'a physical or mental condition or illness that restricts a person in his or her (their) ability to move or use his or hers (their) senses' (p. 228). Essentially, disability can sit within both medical and social models. The medical model of disability, based on deficit and cure, aims to diagnose differences that are deemed to be outside of what is normative. While the social model of disability is a framework that understands disability as a result of societal barriers and attitudes.

Armstrong (2010) posits that 'being at the right place at the right time seems to be critical in terms of defining whether you'll be regarded as gifted or disabled' (p. 15).

This has been reinforced by Oates and Moores' ideas (2024), citing the importance of 'divergent minds and bodies and to situate this in the more-than-personal realm of the cultural and sociopolitical' (p. 63).

In the 2025 diagram I have chosen to use Goodley's (2018) idea of dis/ability as a way of accounting for the co-construction of the two identities, seeing disability and ability on a continuum, rather than as binary opposites. Thus, questioning ableist assumptions and honouring both the able-bodied and disabled self, which can ultimately be self-defined.

Neurodiversity

Neurodivergence has also been medicalised and treated. And, similar to disability, can be viewed through the social model of disability, where neurodivergence is seen as stemming from a society that doesn't accommodate varying needs. Arguably, humans exhibit a wide range of neurodiversity.

It can be said that people with the same brain differences are regarded completely differently dependent on the social, cultural, and political context. Certainly capitalist supremacy has, and is deeply contributing to discrimination against those outside the realm of the neurotypical mind and body (Chapman, 2023).

In this reflection, separating neurodiversity and dis/ability is a complex process in understanding the interconnected nature of both constructs medically and societally.

I have separated these social constructs in P_2, inviting autonomy in the reader to reflect on where they position their dis/ability or neurodivergence or both, while accounting for their experience of systemic oppression and evolving social and political awareness.

Ethnic identity

In the 2025 model, I have added the intersectional introject ethnic identity. Ethnic identity opens up identity beyond race, and gives the reader, student, practitioner, and client, the autonomy to define and reflect on their unique identity more specifically – for example, origin (which may include race), history, heritage/s, culture, language/s, spiritual beliefs, nationality or nationalities, etc.

Indeed, each of these could form a distinctly separate intersectional identity, opening up the model to tens of identities.

C_3 located intersectional identities (P_4, A_4, C_4)

C_3 continues to represent transgenerational power and oppression – P_4 locates the oppressor and C_4 the oppressed – demonstrating the lineage of systemic oppression, which could equate to P_4, P_5, P_6, P_7 – C_4, C_5, C_6, C_7, and so on.

A_2 located intersectional identities

A_2 continues to represent integrating cultural selves, owning both the oppressor and oppressed in self, social, and political awareness and social responsibility.

C_2, C_1, C_0, C_{00} located intersectional identities

With regard to C_2, I have reflected further on the 2022 model on C_0 and C_{00}, housed in C_1, where I described both as innate and where I located race, sex, neuro/disability, and generational experience, as in the DNA born into. I have reconsidered these ideas through further reading, research, and dialogue, and my continuing journeying and furthering of social and political awareness.

I have continually tussled with ideas around what is innate and what is constructed, informed by research citing that our ancestral lineage is passed on through DNA (Klosin et al., 2017), and I have wondered if it is possible to separate them. In this, I have considered overlapping P_0 and C_0 Hargaden and Sills (2002), which highlights the intersection between innate and socially constructed. Yet I want to acknowledge a distinction – and account for the impasse between P0 (socially constructed) and C_0 (innate).

I have replaced race with race/ethnicity; sex as sex organ; neuro/disabled as genotype; and generational as generational/lineage, aiming to give further clarity to my ideas.

Race

When citing race as innate, I have tussled with the fact that race is a social construct reinforced by generations of systemic oppression and White supremacy.

And there are many conflicting definitions of race, some citing race as biological, describing physical traits, some as solely a social construct and others stating racial identity as an important factor in belonging.

Ultimately, I have resolved that race has been in our ancestral bodies for centuries, therefore, I have chosen to continue to name it as innate/born into, while also accounting for the intersection between innate and constructed, demonstrated by the impasse between P_0 and C_0 in the original 2022 and 2025 model (see Figures 1, 2, 3 and 4 in Chapter 4).

Ethnicity

Ethnicity refers to heritage, culture, religion, ancestry, and the country where you were born, and can also be based on a group of people who share similar traits.

Subsequently, I have updated C_0 to 'race/ethnicity' (see Figures 1, 2, 3, 4 in Chapter 4), which offers self-agency in defining self through innate identity, informed by and passed on through DNA and ancestral lineage.

Sex and sex organs

In the 2022 model I described sex, as in the sex of a person as innate. While I still stand by this in terms of being born with sex organs, I support the idea that this does not necessarily equate to a gender.

The Trans movement would contest that the sex of a person, as well as gender is assigned at birth. In that male and female sex organs are aligned with two genders of man or woman, and that these ways of being, are aligned with biological ideas, that are informed by social and political constructs. This is further supported by scientific evidence that gender is on a continuum (Castleberry, 2018).

These ideas have been explored and questioned by northern hemisphere society's response to intersex. (See Chapter 5.)

Therefore, I have updated sex to 'sex organ' (see Figures 1, 2, 3, 4 in Chapter 4) to move away from sex equating a gender, to the idea that sex organs do not necessarily ascribe to a gender construct.

Neurodiversity and disability

In the original 2022 model neuro and disability were considered innate, in terms of being born with a mind and body. However, I believe these social constructs of neurodiversity and dis/ability belong in P_2, informed by systemic oppression.

I updated neurodiversity and disability with 'genotype', which refers to the complete set of genes an individual is born with. Genotypes determine which characteristics an individual will possess: the genetic constitution of an organism. 'The genotype determines the hereditary potentials and limitations of an individual from embryonic formation through adulthood' (Editors of Encyclopedia Britannica, 2025).

This supports the idea that we come into the world with a set of genetics, which are then viewed through the social constructs of the time.

Generational/lineage

The use of generational in the 2022 model served to capture transgenerational ancestry. I updated generational to 'generational/lineage', to further highlight bloodline and line of descent.

Personal reflections from 2022 to 2025

Since 2022 to the present day, I have been inquiring and reflecting on my shifting intersectional identity – researching my family history and furthering my knowledge of my transcultural narrative by DNA testing, as well as developing my social, cultural, and political awareness. I continue to do the work around internalised privilege and oppression, unconscious bias, and systemic racism and oppression.

This has resulted in updating some of my intersectional identities in the 2025 version, and, in some, choosing to sit within two constructs. For example, locating within neurodiversity both neurotypical and neurodiverse – as I continue to process my neuro difference. And also, both able bodied and dis/abled as I come to terms with being dis/abled by society – in the way I have been seen when walking with crutches, waiting many years for surgery.

I have now added Queer along with lesbian, which accounts for my progressive political stance, in aiming to include all intersectional gender sex relationship identities, and in my commitment to challenge society's ideas about gender and sexuality.

In separating race and ethnic identity, I have continued to locate being White within race and understand that being British is a nationality located in ethnic identity. I more recently claimed my maternal Irish heritage as a significant part of my ethnic identity (located in C_3 and C_4), along with the influence of being northern and from the Midlands.

And in accounting for cis gender and trans gender, I have now updated my identity of woman to cis woman.

Summary of critique and update

This critique deconstructs and reconstructs the Transcultural and Intersectional Ego State Model of the Self, 2022 to 2025, with the aim of illustrating fast changing social constructs, shifting intersectional identity, informed by life changes, systemic oppression, and the evolving of social, cultural, and political awareness.

This critique and reflection offers another invitation, to own the part we each play in systemic oppression, and to take decisive action in addressing power imbalances and systemic racism and oppression in our consulting rooms, training rooms, education settings, organisations, community, and outside spaces.

References

Armstrong, T. (2010). *The power of neurodiversity*. MA, USA: De Capo Press.

Baskerville, V. (2022). A transcultural and intersectional ego state model of the self: The influence of transcultural and intersectional identity on self and other. *Transactional Analysis Journal, 52*(32), 1–16. http://doi.org/10.1080/03621537.2022.2076398

Castleberry, J. (2018). Addressing the gender continuum: A concept analysis. *Journal of Transcultural Nursing, 30*(4). https://doi.org/10.1177/1043659618818722

Chapman, R. (2023). *Empire of normality: Neurodiversity and capitalism*. London: Pluto Press. https://doi.org/10.2307/jj.8501594

Collins. (2020). *English Dictionary and thesaurus: Essential edition*. Glasgow, Scotland: Collins.

Editors of Encyclopedia Britannica. (2025). https://www.britannica.com/science/genotype (accessed May 2, 2025).

Goodley, D. (2018). The dis/ability complex. *Journal of Diversity and Gender Studies*. https://doi.org/10.11116/digest.5.1.1

Goodley, D., Lawthom, R., Liddiard, K., & Runswick-Cole, K. (2019). Provocations for critical disability studies. *Disability & Society, 34*(6), 972–997. https://doi.org/10.1080/09687599.2019.1566889

Hargaden, H., & Sills, C. (2002). *Transactional analysis: A relational perspective*. London: Brunner-Routledge.

Jusik, P. (2022). Systemic oppression and cultural diversity: Putting flesh on the bones of intercultural competence. *Transactional Analysis Journal, 52*(3), 209–227. https://doi.org/10.1080/03621537.2022.2076981

Kliman, J. (2010). Intersections of social privilege and marginalization: A visual teaching tool. In *Expanding our social justice practices: Advances in theory and training* [special issue]. AFTA (American Family Therapy Academy), 6(39–48). Monograph Series.

Klosin, A., Casas, E., Hidalgo-Carcedo, C., Vavouri, T., & Lehner, B. (2017). Transgenerational transmission of environmental information in *C. elegans*. *Science, 356*(6335), 320–323. https://pubmed.ncbi.nlm.nih.gov/28428426

Oates, S., & Moores, J. (2024). What is psychological and what is neurological? A political and phenomenological exploration of neurodivergent identity and encounters with thirdness. *Transactional Analysis Journal, 54*(1), 63–77. https://doi.org/10.1080/03621537.2023.228657

Oliver, M., & Barnes, C. (2012). *The new politics of disablement*. London: Palgrave.

Rupchand, F., & Kormann, S. (2024). Intersubjective discoveries on parenting autistic sons: Challenges to ableist, normative narratives of deficit. *Transactional Analysis Journal, 54*(1), 31–46. https://doi.org/10.1080/03621537.2024.2286580

Glossary of terms

Activism: Activism advocates for a cause/a group of people, raising awareness and serving to challenge discriminations and inequalities, with the aim to create change – by standing up for injustices including racial, social, climate justice, and environmental protection – through protest, demonstration, advocacy, and community.

Ally: An ally is a person who stands up for the rights of others, by walking alongside, by advocating for the other – understanding that all oppression is connected. And that one oppression is symptomatic of all oppressions.

Ancestry: Family history and lineage/heritage/ethnic roots and geographical location/s.

Capitalist supremacy: An economic system/society in which private ownership of capital goods, and a free market, hold unquestioned dominance, or influence, rather than state-controlled distribution of resources.

Cis gender: A person's gender is aligned with the sex they were assigned at birth.

Cis gaze: Viewing a transgender person from a cis perspective/frame of reference, risking unconscious bias and prejudice.

Climate justice: Climate justice is linked with an agenda for human rights and international development, and sharing the benefits and burdens associated with climate stabilisation, as well as concerns about the impacts of climate change (ClimateJust, 2025).

Code switching: Code switching conscious and unconscious – is a way of adapting or assimilating in different relationships and contexts. Code switching may include masking parts of self, hiding parts of self, or killing off parts of self to survive or feel safe.

Colonisation: The process of one country or group gaining control and supremacy, when one way of being is recognised as 'superior'. As in the process of sending people to live in and govern another country for example, taking over and governing another country or social group, where one group is deemed as superior.

Colonise: The process of control and supremacy, when one way of being is recognised as 'superior'.

Critical disability studies: Challenges traditional ideas, bringing an intersectional approach and centres the experience of disabled people, considering social, cultural and political contexts – including societal barriers, ableism and rights – defining disability as a social construct.

Critical race theory: 'An intellectual and social movement and a loosely organised framework of legal analysis based on the premise that race is not a natural, biologically grounded feature of physically distinct sub groups of human beings but socially constructed' (Duignan, 2025).

Decolonisation: The process of relinquishing control and supremacy, when one way of being, is recognised as 'superior'. The action of undoing colonisation, restoring autonomy and indigenous perspectives – challenging power structures.

Deconstruction: To deconstruct is to break something down into parts in order to better understand its meaning, to 'reduce something to its constituent parts in order to reinterpret it' (OED, 2012); 'in popular usage the term [deconstruction] has come to mean a critical dismantling of tradition and traditional modes of thought' (Encyclopedia Britannica, 2025).

Dis/abled: The slash highlights the complexity and nuances of disabled and able bodied identity, challenging the binary – the fluidity between disability and ability.

Discrimination: Refers to the disadvantage/mistreatment/bias and oppression of a social group based on prejudice.

Embodied: A way of being, an embracing and a lived experience – an embodiment of beliefs, ideas values that are experienced and lived through mind, body, psyche, soul and being – through the veins, not as an add-on.

Epigenetics: Refers to the study of how the environment and other factors can change the way that genes are expressed, without altering the basic DNA code.

Ethnic identity: Refers to and opens up identity beyond race, allowing the autonomy to define and reflect on unique identity more specifically – for example, origin (which may include race), history, heritage/s, culture, language/s, spiritual beliefs, nationality or nationalities, etc.

Ethnicity: Refers to heritage, culture, religion, ancestry, and the country where you were born; and can also be based on a group of people who share similar traits.

Gender fluid: A person whose gender is not fixed and may shift over time.

Gender mispronouning: When an individual's preferred pronouns are not used or respected – mispronouning is an act of discrimination and can cause harm. Asking everyone their pronouns is an inclusive action, a way of including and honouring all gender identities. Mispronouning is an act of transphobia.

Gender non-conforming: A person whose gender identity/expression does not conform to societal norms/expectations.

Gender pronouns: Pronouns describe the autonomous gender of an individual – not the assumed gender based on sex organs, physical being, or gender stereotypes. Pronouns may be aligned with gender assigned at birth, or may be the congruent gender of an individual. Pronouns include: I, you, we, us, he, him, his, she, her, hers, they, them, theirs, it, its, our, your.

Genotype: Describes an organism's complete set of genes – genetic makeup/traits

GSRD: Gender, Sexuality and Relationship Diversity (GSRD) is an inclusive term accounting for the breadth and diversity of gender, sexuality, and relationship identities.

Heritage: Identity which draws on culture/cultures/ancestral roots/nationality/s/customs/ values and legacy.

Imperialism: 'A nation's or state's policy and practice of extending dominion through land and territory taking; or gaining economic and political control over other areas and peoples' (Haines, 2019).

Indigenous: A native group of people, original habitants of a land, descendants – those existing on a land before the onslaught of colonisation.

Internalised systemic oppression: An individual unconsciously internalises both privilege and oppression influenced by systemic oppression – for example, cis women may internalise misogyny and cis men patriarchy, along with a White person internalising supremacy.

Intersection: Where an individual's identities intersect – come together or cross and converge – forming a unique combination of intersectional identity; and, in relationship, the intersection/s identify the engagement in systemic enactment.

Intersectional self: The self that accounts for the multiple selves we hold in our psyche, soul, and DNA informed by each person's unique identity and lineage of privilege and oppression.

Intersectionality: 'The interconnected nature of social categorizations such as race, class, gender, regarded as creating overlapping, interdependent systems of discrimination or disadvantage' (Crenshaw, 1989).

Intersects or intersections: Cultural and social identities – including present, historical, and ancestral parts of self.

Lineage: Bloodline and line of descent.

Male gaze: The way that women can be perceived by cis men – represented and objectified through a masculine/patriarchal perspective.

Marginalisation: The act of treating someone or something as if they are marginal, i.e., not central, not important – discriminated against/oppressed.

Microaggression: Microaggressions are forms of everyday oppression that tend to go unseen and unacknowledged (Cousins & Diamond, 2021) – but felt deeply as an act of discrimination. 'Subtle, stunning and often automatic non-verbal exchanges which are put-downs' (Pierce et al. 1978, in Cousins & Diamond, 2021).

Neurodivergence: Refers to the different ways a person's brain processes information. 'People who are neurodivergent have brains which operate and develop differently to those who are neurotypical [or perceived as normative]. These differences may occur in cognition, perception, information, processing, attention, memory, sequencing, emotion, mood, sociability and other mental functions' (Widdowson, 2024).

Non-binary: Describes a gender identity that does not fit the system binary of male and female.

Normative or normative construct: Mainstream society decides what is normative through the lens of privilege and power – deciding standards of behaviour, one way of being – inviting conformity and social control which serves to uphold supremacies.

Othered: An experience of being discriminated against, unseen, perceived as less than – an act of racism, transphobia, misogyny, ableism, and so on – this may be conscious or unconscious, and experienced somatically.

Patriarchal supremacy: A system/society in which men hold a position of unquestioned power, authority, dominance, or influence.

Polygamous: In relationship with consenting multiple partners through marriage or contracting.

Privilege: A special authority and unearned advantage/rights given to/possessed by a person or group due to intersectional positioning informed by discrimination.

Queer: A reclaimed slur – now a political stance/identity across all gender, sex, relationship, and identity.

Queer theory: Refers to theory challenging binary thinking, based on the ideas that gender is fluid flexible and subject to change.

Race: There are many conflicting definitions of race, some citing race as biological, describing physical traits, some as solely a social construct, and others stating racial identity as an important factor in belonging.

Racial justice: Refers to fair and equal treatment of all races, addressing systemic racism.

Racism: The prejudice, discrimination, bias, mistreatment, violence towards, and oppression of people of colour created by generations of systemic oppression and White supremacy.

Radical: Progressive and revolutionary thinking – characterised by independence of, or departure from what is usual or traditional; progressive, unorthodox, or innovative in outlook, conception, design, etc., esp. of change or action: going to the root or origin; touching upon or affecting what is essential and fundamental; thorough, far-reaching (OED, 2025).

Radical psychiatry: 'The central principle of radical psychiatry is that psychiatric problems are manifestations of alienation that results from oppression that has been mystified in the isolated individual. Mystification involves cultural discounting or justification of oppression' (Widdowson, 2024).

Social construct: An idea or concept in society that is the result of human collective agreement (i.e., it is socially constructed) rather than something that exists in objective reality.

Social justice: Refers to justice and rights for all social groups including race, gender, GSRD, disability, class, etc.; advocating for awareness and policy change.

Supremacy: A position of oppression – unquestioned authority, dominance, or influence; normally associated with White, patriarchal, capitalist supremacy.

Systemic: Referring to the whole of a system – organisation and so on – not just some elements of it – for example, social, cultural, political, and historical influences.

Systemic enactment: Where individuals unconsciously engage in systemic relating – enacting systemic power dynamics in the therapeutic/education encounter.

Systemic oppression: Refers to society's systems and structures/policies, i.e., an institutionalised system, which determines which groups are oppressed – resulting in inequalities, marginalisation, disadvantage/mistreatment, and oppression of certain social and cultural groups.

Systemic racism: A system that is inherently racist, embedded in institutions and policies – furthering racism.

Trans: A Trans/transgender person is someone who has a gender identity different from that typically associated with the sex organs they were assigned at birth. A non-binary person may also identify as Trans.

Transcultural: Involves, encompasses, or combines elements of more than one culture/multiple cultures.

Transgenerational trauma: Or intergenerational trauma – trauma that is passed on through generations, affecting descendants who may not have directly experienced the trauma.

White fragility: Denial and minimising racism resulting in discomfort, defence and anger, often disrupting the possibility of dialogue and responsibility (DiAngelo, 2018).

White gaze: Refers to the perspective of a person who identifies themselves as White, and sees their view as normative – and ultimately unconsciously imposes a White frame of reference resulting in discrimination.

White psychosis: A delusional belief that Whiteness is superior (Andrews, 2024).

White supremacy: Systems of power that enforce the supposed supremacy and dominance of White people and whiteness.

References

Andrews, K. (2024). *The psychosis of whiteness: Surviving the insanity of a racist world.* London: Penguin Random House.

ClimateJust (2025). https://www.climatejust.org.uk/what-climate-justice (accessed: July 9, 2025).

Cousins, S., & Diamond, B. (2021). *Making sense of microaggressions.* UK: Open Voices Publishers.

Crenshaw, K. (1989). 'Demarginalizing the intersection of race and sex: A Black feminist critique of antidiscrimination doctrine, feminist theory and antiracist politics.' *University of Chicago Legal Forum*, Issue 1, Article 8. https://chicagounbound.uchicago.edu/cgi/viewcontent.cgi?ar-ticle=1052&context=uclf

DiAngelo, R. (2018). *White fragility.* Boston: Beacon Press.

Duignan, B. (2025). 'Critical race theory' entry written for *Encyclopedia Britannica*, https://www.britannica.com/topic/critical-race-theory (updated June 18, 2025) (accessed: July 9, 2025).

Encyclopedia Britannica (2025). 'Deconstruction' https://www.britannica.com/topic/deconstruction (accessed: February 2, 2025).

Haines, S. K. (2019), cited in Mullan, J. 2023, *Decolonizing therapy*. New York: WW. Norton & Co.

OED (2012). *Oxford English Dictionary* 'Deconstruct'. Oxford: Oxford University Press.

OED (2025). *Oxford English Dictionary* 'Radical'. https://www.oed.com/dictionary/radical_adj?tl=true#27278303 (accessed: July 9, 2025).

Pierce, C. M., Carew, J., Pierce-Gonzalez, D., & Willis, D. (1978), cited in Cousins, S. & Diamond, B. (2021). *Making sense of microaggressions*. UK: Open Voices Publishers.

Widdowson, M. (2024), *Transactional analysis: 100 key points and techniques* (p. 149). Abingdon, Oxon: Routledge.

Bibliography

Ababio, B., & Littlewood, R. (2019). *Intercultural therapy: Challenges, insights and developments*. Hove, East Sussex: Routledge.

Abram, D. (1996). *The spell of the sensuous: Perception and language in a more-than-human world*. London: Penguin Random House.

Ahmed, N. (2021/22). Research project 2. *The Transactional Analyst 12*(1), Winter.

Ahmed, N., Baskerville, V., Neish, G., & Nelson, V. (2023). UKCP research project final report: Inclusivity and exclusivity in training – The trainees' experience. *The Transactional Analyst, 13*(1), Winter.

Aldridge, B., & Stilman, R. (2024). Unmasking neurodiversity: Revisiting the relationship between core self and sense of self to examine common neurodivergent script decisions. *Transactional Analysis Journal, 54*(1), 47–62. https://doi.org/10.1080/03621537.2024.2286576

Alleyne, A. (2011). Overcoming racism, discrimination and oppression in psychotherapy. Cited in Lago, C. (2011). *The handbook of transcultural counselling and psychotherapy*. NY: Open University Press.

Altman, N. (2021). *White privilege: Psychoanalytic perspective*. Oxon: Routledge.

American Psychoanalytic Association. (2023), The Holmes Commission on Racial Equality in American Psychoanalysis. https://apsa.org/wpcontent/uploads/2023/06/Holmes-Commission-Final-Report-2023Report-rv6-19-23.pdf?ver

Andrews, K. (2024). *The psychosis of whiteness: Surviving the insanity of a racist world*. London: Penguin Random House.

Armengol, J. M. (2012). In the dark room: Homosexuality and/as blackness in James Baldwin's Giovanni's room. *Signs, 37*(3), 671– 693. http://doi.org/10.1086/662699

Armstrong, T. (2010). *The power of neurodiversity*. MA, USA: De Capo Press.

Arnold, C. (2022/23). 'What's the point of research?' *New Psychotherapist*. Issue 82: Winter.

Bainbridge, C. (2020). *Why social constructs are created*. Verywellmind. (Accessed July 20, 2021). https://www.verywellmind.com/definition-of-social-construct1448922

Baker, J. (2024). Time for a change? A review of transactional analysis psychotherapy training and examinations with consideration to adopting a more inclusive and non-discriminatory approach. *Transactional Analysis Journal, 54*(1), 78–90. https://doi.org/10.1080/03621537.2023.2286577

Baldwin, J. (1953/2001). *Go tell it on the mountain*. London: Penguin Random House.

Baldwin, J. (1956). *Giovanni's room*. New York: Dial Press; London: Penguin Classics, (2007).

Baldwin, J. (1962) Quote from *New York Times,* January 14, 1962.

Baldwin, J. (1972) *No name in the street*. (Penguin Modern Classics, 2024). London: Penguin Random House.

Baldwin, J. (1990). (2017 edition). *The fire next time*. London: Penguin Random House.

Baldwin, J., & Peck, R. (1979, 2017) *I am not your negro*. London: Penguin Random House.

Ballet Black. (2023). https://balletblack.co.uk/events/barbican-2023-balletblack-pioneers/

Barker, M. J. (2016). *Queer: A graphic history*. London: Icon Books.

Barker, M. J., & Iantaffi, A. (2019). *Life isn't binary*. London: Jessica Kingsley.

Baskerville, V. (2021). Evolving an inclusive training. *The Transactional Analyst, 11*(4): Autumn

Baskerville, V. (2021). Research project [1]. *The Transactional Analyst, 11*(4): Autumn.

Baskerville, V. (2022). A transcultural and intersectional ego state model of the self: The influence of transcultural and intersectional identity on self and other. *Transactional Analysis Journal, 52*(32). http://doi.org/10.1080/03621537.2022.2076398

Baskerville, V. (2022). Research project 3. *The Transactional Analyst, 12*(2), Spring.

Baskerville, V. (2022). Research project. *The Transactional Analyst, 12*(4), 4.

Baskerville, V. (2022/23). UKCP research project final report. *The Transactional Analyst, 13*(1), Winter.

Baskerville, V. *et al* (2022). Amplified voices: Students and essay writing – Lauryn McKinsonEnglish, crena watson, julia Pool, caroline matthews, jubriel hanid, rosa trout,Mayuri patel, clodagh McCahill, shabazz Nelson. *The Transactional Analyst, 12*(3), Summer 2022.

Baskerville, V. (2023). Deconstructing and reconstructing the curriculum. *The Transactional Analyst, 13*(2), Spring.

Baskerville, V. (2023). 'The unseen: How many trainees are feeling left out?' *The New Psychotherapist*, UKCP Magazine, issue 83, Summer 2023.

Baskerville, V. (2023) Book review: Intersections of privilege and otherness in counselling and psychotherapy. *New Psychotherapist*, Summer.

Baskerville, V. (2024) Amplified voices: Queer community and allies. *The Transactional Analyst, 14*(2), Spring/Summer 2024.

Baskerville, V., & Adejumo, L. (2022). Amplified voices: Luq adejumo. *The Transactional Analyst, 12*(4), Autumn 2022.

Baskerville, V., & Douglas, M. (2021a). 'Intersectionality in TA training'. *ITAA The Script* 2021-04.

Baskerville, V., & Hunt, B. (2023). Amplified voices: Blythe hunt. *The Transactional Analyst, 13*(3), Summer.

Baskerville, V., & Kannathasan, N. (2023) Book review: The psychology of supremacy: Imperium by dwight turner. *The Transactional Analyst, 13*(4), Autumn.

Baskerville, V., & Khader, N. (2022). Amplified voices: Nada khader. *The Transactional Analyst, 12*(2), Spring.

Baskerville, V., & Minikin, K. (2023). Amplified voices: Karen minikin. *The Transactional Analyst, 13*(1), Winter.

Baskerville, V., & Nelson, S. (2021). 'Intersectionality focus group report'. *ITAA The Script* 2021-07.

Baskerville, V., Nelson, S. & Ngozi, E. (2022). On the frontline, in conversation with Esther Ngozi. *The Transactional Analyst, 12*(1), Winter 2022.

Batts, V. A. (1982). Modern racism: A TA perspective. *Transactional Analysis Journal, 12*(3), 207–209. https://doi.org/10.1177/036215378201200309

Batts, V. A. (1983). Knowing and changing the cultural script component of racism. *Transactional Analysis Journal, 13*(4), 255–257. https://doi.org/10.1177/036215378301300416

BBC. (2009). https://www.bbc.co.uk/stoke/content/articles/2009/02/14/history_mining_staffordshire_feature.shtml

Beetham, T. (2019). Intersectionality and social justice. *Therapy Today, 30*(3).

Belkin, M., & White, C. (2020). *Intersectionality and relational psychoanalysis: New perspectives on race, gender and sexuality*. New York: Routledge.

Berne, E. (1961). *Transactional analysis in psychotherapy. A systematic individual and social psychiatry*. New York: Grove Press.

Berne, E. (1962, 1976). Classification of positions, *Transactional Analysis Bulletin, 1*(3).

Berne, E. (1964). *Games people play*. New York: Grove Press.

Berne, E. (1966). *Principles of group treatment*. Oxford: OUP.

Berne, E. (1968). *A layman's guide to psychiatry and psychoanalysis* (3rd ed). New York: Simon & Schuster. (Original work published 1947 as 'The mind in action').

Berne, E. (1972). *What do you say after you say hello?* New York: Grove Press.

Bhagavad Gita Holy Book. (2003). *Penguin classics*. London: Penguin Random House.

Bondi, L., & Fewell, J. (2017). Getting personal: A feminist argument for research aligned to therapeutic practice. *Counselling and Psychotherapy Research, 17*(2), 113–122.

Brod, H. (1989), Work clothes and leisure suits: The class basis and bias of the men's movement. In Michael S. Kimmel, & Messier (Eds.), *Men's lives* (p. 280). New York: Macmillan.

Castleberry, J. (2018). Addressing the gender continuum: A concept analysis. *Journal of Transcultural Nursing, 30*(4). https://doi.org/10.1177/1043659618818722

Chandler, D., & Munday, R. (2011). Queer theory. *A dictionary of media and communication*. Oxford: Oxford University Press.

Chapman, R. (2023). *Empire of normality: Neurodiversity and capitalism*. London: Pluto Press. https://doi.org/10.2307/jj.8501594

Chin, S. (2014). 'All oppression is connected' [Video]. https://www.pbslearningmedia.org/resource/fp17.lgbtq.oppression/alloppression-is-connected/.

Chin, S. (2014). 'Why am I not surprised'. http://whyaminotsurprised.blogspot.com/2014/07/staceyann-chin-all-oppression-is.html

Chin, S. (2019). *Crossfire: A litany for survival*. Chicago: Haymarket Books.

Chinnock, K. (2011). Relational transactional analysis supervision. *Transactional Analysis Journal, 41*(4), 336–350. https://doi.org/10.1177/036215371104100410

Chinnock, K., & Minikin, K. (2015). Power and the colonizing process. *The Transactional Analyst, 6*(2), Spring.

Clarkson, P. (1987). The bystander role. *Transactional Analysis Journal, 17*(3), 82–87. https://doi.org/10.1177/036215378701700305

Clarkson, P. (1993). Bystander games. *Transactional Analysis Journal, 23*(3), 158–172. https://doi.org/10.1177/036215379302300307

Clarkson, P. (2003). *The therapeutic relationship*. (1992, 1st ed.). London: Wiley.

COE. (2024). https://www.coe.int/en/web/compass/hre-and-activism

Coleman, A. L. (2019). 'What's intersectionality? Let these scholars explain the theory and its history'. *Time Magazine*. March 28, 2019 (updated March 29, 2019). https://time.com/5560575/intersectionalitytheory/

Collins, P., & Bilge, S. (2020). *Intersectionality*. Cambridge UK: Polity Press.

Cornell, W., & Hargaden, H. (2005). *From transactions to relations: The emergence of a relational tradition in transactional analysis*. Chadlington, Oxfordshire: Haddon Press.

Cornell, W. F. (1988). Life script theory: A critical review from a developmental perspective. *Transactional Analysis Journal, 18*(4), 270–282. https://doi.org/10.1177/036215378801800402

Cornell, W. F. (2018). If it is not for all, it is not for us: Reflections on racism, nationalism, and populism in the United States. *Transactional Analysis Journal, 48*(2), 97–110. https://doi.org/10.1080/03621537.2018.1431460

Cornell, W. F. (2024). In these dark times: Exploring our values as transactional analysts. *Transactional Analysis Journal, 54*(2), 114–125. https://doi.org/10.1080/03621537.2024.2327266

Cousins, S., & Diamond, B. (2021). *Making sense of microaggressions*. UK: Open Voices Publishers.

Crenshaw, K. (1989). 'Demarginalizing the intersection of race and sex: A Black feminist critique of antidiscrimination doctrine, feminist theory and antiracist politics.' *University of Chicago Legal Forum*, Issue 1, Article 8. https://chicagounbound.uchicago.edu/cgi/viewcontent.cgi?ar-ticle=1052&context=uclf

Crenshaw, K. (2019). 'Reach everyone on the planet': Kimberlé Crenshaw and intersectionality (Gunda Werner Institute in the Heinrich Böll Foundation and the Centre for Intersectional Justice, Eds.). https://www.boell.de/sites/default/files/crenshaw_-_reach_everyone_on_the_planet_en.pdf

Czyzselska, J. C. (2022). *Queering psychotherapy*. London: Karnac Books.

Dajani, K., & Rozmarin, E. (2024). 'Crossing divides'. *Room: A sketchbook for analytic action* 2.24; https://analyticroom.com/speakingofhome/

Dhananjaya, D. (2022). We are the oppressor and the oppressed: The interplay between intrapsychic, interpersonal, and societal intersectionality. *Transactional Analysis Journal*, *52*(3), 244–258. https://doi.org/10.1080/03621537.2022.2082031

DiAngelo, R. (2018). *White fragility: Why it's so hard for white people to talk about racism*. London: Penguin Random House; Boston, US: Beacon Press.

Digital Poverty Alliance. (2022) https://digitalpovertyalliance.org/uk https://digitalpoverty alliance.org/uk-digital-poverty-evidence-review-2022/introduction-myths-and-shifts/digital-poverty-evidence-review-2022/introduction-myths-and-shifts/

DK. (2024). *The philosophy book*. London: Dorling Kindersley.

Drego, P. (1983). The cultural parent. *Transactional Analysis Journal*, *13*(4), 224–227. https://doi.org/10.1177/036215378301300404

EATA, ITAA. (2024). Joint Common Mission Statement. https://eatanews.org/eata-itaa-common-mission-statement/

Eddo-Lodge, R. (2017). *Why I'm no longer talking to white people about race*. London: Bloomsbury.

Ellis, E. (2021). *The race conversation*. London: Confer.

English, F. (1969). Episcript and the "hot potato" game. *Transactional Analysis Bulletin*, *8*(32), 77–82.

Erskine, R. G. (1980). Script cure: Behavioral, intrapsychic and physiological. *Transactional Analysis Journal*, *10*(2), 102–106. https://doi.org/10.1177/036215378001000205

Erskine, R. G. & Zalcman, M (1979). The racket system. *Transactional Analysis Journal*, *9*(1), 51–59. https://doi.org/10.1177/036215377900900112

Falicov, C. (1995). Training to think culturally: A multidimensional comparative framework. *Family Process*, *34*, 373–388. https://doi.org/10.1111/j.1545-5300.1995.00373.x

Federn, P. (1926). Some variations in ego-feeling. *International Journal of Psychoanalysis*, *7*, 434–444.

Filipache, I. (2022). Shattered dignity and unsymbolized past: Facing the legacy of a totalitarian system. *Transactional Analysis Journal*, *52*(3), 178–192. https://doi.org/10.1080/03621537.2022.2076416

Fine, M., Torre, M. E., Oswald, A. G., & Avory, S. (2021). Critical participatory action research: Methods and praxis for intersectional knowledge production. *Journal of Counselling Psychology*, *68*(3), 344.

Flores, M. (2016). 'bell hooks – intersectional feminist'. https://info.umkc.edu/womenc/2016/01/04/bell-hooks-intersectionalfeminist/

Ghandi, M. (1931). 'Lincoln Heights Tour' Speech, NY.

Gheorghe, N., Brunke, M., Deaconu, D., Gheorghe, A., & Ionas, L. (2019). All my parents: Professional transgenerational trauma in the TA community. *Transactional Analysis Journal*, *49*(4), 263–278. https://doi.org/10.1080/03621537.2019.1649847

Goffe, T. L. (2025). *Dark laboratory – On Columbus, the Caribbean and the origins of the climate crisis*. London: Penguin Random House.

Goodley, D. (2018). The dis/ability complex. *Journal of Diversity and Gender Studies*. https://doi.org/10.11116/digest.5.1.1

Goodley, D., Lawthom, R., Liddiard, K., & Runswick-Cole, K. (2019). Provocations for critical disability studies. *Disability & Society, 34*(6), 972–997. https://doi.org/10.1080/09687599.2019.1566889

Hardy, K. V., & Laszloffy, T. (2002). Couple therapy using a multicultural perspective. In A. S. Gurman & N. Jacobson (Eds.), *Clinical handbook of couple therapy* (3rd ed., pp. 569–593). New York: Guilford Press.

Hargaden, H., & Sills, C. (2002). *Transactional analysis: A relational perspective*. East Sussex: Brunner-Routledge.

Hart, A. (2017). From multicultural competence to radical openness: A psychoanalytic engagement of otherness. *The American Psychoanalyst, 51*(1), 12–13, 26–27. https://apsa.org/wp-content/uploads/apsaa-publications/vol51no1-TOC/html/vol51no1_09.xhtml

Hawkins, P., & Shohet, R. (2012). *Supervision in the helping professionals*. Fourth Edition. London: Open University Press.

Hines, S. (2022). *Is gender fluid?: A primer for the 21st century*. London: Thames & Hudson Ltd.

Hooks, B. (1981). *Ain't I a woman?: Black women and feminism*. London: Pluto Press.

Hooks, B. (1994). Love as the practice of freedom (chapter 20). In *Outlaw culture: Resisting representations*. New York & East Sussex: Routledge; e-book 2015. https://doi.org/10.4324/9780203822883

Hooks, B. (1999). *All about love: New visions*. New York: William Morrow & Company.

IARTA. (2025). Steering Group. https://www.relationalta.com

Isaacs, R. (2020). *More-than-human geographies*. Wiley Online Library. https://doi.org/10.1002/9781118786352.wbieg2041

ITAA. (2014). ITAA Code of Ethics - ITAA Code of Ethical Conduct and ITAA Ethics Procedures Manual. https://itaaworld.com/wpcontent/uploads/2023/05/12-5-14-Revised-Ethics_0.pdf

Jacobs, M. (1988). *Psychodynamic counselling in action*. London: Sage.

Jusik, P. (2022). Systemic oppression and cultural diversity: Putting flesh on the bones of intercultural competence. *Transactional Analysis Journal, 52*(3), 209–227. https://doi.org/10.1080/03621537.2022.2076981

Karpman, S. (1968). Fairy tales and script drama analysis. *Transactional Analysis Bulletin, 7*(26), 39–43.

Khan, M. (2023). *Working within diversity. A reflective guide to antioppressive practice in counselling and psychotherapy*. London: Jessica Kingsley Publishers.

King, M. L. Jr. (1963). Excerpt I had a dream speech. Washington, DC.

Kliman, J. (2005). Many differences, many voices: Toward social justice in family. Toward social justice in family therapy. In M. P. Mirkin, K. Suyemoto, & B. Okun (Eds.), *Psychotherapy with women: Exploring diverse contexts and identities*. New York: Guilford.

Kliman, J. (2010). Intersections of social privilege and marginalization: A visual teaching tool. In *Expanding our social justice practices: Advances in theory and training*. [special issue.]. AFTA (American Family Therapy Academy), *6*(39–48). Monograph Series.

Klosin, A., Casas, E., Hidalgo-Carcedo, C., Vavouri, T., & Lehner, B. (2017). Transgenerational transmission of environmental information in *C. elegans*. *Science, 356*(6335), 320–323. https://pubmed.ncbi.nlm.nih.gov/28428426

Kohut, H. (1971). *The analysis of the self*. New York: International Universities Press.

Lago, C. (2011). *The handbook of transcultural counselling and psychotherapy*. New York: Open University Press.

Leong, C., & Graichen, R. (2024). Decentering neuronormativity: A transactional analysis impasse theory perspective for understanding ADHD masking and authentically honoring the da Vinci archetype within. *Transactional Analysis Journal*, *54*(1), 91–106. https://doi.org/10.1080/03621537.2024.2286581

Lorde, A. (1982). Learning from the '60s', Malcolm X Weekend, Harvard University. https://www.blackpast.org/african-american-history/1982audre-lorde-learning-60s/

Lorde, A. (1983). There is no hierarchy of oppressions. *Homophobia and education*. Bulletin. New York: Council on Interracial Books for Children. Retrieved on December 29, 2021, from https://theanarchistlibrary.org/library/audre-lorde-there-is-no-hierarchyof-oppressions https://sites.williams.edu/engl113-f18/marr/there-is-no https://sites.williams.edu/engl113-f18/marr/there-is-no-hierarchy-of-oppression/hierarchy-of-oppression/

Lorde, A. (1997). *The cancer journals*. San Francisco: Aunt Lute Books.

Lorde, A., (2007), *Sister outsider: Essays & speeches by audre lorde* (pp.134–144). Berkeley: Crossing Press; cited in BlackPast, B. (2012, August 12).

Lorde, A. (2017). *Your silence will not protect you*. San Jose: Silver Press.

Lorde, A. (2018). *The master's tools will not dismantle the master's house*. London: Penguin Random House.

Mandela, N. (1990). Excerpt from Mandela Speech to Joint Meeting of Congress.

Marshall, H. (2023). A place for the ecological third: Eco-TA in therapeutic practice. *Transactional Analysis Journal*, *53*(1), 93–108. https://doi.org/10.1080/03621537.2023.2152567

Marshall, H., & Barrow, G. (2020). Launching eco-TA: A movement of our time. *The Transactional Analyst*, *10*(2), Spring 2020.

Marshall, H., & Barrow, G. (2023). Revisiting ecological transactional analysis: Emerging perspectives. *Transactional Analysis Journal*, *53*(1), 7–20. https://doi.org/10.1080/03621537.2023.2152528

Marshall, H., & Jordan, M. (2010). Taking counselling and psychotherapy outside: Destruction or enrichment of the therapeutic frame? *European Journal of Psychotherapy and Counselling*, *12*(4), 345–359.

McLuhan, T. C. (1971/1992). *Touch the earth: A self portrait of Indian existence*. Victoria, Canada: Promontory Press.

Menninger, K. (1958). *Theory of psychoanalytic technique*. New York, NY: Basic Books.

Minikin, K. (2011). Transactional analysis and the wider world: The politics and psychology of alienation. In Fowlie, H., & Sills, C. (Eds.) *Relational transactional analysis: Principles in practice*. London: Karnac Books.

Minikin, K. (2016). The mind of our state and the state of our minds. *The Transactional Analyst*, *6*(3), Summer.

Minikin, K. (2018). Radical relational psychiatry: Toward a democracy of mind and people. *Transactional Analysis Journal*, *48*(2), 111–125. https://doi.org/10.1080/03621537.2018.1429287

Minikin, K. (2021). Relative privilege and the seduction of normativity. *Transactional Analysis Journal*, *51*(1). https://doi.org/10.1080/03621537.2020.1853349

Minikin, K. (2023). *Radical-relational perspectives in transactional analysis psychotherapy: Oppression, alienation, reclamation*. London: Routledge.

Minikin, K. (2023). Commentary on "War: A transactional group analysis" by Keith tudor. *Transactional Analysis Journal*, *53*(4), 323–327. https://doi.org/10.1080/03621537.2023.2251841

Minikin, K. (2024). The personal and the political. *Transactional Analysis Journal*, *54*(2), 126–135. https://doi.org/10.1080/03621537.2024.2323870

Minikin, K. (2024). Leadership, intersectionality, and feminism: Radicalrelational perspectives. *Transactional Analysis Journal*, *54*(3), 203–215. https://doi.org/10.1080/03621537.2024.2359286

Minikin, K., & Cottier, F. (2018). August – Partitions: Divided country, divided people and divided minds. *Psychotherapy and Politics International*. *16*(2).

Minikin, K., & Rowland, H. (2022). Letter from the coeditors: Systemic oppression: What part do we play? *Transactional Analysis Journal*, *52*(3), 175–177. https://doi.org/10.1080/03621537.2022.2080263

Moiso, C. (1985). Ego States and transference. *Transactional Analysis Journal*, *15*(3), 194–201. https://doi.org/10.1177/036215378501500302

Morgan, K. (2017). 'Britain in the Seventies – Our unfinest hour?', Revue Française de Civilisation Britannique [Online], XXII- Hors série | 2017, Online since 30 December 2017, connection on 16 February 2023. http://journals.openedition.org/rfcb/1662

Morrison, T. (1998). 'Toni Morrison beautifully answers an "illegitimate" question on race' (Jan. 19, 1998) | Charlie Rose. https://www.youtube.com/watch?v=-Kgq3F8wbYA

MoU. (2017, 2022). https://www.bpc.org.uk/professionals/registrants https://www.bpc.org.uk/professionals/registrants-hub/guidance/memorandum-of-understanding-on-conversion-therapy-in-the-uk/hub/guidance/memorandum-of-understanding-on-conversion-therapy; https://www.bpc.org.uk/professionals/registrants-hub/guidance/memorandum-of-understanding-on-conversion-therapy-in-the-uk/in-the-uk/

Mullan, J. (2023). *Decolonizing therapy – Oppression, historical trauma, and politicizing your practice*. New York: W.W. Norton & Co.

Mulvey, L. (1975). Visual pleasure and narrative cinema. *Screen*, *16*, 618.

Napikoski, L. (2019). 'Biography of Adrienne Rich, feminist and political poet' August 4, 2019. https://www.thoughtco.com/adrienne-rich https://www.thoughtco.com/adrienne-rich-biography-3528945biography-3528945

Naughton, M., & Tudor, K. (2006). Being white. *Transactional Analysis Journal*, *36*(2), 159–171. https://doi.org/10.1177/036215370603600208

Norris, C. (2002). *Deconstruction: Theory and practice* (New Accents 3rd ed.). Abingdon: Routledge.

Oates, S., & Moores, J. (2024). What is psychological and what is neurological? A political and phenomenological exploration of neurodivergent identity and encounters with thirdness. *Transactional Analysis Journal*, *54*(1), 63–77. https://doi.org/10.1080/03621537.2023.228657

Obama, M. (2018). *Becoming*. New York: Crown Publishing/Penguin Random House.

Oliver, M. (1983). *The politics of disablement*. London: Palgrave MacMillan.

Oliver, M., & Barnes, C. (2012). *The new politics of disablement*. London: Palgrave.

Orange, D. (2017). *Climate crisis: Psychoanalysis and radical ethics*. Oxon: Routledge

Ostberg, R. (2024, June 13). 'James Baldwin'. *Encyclopedia Britannica*. https://www.britannica.com/biography/James-Baldwin

Pandya, A. (2024). System imago: A new perspective on leadership and power. *Transactional Analysis Journal*, *54*(3), 216–230. https://doi.org/10.1080/03621537.2024.2359287

Pappas, S. (2023). A tangled web. *Scientific American Magazine*, *328*(5), May 2023.

PBS. (2006). https://www.pbs.org/wnet/americanmasters/james-baldwin https://www.pbs.org/wnet/americanmasters/james-baldwin-about-the-author/59/about-the-author/59/

PBS. (2012). 'Slavery by another name'. https://www.pbs.org/tpt/slavery https://www.pbs.org/tpt/slavery-by-another-name/themes/life-coal-mine/by-another-name/themes/life-coal-mine/

Poetly. (2021). Obituary tribute to bell hooks. https://poetly.substack.com/p/poems-from-bell-hooks-when-angels

Poetryfoundation. (2024). https://www.poetryfoundation.org/poets/audre; https://www.poetryfoundation.org/poets/audre-lordelorde (accessed August 2024).

Poetryfoundation. (2024). https://www.poetryfoundation.org/poets/adrienne-rich

Powell, D., Dada, M., & Yaprak, R., (2015). 'Black and minority ethnic (BME) trainee counsellors reflections on their training and implications for practice', Lewisham Counselling & Training Associates.

Powell, J. (2015). John A. Powell & Bell Hooks: Dialogue at the othering & belonging conference 'Belonging Through Connection, Connecting Through Love: Oneself, the Other, and the Earth'. https://youtu.be/0sX7fqIU4gQ?si=LLd-73TyCX8_6l7i

Project TA 101. (2025). ITAA, USATAA, Southeast Institute, IESA committee begun 2018. Retrieved 29/5/25 from https://itaaworld.com/about-ta/project-ta-101/

Research Team Interviews. (2021). https://www.dropbox.com/s/dkh23gzj6dbawld/Introducing%20Research%20Project.mp4?dl=0

Rich, A. (1973; 1994). *Diving into the wreck, reissue: Poems 1971-1972*. New York: W.W. Norton.

Rich, A. (1979). What does a woman need to know?. Speech Smith College. https://www.coursehero.com/file/66234961/Adrienne-Rich-What-Does-a-Woman-Need-to-Know-TPO-4-71-76pdf/

Rich, A. (1980). Compulsory heterosexuality and lesbian existence. *Signs: Journal of Women in Culture and Society* (University of Chicago Press Journals), *5*(4), 631–660. http://doi.org/10.1086/493756.

Rich, A. (1984). *Sources*. Woodside, California: Heyeck Press.

Rich, A. (1995). *Dark fields of the republic*. New York: W.W. Norton & Co.

Rich, A. *(*1995*)*. *On lies, secrets, and silence: Selected prose 1966-1978*. New York: W.W. Norton & Co.

Rich, A., & Gilbert, S. M. (2019). *Culture, politics, and the art of poetry: Essential essays*. New York: W.W. Norton & Co.

Romero, M. (2018). *Introducing intersectionality*. Cambridge, UK: Polity Press.

Rowland, H., & Cornell, W. F. (2021). Gender identity, queer theory, and working with the sociopolitical in counseling and psychotherapy: Why there is no such thing as neutral. *Transactional Analysis Journal, 51*(1), 19–34. https://doi.org/10.1080/03621537.2020.1853347

Rupchand, F., & Kormann, S. (2024). Intersubjective discoveries on parenting autistic sons: Challenges to ableist, normative narratives of deficit. *Transactional Analysis Journal, 54*(1), 31–46. https://doi.org/10.1080/03621537.2024.2286580

Schiff, A. W., & Lee Schiff, J. (1971). Passivity. *Transactional Analysis Bulletin, 1*(1), 71–78. https://doi.org/10.1177/036215377100100114

Schiff, J. Cathexis Institute. (1975). *Cathexis reader: Transactional analysis treatment of psychosis*. New York: Harper & Row.

Schiff, S. (1977). Personality development and symbiosis. *Transactional Analysis Bulletin, 7*(4), 310–316. https://doi.org/10.1177/036215377700700407

SCOPed. (2025). https://www.bacp.co.uk/about-us/advancing-theprofession/scoped/

SFGMC. (2022). https://www.sfgmc.org/blog/aids-crisis-1980s

Shadbolt, C. (2009). Sexuality and shame. *Transactional Analysis Journal, 39*(2), 163–172. https://doi.org/10.1177/036215370903900210

Shadbolt, C. (2012). The place of failure and rupture in psychotherapy. *Transactional Analysis Journal, 42*(1), 5–16. https://doi.org/10.1177/036215371204200102

Shadbolt, C. (2017). Dancing in a different country: When the personal is professional. *Transactional Analysis Journal, 47*(4), 264–275. https://doi.org/10.1177/0362153717719030

Shadbolt, C. (2018). The sorrow of ghosts: The emergence of a traumatized parent ego state. *Transactional Analysis Journal, 48*(4), 293–307. https://doi.org/10.1080/03621537.2018.1505127

Shadbolt, C. (2022). The many faces of systemic oppression, power, and privilege: The necessity of self-examination. *Transactional Analysis Journal, 52*(3), 259–273. https://doi.org/10.1080/03621537.2022.2076411

Shafak, E. (2021). *The island of missing trees*. London: Penguin Books.

Shivanath, S., & Hiremath, M. (2003). The psychodynamics of race and culture. In Sills, C. & Hargaden, H. (Eds.), *Ego states (key concepts in transactional analysis: Contemporary views)* (pp. 169–184). Worcester: Worth Publishing.

Smith, K. (2021). 'Exploring Audre Lorde's intersectionality'. https://www.facinghistory. org/ideas-week/exploring-audre-lordes https://www.facinghistory.org/ideas-week/exploring-audre-lordes-intersectionalityintersectionality

Stark, M. (2000). *Modes of therapeutic action*. Northvale: Jason Aronson.

Steiner, C. (1966). Script and counterscript. *Transactional Analysis Bulletin, 5*(18), 133–135.

Steiner, C., Wyckoff, H., Marcus, J., Lariviere, P., Goldstine, D., & Schwebel, R.; Members of the Radical Psychiatry Center. (1975). *Readings in radical psychiatry*. New York: Grove Press.

Subramaniam. (2010). Cited in chapter: '*Gender and sexism*'. https://pressbooks.umn.edu/ interculturaldialogues/chapter/chapter-7gender-and-sexism/

Taylor, F. (2023). *Unruly therapeutic: Black feminist writings and practices in living room*. New York: W.W. Norton & Co.

Thomas, L. (2022). *The intersectional environmentalist: How to dismantle systems of oppression to protect people+planet*. London: Souvenir Press.

Thompson, N. (1998). *Promoting equality: Working with diversity and difference*. London: Red Globe Press.

Tilden, J. (2021). *Queering your therapy practice*. London: Routledge.

Tilney, T. (1998). *Dictionary of transactional analysis*. London: Whurr Publishers.

Totten, T., & Neely, N. (2021). Season 4 - Between us: A psychotherapy podcast: Episode 40: Radical openness: D/@betweenusapsychotherapypod6335.

Tudor, K. (2016). We are: The fundamental life position. *Transactional Analysis Journal, 46*(2), 164–176. https://doi.org/10.1177/0362153716637064.

Tudor, K. (2024). *Transactional analysis proper and improper: Selected and new papers*. Abingdon: Routledge.

Tudor, K., Green, E., & Brett, E. (2022). Critical whiteness: A transactional analysis of a systemic oppression. *Transactional Analysis Journal, 52*(3), 193–208. https://doi.org/10. 1080/03621537.2022.2076394

Tudor, K., & Summers, G. (2000). Co-creative transactional analysis. *Transactional Analysis Journal, 30*(1), 23–40. https://doi.org/10.1177/036215370003000104

Turner, D. (2021). *Intersections of privilege and otherness in counselling and psychotherapy*. London: Routledge.

Turner, D. (2023). *The psychology of supremacy: Imperium*. London: Routledge.

Turner, D. (2025). *Decolonising counselling and psychotherapy: Depoliticised pathways towards intersectional practice*. London: Routledge.

UK Digital Poverty Evidence Review. (2022). https://digitalpovertyalliance.org/wp-content/ uploads/2022/06/UKDigital-Poverty-Evidence-Review-2022-v1.0-compressed.pdf

UKCP. (2017). Standards of Education and Training. https://www.psychotherapy.org.uk/ media/03olj3jw/ukcp-adult-standards-of-education-and-training-2017.pdf

Universal Declaration of Human Rights. (1948). https://www.un.org/en/about-us/universal-declaration-of-human-rights

Vaid-Menon, A. (2020). *Beyond the gender binary*. New York: Penguin Workshop.

Vaid-Menon, A. (2021) *Your wound, my garden*. Audible Studios (2023).

Vaid-Menon, A. (2021) *Femme in public*. https://www.alokvmenon.com/writing

Vaid-Menon, A. (2022). 'Alok: The urgent need for compassion'. *Man Enough*. https:// youtu.be/Tq3C9R8HNUQ

Vaid-Menon, A. (2022). 'Have the courage to break your own heart': Keynote – Creating Change conference: National LGBTQ Taskforce.

Wells, M. (2012). From fiction to freedom: Our true nature beyond life script. *Transactional Analysis Journal*, *42*(2). https://doi.org/10.1177/036215371204200208

Wells, M. (2018). *Sitting in the stillness: Freedom from the personal story*. Hampshire, UK: Mantra Books.

Widdowson, M. (2024). *Transactional analysis: 100 key points and techniques*. London: Routledge.

Williams, J. (2021). *Climate change is racist*. London: Icon Books Ltd.

Wong, A. (2020). *Disability visibility: First person stories from the twentyfirst century*. USA: Crown Books.

Woodstreetradio. (2020). https://woodstreetradio.radiostream321.com/

Woollams, S. J., & Brown, M. (1978). *Transactional analysis*. Huron Valley: Huron Valley Institute Press.

Woollams, S. J., & Huige, K. A. (1977). Normal dependency and symbiosis. *Transactional Analysis Journal*, *7*(3), 217–220. https://doi.org/10.1177/036215377700700303

Yehuda, R., & Lehrner, A. (2018). Intergenerational transmission of trauma effects: Putative role of epigenetic mechanisms. *World Psychiatry*, *17*(3), 243–257. https://doi.org10.1002/wps.20568

Zahid, N., & Cooke, R. (Eds.) (2023). *Therapists challenging racism and oppression – The unheard voices*. Monmouth, UK: PCCS.

Index

For Product Safety Concerns and Information please contact our EU
representative GPSR@taylorandfrancis.com
Taylor & Francis Verlag GmbH, Kaufingerstraße 24, 80331 München, Germany

www.ingramcontent.com/pod-product-compliance
Lightning Source LLC
Chambersburg PA
CBHW052002270326
41929CB00015B/2751